MW01533716

FINE LINES: Spring 2025
Volume 34 Issue 1
Edited by David Martin and Kristen Martin

9905 Rockbrook Road
Omaha, NE 68124
www.finelines.org

ISBN: 979-8-3163-9473-9

Fine Lines, Inc. is a 501 (c) 3 non-profit corporation.
EID: 47-0832351
All donations are tax-deductible.

Cover photograph *Sunrise Praise* by Cindy Goeller

Fine Lines logo designed by Kristy Stark Knapp, Knapp Studios
Book and cover design by Michael Campbell, MC Writing Services

~ Spring 2025 ~

VOLUME 34 ISSUE 1

Edited by David Martin
and Kristen Martin

CONTENTS

ABOUT *FINE LINES*

Fine Lines is published by *Fine Lines,* Inc., a 501 (c) 3 non-profit corporation. David Martin is the managing editor. In this quarterly publication, we share poetry and prose by writers of all ages in an attempt to add clarity and passion to our lives. Support is provided through donations, all of which are tax deductible. Join us in creating the lives we desire through the written word.

Composition is hard work. We celebrate its rewards in each issue. Share this publication with others, who love creativity. We encourage authors and artists of all ages. Our national mailing list reaches every state. Increased literacy and effective, creative communication are critical for all.

Fine Lines editors believe writing of life's experiences brings order to chaos, beauty to existence, and celebration to the mysterious.

DONATIONS

Contributions are tax deductible. When you support *Fine Lines,* we send e-letters with *Fine Lines* news, upcoming events, the inside scoop on special issues, and provide copies to students, who have no means to buy this publication. You will add to their literacy, too.

We offer two methods of payment for your *Fine Lines* donations:

- U.S. residents should make checks payable to *Fine Lines.* Please include your name, address, and email with your donation, and send to:

Fine Lines

9905 Rockbrook Road

Omaha, NE 68124

- Click DONATE on our home page: www.finelines.org

SUBMISSIONS

- We accept submissions via email, file attachments, CDs formatted in MS Word for PCs, and laser-printed hard copies.
- Editors reply when writing is accepted for publication, and if a stamped, self-addressed envelope or email address is provided.
- Submissions must not include overt abuse, sexuality, profanity, drugs, alcohol, or violence.
- Do not send "class projects." Teachers may copy *Fine Lines* issues for their classes and submit student work for publication, when they act as members and sponsors.
- Address changes and correspondence should be sent to the *Fine Lines* email address: fine-lines@cox.net

We encourage readers to respond to the ideas expressed by our authors. Letters to the editor may be printed in future issues, after editing for length and clarity. Reader feedback is important to us. We support writers and artists with hope and direction. Write on.

"The obstacle in the path becomes the path."

RYAN HOLIDAY

Fine Lines
35
Years

PANGUR BAN

Robin Flower, an 8th century monk, wrote this poem in Gaelic.

I and Pangur Ban, my cat
'Tis a like task we are at;
Hunting mice is his delight
Hunting words I sit all night.

Better far than praise of men
'Tis to sit with book and pen;
Pangur bears me no ill will,
He too plies his simple skill.

'Tis a merry thing to see
At our tasks how glad are we,
When at home we sit and find
Entertainment to our mind.

Oftentimes a mouse will stray
In the hero Pangur's way:
Oftentimes my keen thought set
Takes a meaning in its net.

'Gainst the wall he sets his eye
Full and fierce and sharp and sly;
'Gainst the wall of knowledge I
All my little wisdom try.

When a mouse darts from its den,
O how glad is Pangur then!
O what gladness do I prove
When I solve the doubts I love!

So in peace our tasks we ply,
Pangur Ban, my cat, and I;
In our arts we find our bliss,
I have mine and he has his.

Practice every day has made
Pangur perfect in his trade;
I get wisdom day and night
Turning darkness into light.

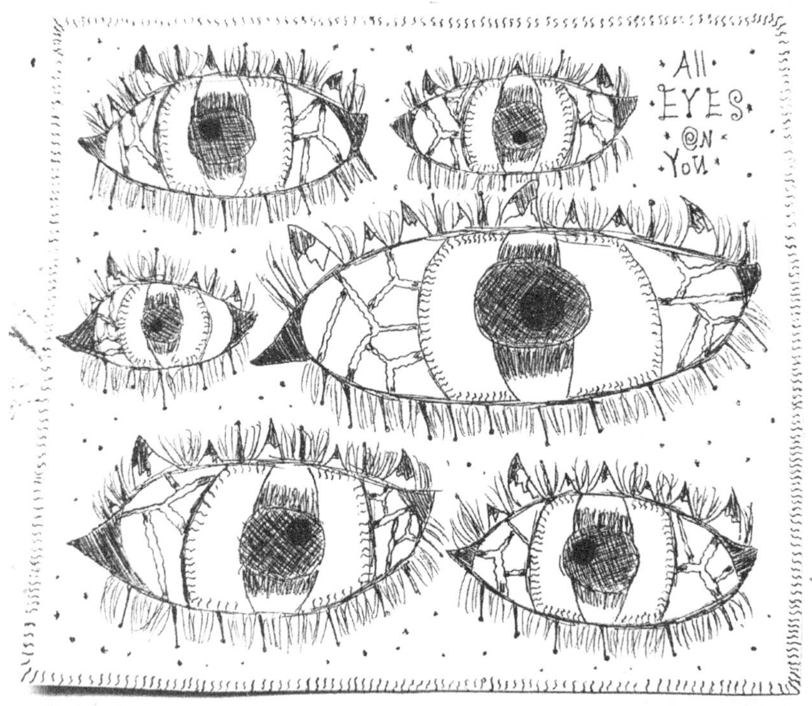

All Eyes on You
Ink drawing by 11-year-old Olivia Bottlinger

Eyes Like Hers

EUNICE AMBRIZ
Council Bluffs, Iowa, Community School Student

Today, I woke up at sunrise. I stretched out my legs and looked behind me. I saw that you were still there. It's been a few months since you adopted me. I thought I would spend the rest of my life in the shelter. I remember clearly how you walked up to me, placed your wrinkly finger on the glass, and looked at me with such kind, thoughtful eyes. I've never seen such gentle eyes before. I purred loudly and clung onto you, when you held me for the first time. I was so desperate for you to take me with you. I dug my claws through your wool sweater and into your skin. When you cried out in pain, a lady wearing all gray reached out to grab me, but you refused to let me go.

"No, no she's just a baby," you said calmly. That same day, I was adopted, and we've been inseparable ever since.

I followed you everywhere you went, and I often left hairballs, fur, and vomit on the couch and carpet floors, but you never scolded me. I always slept in your bed during the winter time. It was toasty, spacious, and soft; the scent of cinnamon always lingered. I never liked that scent, but I never left your bed, if it meant that I would stay by your side.

Sometimes, you woke up at the same time as I did, and we would have breakfast together, but ever since you fell sick, you've been waking up at the hour of my lunch time. Lately, there have been more and more orange cylinders with white substances inside them. I knew they weren't treats for me, since they smelled nothing like tuna, but I always saw you taking them every single day. I assumed they were for you, anyway, because my treats always came in a brown bag. The days were shorter, during this time of year.

"Come here, Daisy. Let's watch our movie, while I knit you a scarf." My favorite part of the day was when it was movie time. You played the same movie every day, but I didn't mind, since I would sleep the entire time. I laid on your lap, while you knitted my scarf. This was our daily routine for the winter: waking up, eating, knitting, and sleeping once again. On some days, you would go outside. It always made me worry every time you left. Once, I tried to stop you from leaving, but you nudged me away and walked out the door, but then you would always come back with a brown bag and treats just for me.

The following morning, I decided to get up and have breakfast. I waited a while for you to get up, but hours seemed to fly by, and you didn't open your eyes. I called for you, but there was no answer. I licked your nose, and there was no answer. I tried my last resort, which was nibbling at your ear, but you didn't flinch. I waited for what seemed like forever, but there wasn't a single movement from you at all. Once it was dinner time, that was when I started to worry. I went inside your room, and you hadn't moved.

I was starving, and I tried to call your name a little louder, but there was nothing, not a grunt, or a sigh. Suddenly, a person burst through the door, which startled me. I ran to hide inside your closet. I poked my head out a little and saw that the person was your son. I remember him a little, a tall man with an odd amount of fur around his mouth and cheeks, who always had treats and toys for me, whenever he visited. I liked that he had your kind eyes, but when he burst through the door, his eyes widened, and they seemed frightened.

I heard him call your name but a lot louder than I did. "Mom? Mom? Are you okay? Can you hear me?" I heard him say.

The next thing I knew, there were three people dressed in orange with gray stripes. They had blue hands, and they burst inside the house the same way your son did. I saw them put a weird white stick in your mouth, and they put their hands on your chest, as they aggressively started pushing. It was terrifying, and I wanted you to wake up so you could see how many people broke inside our house.

Then, your son approached me and grabbed me quickly. I didn't even have time to react. He took me out to the living room, and he started petting me and speaking to me softly.

"It's okay Daisy, It's okay" he said, although he was trying to comfort me. It seemed like he needed more comfort himself.

I saw the orange people with blue hands take you away on a bed with wheels. I tried to wiggle out of your son's arms, but he held me tightly. It was the last time I saw you. Your skin was more blue, and your kind gentle eyes never opened.

Your son held me closer, and I heard him cry into my fur, as he placed me on the ground. He sniffled and sighed deeply, as he gave me a head scratch, then he pulled out what I just learned recently is called a "phone" and spoke into it. I went to your room and sat wondering when you would come back.

Three days have gone by. I refused to eat, and you still haven't returned home. By this hour, we would be on the couch together with me on your lap and you knitting my seventh scarf. One more day passed, and I heard the door open, abruptly. I was too weak to check who had come, but it was your son, once again.

"Let's go, Daisy," he said, as he brought in my cage and opened it, gesturing me to go in. I turned away, refusing to go, but your son forced me inside. He took me to a place that was nothing like the vet's. Everything smelled differently.

"This is your new home, now. I just know mother loved you so much," your son spoke, quietly. He left the room for a moment, and it struck me, then, that you weren't coming back.

As I lay on the couch, your son sat beside me. He stroked my back, slowly. I turned to look at him and saw almost an exact resemblance of your gentle brown eyes, subtle fingers, and soft smile. His presence was comforting and quiet, though it wasn't exactly yours. Still, maybe with time, I'd come to accept it and cherish him, too.

Dizzy Party

DUANE ANDERSON

One by one, the brothers and sister
started spinning around in circles
after eating cookies and ice cream sandwiches

laced with pure sweetness to their taste buds,
making them go dizzy as they spun around.
Sister falls down, then gets up,

the brothers one fall down, then get up,
only to continue to spin and spin,
a circus of dizziness surrounding them.

Join in on the silliness if you wish,
but as for myself, I will just sit back and watch
as the dizzy party continues.

I'm Taken

DUANE ANDERSON

After the house had been up for sale for weeks,
it finally sold, maybe sold for a pot of gold,
sold for cash, sold for bit coin,
or even swapped for a bowl of magic beans,
and instead of placing a "Sold" sign in the yard,

a sign stating "I'm Taken" was put up,
followed with "Yay! This house just became a home,"
but maybe they should have waited a little longer,
until someone moved in, and then,
just maybe, it would become a home again,

and the words of "I'm Taken," did it
mean the house was taken hostage,
and needed help from someone to free it,
or "I'm Taken," ready to play on someone else's team,
so get lost, and find another house to choose from,

wishing anyone good luck with that since there
wasn't another gem in the area like it,
but no matter the sign preferred,
someone was definitely moving in, and as good neighbors,
we will welcome them into the neighborhood.

Sweet Iced Tea

DANIEL BARBARE

Shorter than the day
a friend's visit
seemed as quick
as a knock on the
glass door
if only the Christmas
lights could glow
and we could
get a refill on the iced
sweet tea.

"The purpose of human life is to serve and to show compassion and the will to help others."

ALBERT SCHWEITZER

I Must

DAVID BARNES

Stress decreases when I begin to think of something to write. The time used to organize a story or essay keeps unnecessary, maybe troubling, thoughts away.

This process came to me late in life, the actual writing process, but looking back, I've been mentally writing for years in my mind, as I sat and watched or drove the many miles required for my job. I've been observing people, scenes, panoramas, and using my imagination since a young boy.

I simply didn't realize that putting these thoughts on paper would matter to me or to anyone. Now I know. I write because I must.

Is a Writer an Artist?

DAVID BARNES

Is a writer an artist? To be clear a writer for this essay is one who puts words to paper for a purpose. The writing could be to tell a story, write a poem, inform, or state an opinion.

Word doodlers are not included in this assessment just as picture doodlers wouldn't be included if oil, watercolor, or pen and ink were examined. Whatever the degree of ability, writers are those who intend to place a part of themselves on paper for all to see.

This argument or conversation has been floating the ether for years and years. Is an artist only one who paints, draws, or sculpts? To perform these arts takes skill, practice, and imagination.

The same can be said, precisely, about the writer. The more words the author puts to paper the better they become. Figuring out how to make a sentence jump alive in a reader's mind is nothing less than an art. Nearly anyone can write a two-dimensional sentence. But to describe a street scene with people, traffic noise, odors of diesel and mud is exceptionally hard to do if one wants the scene to be a living being.

When I see Monet's or Pissarro's Paris street scenes words leap in my mind. Of course, the beauty of the painting and the skill of the artist is foremost. But there is an additional component of enjoying these paintings, at least for me. I imagine walking with the people depicted and taking part in the life of those times. Words in my imagination make the paintings complete for me.

A writer can accomplish the same objective as the painter. The writer can construct the same scene with words. We paint with words. The trick, if it can be called that, is to provide enough detail for a reader's imagination to fully engage with the page. Too little description and interest flags. Too much detail and the reader is many time lost in a morass of unnecessary vocabulary. While reading a story like this the reader may have to reread sentences to try to determine what the writer intended to pass along. Balance and timing is what the writer strives toward.

When I look at paintings that give me a pleasing experience, I see stories that could be written, people walking along and talking; people jumping out of the way of a splash of water caused by a fast-moving horse cart or trolley; a woman and man standing shoulder to shoulder looking over the side of a bridge with a rushing river underneath.

Writers can take a notion from thin air or a photograph or a watercolor and tell any kind of tale they wish. It could be true, based on truth, or complete fabrication. The only parameters are those set by the skill of the person with the pen. Isn't this exactly the same as the limits on the composer or the painter?

Writers are artists in all the same ways painters, sculptors, and composers are. The purpose is the same for all who call themselves artists. We strive to convey ideas to others. We attempt to make other think and sometimes opine. We simply paint with words.

Dear Big Brother

DAVID BARNES

Dear Big Brother,

It's been a couple of weeks since we last talked on the phone. If you recall, we had a nice conversation like always. Even with time in between, it's just like we were sitting side by side yesterday. But that's how it is when you're close to someone.

Jeff called me early Monday morning and told me you've moved on. I won't be able to hear your voice again, for a while anyway. Don't think that just because you can't talk to me that I will stop talking to you.

My thoughts right now are like lightning bolts. They fly everywhere and just when one ends another bursts in my memory. We had some real fun when I was a boy. We rode together in the red '59 Impala with that white convertible top. Laughing and going nowhere in particular. Then we took it to Grace Elementary School, so you and your softball team could practice. I believe this was the first time I ever saw a group of grown men having as much fun as us kids.

I remember taking a bus from north Asheville to downtown, so I could watch you working as a DJ. You spun those 45s, read that copy, and talked to the microphone like it was a close friend. I'll never forget those hours watching you there. But when you let me come into the control room and sit right there, while it was all happening, were the best times!

You interceded with management; often trying to get some semblance of a reduced sentence from her. Many times, you succeeded, but those times, when management had enough of me, you stayed with me for a while so I could calm down.

We had golf, basketball in the driveway, teaching me and the neighbor kids the Iowa single-wing offense in the street, and helping me with my bad temper. There was my first taste of Pabst Blue Ribbon after a round of golf at Beaver Lake Golf Course. You asked if I'd like a sip just after Dad went inside the house. After nodding, yes, you handed it to me and said, "Hurry up!"

When I gave you the mumps. you didn't get angry with me and did your radio show from our bedroom. I wanted to go in to watch but household management declined permission.

No matter where you are or where I am, we are buddies. Big brother and little brother doesn't quite tell the whole tale. Miles of separation make no difference. We love each other, and we always will. I'll continue recalling our experiences together. Someday, we'll sit down and have another PBR, maybe with Dad. In the meantime, expect incoming conversations.

"... and the party never ends."

Little Brother

The Last Note

DAVID BARNES

The first time I heard the song was on a cloudy, cool, and damp afternoon in a quiet neatly kept field of grass and marble. At the edge of the field were oaks and maples just beginning to show their leaves. The white of a few dogwoods tried to brighten the woods that lay just beyond a low stone wall on two sides of the field. The sound of cars driving past the cemetery and a few whispers were the only background noises to sadness and memories.

A friend of mine had been murdered, shot in the back seven times, and was now being laid to rest. Before becoming a police officer Al was a member of the United States Army. An honor guard was there to give his widow the U.S. flag and express their condolences. A 21-gun salute must have been declined, at least I have no memory of it. *Taps* was played.

Before this service the only time I ever heard *Taps* was in grade school when we learned songs related to our country's history and in the movies. I wasn't prepared for the wave of emotion that hit me as *Taps* was played by a bugle at Al's funeral. I dared not look at anyone because my eyes had filled with tears. This shouldn't be. Al was a cop and so was I. He had been a member of the force for years. I had been one for only four months but I wanted to be what he would expect, not stand there with tears in my eyes. I did sneak a look at the cop next to me who had several years of experience. He wiped his eyes and then looked straight ahead. Soon the last note drifted away and we began leaving. No one, then or later, talked about being sad at the service. Maybe the cop I saw wipe his eyes and me were the only ones affected.

As years passed, more cop friends were murdered and more funerals were held. At each one, whether the cop had been a military veteran or not, *Taps* was played. Each time my eyes welled up. As I obtained more years of experience, I wasn't fearful of looking at the faces of other cops during funeral services. Most times other cops wiped their eyes so no one would see.

My career passed and now retired I've thought about my friends who were killed and thought about cops whose bodies were the focus of crime scenes I worked. Mostly my sadness now is inside where memories live. But *Taps* continues to cause me to react the way it did at Al's service. Recently I saw a televised service of one of four U.S. Marshal's Task Force agents who were ambushed and murdered. As usual *Taps* was there. As usual, my eyes watered. I began wondering why the song impacts me the way it does.

Lights Out was the predecessor to *Taps*. It was a bugle call to officially end the day for U.S. Army soldiers up to and during the Civil War. One general decided his soldiers deserved a better song so he edited *Lights Out*. As a result *Taps* soon became the standard for the Army. At about that same time, funeral services with full military honors became problematic. Part of a traditional full honors service includes a 21-gun salute, or three volleys of seven rifles. Some of the services in the Civil War were held in close proximity to Confederate troops and a rifle volley might well cause a misunderstanding and return gunfire. The decision was made that *Taps* be played instead of the rifle salute. The song was so moving it became an on-going part of military tradition. Now I understood how its use at funerals originated and why it is used even today.

The words to Taps are haunting to me. Of course there are more words than these in the song. But the first verse is the one that my mind hears at funerals:

Taps

Day is done, gone the sun,
From the lake, from the hills, from the sky:
All is well, safely rest,
God is nigh.

I believe that each time *Taps* is played at a funeral service of a cop, other cops lose a piece of themselves. That piece travels on the last note of the song and goes into eternity with the person being interred. Bit by bit, piece by piece, every cop changes after the last note.

I wonder if the bits of ourselves we give away are replaced by fragments that are part of the cynicism and numbness we accumulate. But no matter. When my eyes well up at the playing of *Taps* I struggle to keep the tears from dropping to the ground. Instead, I give a piece of me to the cop being interred as a parting tribute.

This is a personal sentiment. Others may simply hear the song and deal with the sadness and loss in their own way. They may not realize the tribute they are giving.

The Price

DAVID BARNES

My name is Detective Sergeant Will Travers. I've been a copper for close to twenty years and currently conduct special investigations with a team of two detectives from the police department, along with two deputies from the Sheriff's Office. Special Investigations is a catch-all unit. If the powers that be decide something needs special attention, it's sent to us. Case in point: this fugitive that the whiner and I are trying to find.

How long have we been sitting in this dark hotel room? I gave my head a small shake. I didn't want to take my eyes off of the scope to look at my watch, and it wouldn't matter, anyway. We'd be here until we saw our target, or he was seen elsewhere. In my peripheral, I saw movement. It was the deputy assigned to me from the Watson County Sheriff's Office, and I was a thread's width away from throwing him out the window. I already stopped myself at least once from pushing him out and swearing he fell. He kept whining about the room, the smell in the room, and the hours we've already spent on this surveillance. Tiresome and unnecessary verbiage. This is precisely why I prefer to work by myself.

I started off answering him, but after all these days of close personal contact, now, I ignored him, unless it was work related. Being a part of a Special Investigations Unit wasn't all driving hot cars and dressing like you had more money than sense. Patience and attention to detail were the key elements. I knew if he wasn't the Chief Deputy's personal project, he wouldn't be here, so I slogged on.

While I looked through the spotting scope for our target, his job was to watch the street and adjoining buildings for unusual activity. He alternated scanning with binoculars and simply looking right and left, up and down. The only time he wasn't yapping was when he used the binoculars. I wished he used them more.

"Look at that guy on the bench over there. He sits there smoking a pipe, reading paperbacks, or a darn newspaper. What's he doing there every damn day?"

More whining.

But I smiled to myself. I knew who that guy was. My buddy here wasn't in the need to know that info. I hadn't told the man across the street we were up here, but my bet was, somehow, he knew. That man was a deep source for me, and I had named him The Wizard.

My mind drifted back to the day I first met The Wizard. I was newly assigned to the Detective Bureau and caught a missing persons case. The missing person was a seventeen-year-old girl, who had dropped out of high school, but was in the process of getting a GED through the local community college. I did all the due diligence that came to mind. After several days, there simply was no trace of the girl. As a last measure, I walked the sidewalks connecting Asheville's bars. In the 1970s, these were referred to by us cops as "redneck bars." They were honkytonks. Lots of beer, juke boxes, good ol' boys, and hookers were the norm. Sometimes, runaways ended up making money selling themselves. Though this girl's background pushed me away from that possibility. I showed her picture around and asked questions. Experience told me the hookers would be the ones to give me honest answers, if this young lady had gone to work. After an evening of questions and no answers, I called it a day, but the next day was Saturday and Saturday night more working girls would be in the bars. It was one of my days off, but I went back at about eight o'clock to talk to anyone I'd missed.

At 9:30, there wasn't anyone else to talk to, so I got a beer at Red's Tavern and just listened to the customers' banter. After finishing my beer, I walked back to my car. On the way, a guy I'd seen around the bar area over the years walked by and said just loud enough for me to hear.

"There's a note on your windshield."

After telling me this, he simply kept walking and disappeared among the throng of people looking to have a good time.

He was a smallish man of undetermined age. He had short hair, wore a straw pork-pie hat with a dark blue band, jeans, a clean light blue shirt, and western boots.

When I got back to the car, there was, indeed, a note on the windshield. It read: "The girl you're looking for is being held in a small house on the West End, the bright blue house—11 Park Street. A man called Trashman kidnapped her and is planning on adding her to his stable of working girls."

Using this information, myself, and a couple of cops from the Paddy Wagon went to West End and found her. We charged Trashman with kidnapping and other assorted violations and returned the girl to her family.

I came to call my new source The Wizard, because he provided me with bits of knowledge that often-solved cases for us. He never told me how he came by the information he gave, but it was always nearly perfect. Over the ensuing years, he gave me intelligence on other crimes the P.D. was investigating. I never told anyone about him and never contacted him. He would periodically find me and hand me a note.

Most times we pay informants for information. A person might need help with a charge against them or there would be monetary compensation. Not this guy, he never asked for or accepted any reward.

* * *

As a young man I developed a liking to hats, especially pork-pie hats. I wasn't a big man, and I thought hats gave me a jaunty look. I found that for some reason they also gave me some anonymity. People would see the hat and not my face. This was perfect, as far as I was concerned. I'm shy. I like people, well most people, and I just have difficulty communicating. My introversion must be off the charts. Keeping to myself allowed me to examine the human condition more than most.

While in grade school I noticed the ways our neighbors interacted with each other. I was disturbed by their posturing and the demeaning attitudes toward us. We were not poor, but we had less stuff, fewer material things than our neighbors. It didn't seem to bother anyone in the family. My two brothers and our parents went about their daily lives being pleasant and cordial. This was not returned to them in many cases. It seemed to me that we were not accepted as equals; we were looked down upon by the people on our street.

I once asked my father why people liked to deride others the way they did. As far as he could tell some people measured their happiness against the misery of others. I still remember the sadness in his words and on his face when he explained that to me.

After college I tried to use my psychology degree as a counselor, but since grad school wasn't where I wanted to go, the degree proved unimportant. I have a job in a small bookstore that caters to a niche clientele and pays a decent wage. The hours are really convenient, and my modest home is within walking distance of downtown.

So, I mind my business, most of the time anyway. Detective Travers misnamed me. I'm not a wizard at all. If I were to give myself a nickname, I'd be The Ear. I hear the information others throw away. I spend my time sitting or standing in places where people pass by or gather for a few minutes to talk. No one pays attention to me because I never give them a reason to do so. My bet is they never realize I'm nearby.

"What do I do with the things I hear," you may ask. Once or twice a day, I take the small bag I carry everywhere to the public library. It's right in the middle of downtown and is the one place I don't have to listen to the ups and downs of people who walk by me. My bag is where my active journals are kept. Sometimes, I spend hours writing what I hear. It can be disjointed, but every now and again, a puzzle is solved.

I have a rule. Evil is never ignored. Sometimes, I put a note on someone's car or inside a pocketbook with warnings. What they choose to do with those notes is up to them. I have provided Sergeant Travers information that helped him bring several bad guys, as he calls them, to justice.

In between working and writing, I walk the streets or sit outside a café or use one of the city's benches to listen and watch. What I hear goes into the journals, if it seems interesting.

* * *

Finally, the surveillance detail was over. The target had been arrested elsewhere, and I was now shed of the young deputy. First morning back at the office, I walked down the hall to the Robbery/Homicide squad room to see if my girlfriend was there. Standing at the doorway, the entire squad room could be scanned in less than a minute. There were only ten desks, and they were setup with two facing each other in a single row. The rest of the room held a long table and chairs, a large white board on the wall, and the entries to the Sergeant's and Lieutenant's offices.

My girlfriend wasn't in the office. Someone saw me and said she was out with her partner on a robbery case. Just as I turned to leave, two detectives walked by me going into the office. One held a straw, pork-pie hat. At the same time, I noticed the hat, one of the detectives said, "That little bookstore couldn't have had more than a couple hundred in the till. What was the purpose of knocking that place over?"

Oh crap! Not wanting to give anything away about me and the Wizard, I eavesdropped, as they walked by. Finally, there was nothing more to hear, and I was going to have to do some asking, but I had to tread carefully. Detectives jealously guard their investigations, unless they ask for or are assigned help. This wasn't my first rodeo.

I walked to my girlfriend's desk and wrote her a note that I folded and put under her phone. As I turned to leave, an idea formed.

"Hey boys one of you turning into Popeye Doyle?"

They both looked at me, puzzled.

"You know the NYPD narc, who got the French Connection?"

Still puzzled they looked at each other and shrugged.

"Never mind, it's from an old NYPD case and movie. What's with the new hat?" I asked.

The guy holding the hat looked at it and said, "Nah, it's not ours. Belongs to a vic who got robbed in that little bookstore on Vine Street."

"No way," I said. "Who'd rob that place? There's never anybody in there. I can't see how they stay in business. A perp would be wasting his time there."

"That's exactly what we said. To beat all, they gave the little guy in the store a really bad time. He's in the hospital and may not make it."

I nodded and left them to their jobs. It was a ten-minute drive to the hospital, but I made it in eight. I got his room number from the information desk and took the elevator to the seventh floor. At the ICU, I had to tell the charge nurse who I was, so she'd let me in the room. I found his name on a chart at the foot of his bed, William Prentis.

He was lying there all bandaged up, his face was badly swollen, and he had an oxygen line running to his nose. I sat down in a chair beside his bed and looked around the room. He was hooked up to a couple of machines to monitor heart rate and blood pressure. The room smelled of antiseptic. Every so often, a nurse came in, checked on him, and nodded to me. None of the nurses gave any indication of how badly he was hurt, but I could tell it was bad. After an hour, I stood and patted his arm and left.

I had to be very careful with what I planned to do next. The assigned detectives would give The Wizard's case a solid try, but I could tell from their conversation that if nothing fell together in a couple of days, the case was going to a filing cabinet. There was simply too much work for too few detectives.

I was going to do something I'd never done, since putting on the badge, but The Wizard was going to get justice.

I learned years ago that in court money buys what most people recognize to be a judicial outcome. The lesson also taught that charges, trials, verdicts, and sentencing aren't the only ways for a bad guy to get his proper payment for misdeeds. On the street, many misdeeds are corrected without use of law enforcement or courts. Street people also recognize how money and justice works. Many times, they prefer to work it out beyond the system they don't trust. That's what I had in mind here.

Working the street for a number of years, I had come to trust, almost as much as other cops, a varied stable of street characters. A few had saved my life, and a couple of others owed their lives to me. Of these two or three, I knew one, who had offered to kill a guy who was planning to put a bomb in my car. It took hours of persuasion to convince Jimmy to let me handle the problem. He didn't like it but relented in the end, as long as, I promised I'd call him if the traditional way didn't pan out some day.

I called Jimmy.

He and I met at a picnic area near the French Broad River that afternoon.

"Jimmy, how's everything in your world?" I asked.

He nodded, looked out at the river and didn't say anything for a minute or so. When he looked back at me, he gave me a thumbs up and said, "I'm good. The methadone program you insisted I enter has helped me stay moderately clean."

"Moderately?" I asked.

"Hey man, you know how it goes, I don't shoot up anymore, but that first time high is still on my mind. The program has kept me away from Dilaudid, but I still pop a pill now and again, and there's always pot and Budweiser." He gave me a half smile.

I nodded. Jimmy would never be completely free of the desire to get high. He used various drugs for too long, and his brain thought it needed a chemical assistance to get by. A man with more money would have gone to an in-house program to get his mental condition back on the right track, but he wasn't of that ilk.

Jimmy was a thief, a junkie, a robber, a very dangerous man to some, but he had become my friend. Our relationship began one fall afternoon, when a state narc introduced me to him. We were to begin an undercover operation targeting the drug Dilaudid. Heroin hadn't made it here, at that time, and Numorphan (or "blue morphine" on the street) had just faded as the arm dope of choice. There weren't many big dealers, half a dozen or so, but these folks fed a steady supply of pills to street dealers and thus to junkies in all parts of our small city.

He didn't like me, at first. He was tall and skinny. I was tall and looked like a biker. He told me I was too old to buy any pills. He was wrong. We cleaned up every dealer who was in business at that time dealing Dilaudid.

"How are you doing, Will? I haven't heard from you in a while."

"Jimmy, we haven't talked in exactly one week," I said with a smile.

"Well, that could be a lifetime in my world. You bring any coffee and maybe a donut from Dunkin'?" he asked, as he walked to my car and looked inside.

He opened the driver's door and retrieved a bag and two coffees. He handed me one coffee and pulled the lid on the other. He must have dumped ten sugars in and then added two creams. He didn't offer me any of the donuts because he knew they were all his.

We walked over to a picnic table and sat down. After he'd eaten a couple jelly filled pastries, he laughed and said. "Man, these are almost as good as a buzz I can get from a needle."

We talked small talk, friend to friend conversation, for a few minutes. Then, I told him what I wanted.

"Jimmy, a guy I know has been beaten and robbed. He may not make it, and no one knows who assaulted him. The detectives, who caught the case, have a full plate, and I don't think they're going to go anywhere with this. You know how it goes. No leads and after a while, it's filed away. I want you to find out who did this to him, and then, I want you to help me bring that mutt to justice."

He looked at me for a minute, drank some more coffee, and ate another donut. Then, he looked away and asked, "Is this going to court justice or my kind?"

When he turned back to me, I simply said, "Your kind."

He smiled. “This guy is more than just a vic to you, isn't he?”

“He is,” was all I said.

“Tell me what there is to tell, Will.”

I gave him every detail about The Wizard and what happened except that he helped me for years. Jimmy already figured that out on his own.

Jimmy and I knew just about all of each other's secrets. He is a bad guy, and an informant. But those were technical details that others needed so that a semblance of order, of normalcy, could be observed. Those of us who were down in the gutter, on the street, making cases against drug dealers, had other rules.

Jimmy and I were the same, and we were different. We scratched and clawed through the miasma of the drug underworld trying to make those, who caused the most misery, pay the price of breaking the law. We were different in the way we went about getting the job done. I had rules, the law. I had taken an oath to defend the Federal and State constitutions. Jimmy had done no such thing. He once told me his only real allegiance was to me and what was left of his family. I knew he had no traditional friendships. Being a bad guy meant never trusting, never be yourself, and always be the most feared lion in the savanna. He could relax around me, because he saw me as an equal, albeit an equal with rules.

Jimmy walked over to a trash can and threw in his coffee cup and the donut bag. He came back for my cup, as I finished my coffee, and just before he took it, he looked intently at me. He never said anything and showed no emotion whatsoever. When he took my cup, he turned and walked to the can.

Just before he put it in the trash, he asked, over his shoulder, “Do you realize what this bend in the road we've been on together for years, this new path, might push us toward? You're talking about my world. No guidelines like the civilized world pretends to use. There isn't any jury of twelve citizens. There's just us. There's only two.”

"Jimmy, this man didn't deserve what happened to him. Whoever beat him did so, because he was defenseless. If, by a slim chance, the detectives working the investigation make a case, the District Attorney in charge will find a way to reduce any charges. He has no intention of making crooks pay any true price for their crimes. He sees crime as an ill that the disadvantaged are forced to commit, because of their status in society. He once told me that he hated prosecuting those who steal, because they obviously need what they stole more than the person who owned the loot. Everything's upside down, and I won't be able to look at myself in the mirror, if the mutt who did this isn't shown the error of his ways in a fashion they fully understand. Being illegal isn't a position for me on this, being wrong is."

Jimmy nodded and sat down. "You want me to find out who did this, and then what?"

"Find out who, and let me know. I'll think just a bit after that, but my inclination is to let the street deal with the issue, as the street sees fit. Years ago, an old cop who was supposed to be training me gave me an insight that I rejected at the time.

"Crime is a disease that has always been here. It's just what some people do, if they think they can get away with it. I think there is a cure though. Let the street decide who's wrong and what penalty should be paid."

"This is the only valuable thing he ever taught me, even though I didn't recognize it at the time. The more I saw money interfering with true justice, the more I understood."

Jimmy nodded and simply replied. "I'll be in touch." He turned and walked through the park toward downtown.

Just then, I noticed the day had gone from dark and gray with rain teasing that it would begin soon, to sunny with fast moving clouds. The breeze increased and any chance of rain disappeared. I didn't dislike sunny weather, but my favorite has always been cloudy and cool with snow or rain making a promise to appear. I looked up at the sky and realized I was sad.

Nothing transpired for about a week. The Wizard was better. Jimmy hadn't tried to contact me. The detectives assigned to the investigation shoved the case to the back in the line-up of on-going work. No leads meant nowhere to go; therefore, other cases took priority. I hadn't expected any other outcome, as far as the detectives were concerned. The sheer number of new investigations each week was numbing.

One morning about ten, I was sipping on a cup of office coffee and daydreaming about going trout fishing, when my desk phone rang. The call came through to my private number and not through the secretary.

I answered and heard a familiar voice say, "Same place one hour. Bring coffee and donuts." The call then disconnected.

I sat at my desk wondering, if I really wanted to meet Jimmy. I don't usually deviate from a decision once made, but this one bothered me some. "Law and order—justice and honor" had been my mantra, until this attack on The Wizard. It was harder than I expected to allow this plan to develop. The walk to my car was a bit slower than usual.

Jimmy was sitting on the edge of one of the picnic tables and had what looked like a book of some sort. He was leafing through it, when I walked up with the coffee and donuts. He placed it on the picnic table and reached for his coffee. I placed the bag next to the book and sat down on a bench. Jimmy looked at me, as he sipped his coffee, but didn't say anything at first.

"I found the two idiots who did this." Jimmy maintained his eye contact with me. "This journal was stolen from your guy, when they took the money." He handed it to me.

I leafed through it and read some of the pages. There were notes about people he observed and heard. There were descriptions of street scenes and the weather. It was a running account of The Wizard's life, as he sat and walked around downtown. I couldn't believe how well written it was and how meticulous the details were.

"How did you find them?" I asked.

"They were drinking and bragging, Showing this journal around a couple of bars. I knew one of them really well, by reputation. He's a wanna-be bad guy, a bully. His buddy is the same. I just put a quiet word out, and it didn't take long. They don't have any friends; nobody cares a tinker's damn about either one."

I nodded and leafed through the journal again. I tried to decide if I wanted to know more than Jimmy already told me, but I felt that if I didn't ask, then, it was like hanging Jimmy out. I was all in, and the rest had to be told.

"Where are these guys now Jimmy?"

As the words spilled out, I happened to look at Jimmy's hands. His knuckles were recently scuffed. I nodded again.

"Let's just say they aren't among those crossing the River Styx. They most likely felt, as though they were going to cross, as I made a few special points in my discussion with them, however. Will, you are one of my closest friends, and I'm thinking that you would go to this length to avenge me under similar circumstances, but looking at you now I'm going to make you promise me something."

"What is it, Jimmy?"

"This kind of thing has to be a one off for you. Street justice is not what you're about brother. You are the man with the badge and the honor that goes with the metal. The judicial system in this country is messed up, but it's what keeps people like them and me from overwhelming the common man." He smiled, shrugged, and added, "Or woman."

I sipped my coffee and looked away from Jimmy. He was right. This had to be done to make my world right or as right as it gets. But it had taken a toll on me that I didn't expect and might never fully recover from. Jimmy was a standup guy to me and a force on the street.

I held his gaze and simply replied, "I promise."

"Good," he said. "Now, let's have a donut. By the way, those two fools have decided to move to Charlotte." He looked at his wristwatch. "Right now, they should be getting off of the Trailways bus. I have a friend waiting to greet them, to show them they aren't totally forgotten over here."

We talked about this for a bit, and then, Jimmy stood up, grabbed the remaining donut, and simply walked away. "See you around Will," he said over his shoulder.

I drove back to the office, where the detectives assigned The Wizard's case were talking about William Prentis. He had been released from the hospital.

I walked outside, as quickly as I could without running. I got to the parking lot and looked at the mountains in the distance. Blue and hazy just like always. I walked to my car, got in, and sat there looking out of the windshield. The Wizard was safe, and as far as I was concerned, justice had been served. But at what cost to me? Doing what seemed to be the right thing had taken part of me, and I didn't believe I could get it back. I put my forehead on the steering wheel, and for the first time in years, I cried.

The River

DESIREE BATISTE

Go with the flow, they say
try to let go
Sometimes the pull
is rushing me forward
Cold rollercoaster hands
throw me this way and that
Fear grips until
the inevitable moment
when I am becalmed
Floating as driftwood
without a care in the world
Please stay forever!
Let me just meander aimlessly
in slow peace
Not meant to be
Not for me
Smashing against the rocks
A rude wake-up call
I feign surprise
but suspected all along
I am tossed once more
never knowing when
peace will return
I can't fight it
We're all in it
A part of it
The river of life

The Phoenix

DESIREE BATISTE

Take these broken wings!
Let them fall away
Remove the safety net
Let's see how this story ends

I walk the tightrope with eyes shut tight
feeling the danger, but welcoming it
Expecting the moment when
the ground will rush up to meet me

Will that finally end the years of sadness
comparing myself to those I admire
yet always coming up short?
Surely, the answer is no

For, wherever I may go from here
be it good or bad
I will still be me when I get there
with the same fears and insecurities

I'll always wonder why
true happiness eluded me
Why only doubt and apathy
were my constant companions

Why I couldn't see the beauty within me
Why I couldn't allow love to grow as fast as hate did
Why I thought I couldn't handle any of it
Why I decided to give up, knowing it would change nothing

Knowing then that peace can't be achieved this way
I must open my eyes as I walk this fine line
Ignore the ash and soot surrounding me
I must mend these broken wings!

Being reborn does not come only through death
Our choices can breathe new life into us
I must never forget who I am
I am the Phoenix, and I will rise again!

King of Color
painting by Isaak Olson

Standing on the Edge of Time

DESIREE BATISTE

A cacophony of silence
Inky blackness lights my eyes
Every emotion flows through me at once
Standing on the Edge of Time

The clock holds no power here
Ravaging of our bodies and minds on pause
A place where I go to ponder
Standing on the Edge of Time

The world keeps spinning
Change keeps changing
The one constant I have
Standing on the Edge of Time

Take my hand!
Walk into the whispering blackness with me
From this day on, we'll always be
Standing on the Edge of Time

The edge escapes the changes
It refuses the script
No greater power can be known
than standing on the Edge of Time

"Bizzaro" America

JOSEPH S BENSON, PHD

"Bizzaro" is a comic book character, created as a villain in the *Superman* series. As a character, "Bizzaro" is a defective clone. Attempting to create an army of supermen, Lex Luther's project winds up making a monstrosity. "Bizzaro" shares many of the same powers with Superman, such as invulnerability, superhuman strength and ability to fly. Instead of heat vision and freezing breath like his enemy, "Bizzaro" has freeze vision and breathes flame.

He lives in "Bizzaro" world, a planet shaped like a cube called Earth, where values are the opposite of those in Superman's world. In many ways," Bizzaro" and his world are a mirror image of Superman and Earth. Just as in a mirror reflection, everything is backwards.

In attempting to make some sense of life in our country, I've begun to think of it as at least two opposite factions. One is the American Dream of truth, justice and the American way, where everyone can enjoy life, liberty and the pursuit of happiness. The other component is "Bizzaro" America, where lies criminal behavior and the pursuit of a self-serving, shortsighted agenda is the ideal. In "Bizzaro" America, luxury, decadence and excess are limited to an elite few, at the expense of the rest of society.

On January 6, 2021, when a frenzied mob attacked the United States Capitol, television and print media often used a phrase, "This is not my America." The unfortunate truth is that these insurgents are a significant part of our society. The number of Americans, who distrust their government and blame it for their problems, has grown rapidly. It is also a sad fact that the majority of Americans have ignored and dismissed the anti-establishment segment of society as trivial and lacking power.

There have always been members of any community, who feel left out and overlooked in regard to the rewards of their society. Feelings of isolation and little sense of belonging make people susceptible to manipulation, when a group invites them in. Behavioral and legal standards have become confused during the recent history of the United States.

Beginning with the resignation of President Richard Nixon to avoid impeachment for obstruction of justice, abuse of power and contempt of Congress, America would witness people being relieved of responsibility for their actions. At that time, Vice President Gerald Ford, who was appointed to the position, when the elected VP resigned due to his own legal problems, became an unelected U.S. President. He used the power of that office to pardon Nixon, preventing further investigation and probable conviction.

President Ford went on to grant limited amnesty to those individuals, who chose to leave the country rather than face the chance to be drafted into military service. Draft evasion was punishable with up to a $250,000.00 fine, five years in prison or both. Ford's amnesty plan required those, who applied for it, to complete two years of work in a public service job.

Ford lost the subsequent presidential election to Jimmy Carter. President Carter fulfilled a campaign promise, when he granted full amnesty to military deserters and draft evaders. Estimates range between 30,000 and 100,000 men of draft age, who fled the country to avoid being called to military service. Most of these would now be in their 70s and 80s. That equates to three generations of U.S. citizens, who learned that breaking the law can result in no legal consequences. Many more citizens were aware of this fabricated justice. U.S. citizens who felt disenfranchised were welcomed into the group who believed they are entitled to do as they please. The seeds were sown to germinate the basis for "Bizzaro" America.

The future of the democratic republic that is the United States is unknown. The country was in this position before beginning by the early to mid-19th century. Andrew Jackson's presidency was marked by replacing all federal employees not in Jackson's Democratic Party with people loyal to him. Ultimately the pendulum swung back. In the 1880s, Civil Service Reform established that Civil Service job hiring practices be based on merit, not political favors. Currently, the swing is to the political right. The next few years will establish the political way forward for our country.

"Peace cannot be kept by force; it can only be achieved by understanding."

ALBERT EINSTEIN

A Recommendation of *Albert Camus: From the Absurd to Revolt*

BRET BROKAW

I am no Camus scholar, but I wish to express my appreciation for *Albert Camus: From the Absurd to Revolt,* by John Foley, and the man it is written about. Like never before, John Foley has helped me understand Camus' life and work. Every chapter and paragraph of *Albert Camus: From the Absurd to Revolt* is highly detailed, well organized, and clearly written.

We begin with Camus' first major published essay *The Myth of Sisyphus*. Here Camus is dealing with man's absurd condition. The absurd is Camus' "first principle." In *The Myth of Sisyphus* he writes, "At this point of his effort man stands face to face with the irrational. He feels within him his longing for happiness and for reason. The absurd is born of this confrontation between the human need and the unreasonable silence of the world."

But Camus says, "the realization that life is absurd cannot be an end, but only a beginning. This is the truth that nearly all great minds have taken as their starting point. It is not this discovery that is interesting, but the consequences and rules for action that can be drawn from it." As Foley shows us, for Camus, "The absurd is a method and not a doctrine, but its recognition remains a first necessary step in the development of properly human values." He continues, saying, "... in Camus's analysis, the absurd subject, meditating on his condition, realizes at last this his condition is the common human condition, and crucially, this recognitions gives rise to a solidarity that saves the individual conscious of the absurd from both solipsism and the temptation towards nihilism." Foley ends this chapter on the absurd with a quote from the beginning of Camus' "most important work", *The Rebel*, "In our daily trials rebellion plays the same role as does the "cogito" in the realm of thought: it is the first piece of evidence. But this evidence lures the individual from his solitude. It founds its first value on the whole human race. I rebel—therefore we exist."

Foley next covers Camus' extensive political engagement between the period of writing *The Myth of Sisyphus* and *The Rebel*. Camus was thrown out of the Communist party in 1937 in his home country of Algeria because of his insistence that the local Muslim majority was a cause the party should continue to fight for, despite a change in policy from Moscow. He continued to bring attention to this injustice in the pages of the newspaper *Alger républicain* before its forced closure in 1940. This eventually led Camus to move to Paris to continue working as a political journalist. He joined *Combat*, an underground resistance newspaper. Foley comments, "The experience of Nazi Occupation and indeed the very existence of Nazism itself required Camus to address with greater urgency… the possibility, without the support of God or a regime of absolute values, of establishing an ethical code strong enough to both refute nihilism (of which Camus saw Nazism as exemplary) and justify political action." Camus writes, "… it seemed to me that man must exalt justice in order to fight against eternal injustice, create happiness in order to protest against the universe of unhappiness." Responding to a criticism of Camus' arguments, Foley writes, "Camus, after all, is not arguing that if humankind wants an ethical order, then such an order must exist, but rather that if humankind wants an ethical order, then it is capable of creating one." Another article Camus wrote around this time supports this interpretation, Camus writes, "Nothing is given to man, and the little they can conquer is paid for with unjust deaths. But man's greatness lies elsewhere. It lies in his decision to be greater than his condition. And if his condition is unjust he has only one way of overcoming it, which is to be just himself."

In the post-war, cold war period of France, we see Camus writing against his colleagues' endorsements of communist violence. In a series of articles in newspapers and journals, Camus defends his claim that, "... we must refuse all attempts to theoretically legitimize violence, whether as an absolutist *raison d'Etat* or in the interests of a totalitarian philosophy... In a world where people are occupied with opposing arguments defending the use of terror, I believe it is necessary to impose a limit to violence, to confine it when it is inevitable, to limit its terrifying effects by restricting its excesses. I have a horror of comfortable violence." Camus begins a lengthy series of articles articulating his vision of a moral politics, attempting "to define the conditions for a political position that is modest." He calls the twentieth century, the epoch in which scientific investigation has culminated in the atom bomb, the "century of fear." (Foley also notes, "Writing the day after the attack on Hiroshima, Camus was almost alone among his contemporaries in condemning it.") Camus continues, "... We suffocate among people who think they are absolutely right, whether in their machines or in their ideas. And for all that cannot live without dialogue and the friendship of other human beings, this silence is the end of the world." He also suggests there are many who "doubt that socialism has been realized in Russia or liberalism in America" and "who grant each side the right to affirm its truth but refuse it the right to impose that truth by murder, individual or collective." Foley summarizes what Camus was insisting at this time, "Instead we should aspire to a world in which "murder" is not given theoretical legitimacy. Although it would be "completely utopian to want people to stop killing people", "a much sounder utopia is that which insists that murder be no longer legitimized"... Camus claims that both Marxist and capitalist ideologies are utopian to a far greater extent, in that they are both "based on the idea of progress", and are "both certain that the application of their principles must inevitably bring about a harmonious society", a society in which violence will no longer be necessary. Furthermore, he adds, in their ready use of violence in the cause of an imagined non-violent future, "they are both at the moment costing us dearly."

Foley brings us to *The Rebel*, "Camus's most important book... we find in this essay the most detailed articulation, indeed the culmination, of many of the ideas we have examined in previous chapters. Foley outlines what Camus believes motivates an individual to revolt:

"The rebel is first and foremost one who refuses, who says "no." But, Camus observes, this refusal is also affirmative, because the declaration implies a discourse of value: the rebel must revolt in the name of something. The instant that the slave, or any human being who becomes aware of the weight of oppression on his shoulders, realizes that his master has exceeded certain limits, has trespassed upon certain rights that the slave holds to be inalienable, revolt is born. The rebel affirms the existence of a value, which must be recognized by both slave and master, and a limit to the absolute freedom the master assumes that he should enjoy. "The slave who opposes his master", says Camus, "is not concerned... with repudiating his master as a human being"—"he repudiates him as a master." "If men cannot refer to a common value, recognized by all as existing in each one then man is incomprehensible to man." Accordingly, although the act of revolt is, explicitly, the assertion of a limit that must not be transgressed by the master, it is also, implicitly, an acceptance on the part of the slave not to transgress that limit either (in other words, the slave's revolt is a refusal of both servitude and oppression). Having established this, Camus is able to assert that the solidarity of humankind is based upon revolt, "and revolt, in its turn, can only find its justification in this solidarity." Accordingly, these two mutually generating values of revolt and solidarity present the basis for an ethical understanding of legitimate political action: "We have, then, the right to say that any rebellion which claims the right to deny or destroy this solidarity loses simultaneously its right to be called rebellion and becomes in reality an acquiescence in murder. In the same way this solidarity, except in so far as religion is concerned, comes to light only on the level of rebellion. And so the real drama of revolutionary thought is announced. In order to exist, man must rebel, but rebellion must respect the limit it discovers in itself—a limit where minds meet and, in meeting, begin to exist. Rebellious thought cannot therefore dispense with memory: it is a perpetual state of tension. In studying its actions and its results, we shall have to say, each time, whether it remains faithful to its first noble premise or if, through indolence or folly, it forgets its original purpose and plunges into a mire of tyranny or servitude."

Camus proceeds to analyze "Metaphysical rebellion"—juxtaposing Prometheus and Cain, historical rebellion—beginning with Sade and the regicide of the French revolutionaries' new religion of justice, Hegel—reducing reason to history and endowing it with "a lack of moderation", Marx and state terrorism—"A Utopian Messianism", its "conception of the world is not only false but leads inexorably to murder."

Foley says, "*The Rebel* argues that the history of political or historical rebellion is to a large extent the history of the forgetting of the initial impulse that motivated it: "The slave begins by demanding justice", Camus says, "and ends by wanting to wear a crown"… Camusian revolt, exemplified in Prometheus, therefore finds its validity in its insistence upon limits. And these limits are grounded ultimately upon the consequences of the absurd: "The absurd", Camus noted in *The Myth of Sisyphus,* is "lucid reason noting its limits"… Camus proceeds to examine revolt from the perspective of the two values he suggests are at its heart—freedom and justice—and argues that the values that motivate the rebel's actions, and that his actions are designed to defend, are never absolute. The rebel is not concerned with either absolute justice or absolute freedom: "Absolute freedom is the right of the strongest to dominate. Therefore it prolongs the conflicts that profit by injustice. Absolute justice is achieved by the suppression of all contradiction: therefore it destroys freedom. The revolution to achieve justice, through freedom, ends by aligning them against each other." A legitimate revolutionary act, "a revolutionary action which wishes to be coherent in terms of its origins"... must be "uncompromising as to its means" yet will accept "an approximation as far as its ends are concerned." This he labels a philosophy "of limits" or "*la mesure*"... Although he sees much to admire in Marx... a large part of The Rebel constitutes a sustained critique of the Marxist theory of history, which he characterizes as the invocation of "History" to justify an indifference to the terrible human costs of radical political choices. Camus insists that all our political aspirations should be relative or ameliorative... undergirded by a sense of limits and moderation."

Camus thoroughly assesses assassination and capital punishment as well. Assassination is central in several of his works and Foley believes "that for Camus the following conditions, at least, must be met for an act of killing to be deemed legitimate: (1) The victim is a tyrant. (2) The act must be discriminate... The innocence of civilians is central to Camus's thinking on political violence... (3) The assassination is committed by a rebel in close proximity to his victim, and the assassin must accept full responsibility for his individual action. (4) There is no less violent alternative to assassination.

Foley continues, "One of Camus's most interesting contributions to the question of political violence is his essay on capital punishment, "Reflections on the Guillotine", first published in 1957 (a time when France was actively executing Algerian militants). Whereas, as we have seen, several of Camus's works recognize the legitimacy of political violence in certain circumstances, in this essay he rejects the use of capital punishment, which he considered to be state sanctioned murder, under any and all circumstances. Foley begins this section with a quote from Camus from a letter to a close friend, "After the liberation of Paris, I went to see one of the purge trials. The accused was, to my mind, guilty. However, I left the trial before the end because I ended up on the side of the prisoner; I've never been back to a trial of that kind. In every guilty person, there is some innocence. It is that which makes all absolute condemnation repulsive."

Foley spends a whole chapter addressing Camus's connection with Sartre, a famous intellectual during his time. Although commonly associated together, Camus wrote, again in a letter to his friend, "In spite of appearances I don't feel much in common with the work or the man." And Foley profoundly demonstrates that "their political and philosophical differences were fundamental." At the heart of their disagreement was the problem of legitimate political violence. Sartre was critical of Camus's series of political articles in 1946 and 1947. And Foley notes, "However, the clearest indication of the significance of their political and philosophical differences had already come to pass by this time, with Sartre's founding of *Les Temps modernes* in 1945.

Camus's refusal of the offer of a place on the editorial board has been explained by the fact that by this time he was editor-in-chief of *Combat*. However, it is abundantly clear that Camus did not share the values that *Les Temps modernes* sought to promote, and in January 1946 he publicly stated his fundamental disagreement with the ideas expressed in Sartre's "manifesto" in the inaugural issue of the journal, calling it "unacceptable"... It is hardly surprising given the radically different political positions adopted by Sartre and Camus by this time, as well as their complete awareness of these political differences, that when the time came, *Les Temps modernes* would review *The Rebel* negatively." Camus responded, arguing the reviewer ignored central arguments of the book and "Everything... that deals with the misfortunes and specifically political implications of authoritarian socialism."

For example, Foley says, "The question of whether or not there is a dimension of Marxist philosophy that Camus calls "a Marxist prophecy," and whether or not such a prophecy, if it exists, is not "contradicted today by numerous facts"... Camus interprets [the review's] refusal to respond directly to the discussion of Marxist historicism in *The Rebel* as not only an implicit admission of faith in that doctrine, but also an admission that such a faith was incompatible with the prevailing existentialism of *Les Temps modernes*... Camus argues in *The Rebel* that the sacrifices demanded by Marxist revolution "can only be justified in the context of a happy end to history," and now writes that [the journal's] "professed existentialism would be threatened in its very foundations if [it] accepted a foreseeable end to history." In order to reconcile [its] existentialism with Marxism, at the very least [it] would need "to demonstrate this difficult proposition: history has no end but it has a meaning that, however, does not transcend it. Perhaps, this perilous reconciliation is possible, and I would love to read it."

Camus concludes, as long as this contradiction between the fundamental freedom of the individual and the inexorable progression of history towards its end remains, the political and philosophical perspective of *Les Temps modernes* will remain contradictory, something that is both terribly cruel (because of the reality of those regimes founded on the ideology in question) and terribly trivial (because the contradiction is fundamental to *Les Temps modernes'* political agenda... in his letter responding... Camus asked Sartre to explain how *Les Temps modernes'* implicit faith in Marxist historical determinism did not contradict its founding existentialist principle of radical freedom. This particular point, made more elaborately some years later by Raymond Aron, is ignored by Sartre. (Aron considered Sartre's desired synthesis of existentialism and Marxism to be ultimately "impossible.")."

Foley's final chapter covers Camus and Algeria. Foley begins with, "Camus's attitude to Algerian independence remains highly controversial, but his position can be stated simply: although he believed Algeria was culturally and historically inextricable from France, he loathed the injustice of its system of government, which served the interests of the tiny minority of wealthy European *colons*... What Camus did wish to defend in the face of the demands for Algerian independence was what he called a "new Mediterranean culture", and... an "indigenous culture"... In December 1936, the French

Popular Front government published the *Projet Blum-Viollette,* a bill that proposed giving full French citizenship, including voting rights, to approximately 20,000 Algerian Muslims (about 0.35 per cent of the Muslim population at that time). In the face of the threat of mass resignation by the *pieds-noirs* [people of French and other European descent who were born in Algeria during the period of French rule, like Camus] members of the French parliament and the expressed hostility of the then President of the Republic, Albert Lebrun (who declared that were the plan to succeed the French National Assembly "would become the Tower of Babel and France would be governed by her former subjects"), the project was abandoned… In May 1937 Camus published a manifesto explicitly defending the plan against these attacks, arguing that… the current situation in Algeria was such that its cultural life was being suffocated: "culture could not live where dignity was dying, and a civilization could not flourish under laws which crush it… . One cannot speak of culture in a country where 900,000 inhabitants are denied schools, or of civilization, when it is a question of a people weakened by unprecedented poverty and destitution and bullied by emergency legislation and inhuman regulations"… As "the only means to restore dignity to the Muslim masses was to allow them to express themselves"… the Viollette plan must be defended as "a step toward the attainment of their right to life, which is the most elementary of rights… a stage in the complete parliamentary emancipation of Muslims… a minimum in the work of civilization and humanity which ought to be that of the new France."

Foley remarks, "… at this time Camus was deeply involved, perhaps as much as any other European Algerian, in the campaign for civil rights for Algerian Arabs and Berbers. This political commitment saw Camus, through the 1930s, politically aligned with reformist and moderate nationalists… Furthermore, postcolonial criticism not only tends to disregard Camus's relationship with Algerian nationalists; it also habitually ignores perhaps one of the most spectacular moments in Camus's early career as a political activist: his expulsion from the

Algerian Communist Party (PCA). Camus joined the party in 1935, claiming that his adherence was necessary "in order to remain close to people with whom he identified, the working class of Algiers, whose cause the Communists had annexed"... . However, about this time the Communist Party in Algeria was instructed by Moscow to abandon its pro-Arab militancy. In January 1937... Camus found former comrades being imprisoned..."in the name of a policy approved and encouraged by the [Communist Party]." Camus made his objections to the new policy well known and was soon summoned to party headquarters, where he was asked to amend his position. Instead he reiterated it, "observing that the Party had been right to support Muslim nationalists earlier and it did not have the right to discredit them now, thereby playing into the hands of the colonialists." Camus was advised by friends to resign, but refused, so the party was left with no choice but to expel him. "

"Camus's political activism continued... By 1938 he had joined the socialist newspaper *Algér republicain*... the most significant of Camus's political interventions at this time was his series of articles on the destitution he witnessed among the Berbers of the Kabylie region of Algeria, "Misère de la Kabylie." Prompted by reports in the bourgeois press extolling "the delights of Kabylie", Camus was sent to the region to report accurately on the conditions there..."... I saw children in rags fighting Kabylie dogs for the contents of a dustbin... . The poverty of this village is like the denial of the world's beauty."... The... economic hardship... was massively exacerbated by the total indifference of Algeria's political elite. (The reports were so embarrassing to the colonial government that Camus quickly became *persona non grata* in Algeria. Indeed, [according to Camus's widow] the authorities tried to "buy" Camus's silence before the articles were published.) Articles such as these prompted the authorities to shut down the newspaper at the outbreak of the Second World War in 1939... Camus was by this time so unpopular with the colonial administration that they made it impossible for him to secure work in Algeria, effectively exiling him to

France, where his former editor-in-chief, Pascal Pia, had found him a job as editorial assistant at the popular daily *Paris-Soir*. Although the focus of Camus's political concern during the war, as articulated in his articles in *Combat*, was with the struggle against Nazism, his concern for the rights of Algerian Muslims became prominent again very soon after the liberation of France."

Foley writes, "Coinciding with celebrations in France of VE Day in May 1945, Algerian nationalists paraded, celebrating the European victory over Nazism but also protesting against the… French… and waving the green and white Messaliste flag (now the national flag). Across Algeria… many of the marches turned to violent protests… rioting… resulting in the deaths of about one hundred Europeans. The French army responded with merciless repression: thousands of Muslims (some estimate that as many as seventy-five thousand) were killed. Many consider this mass murder… to constitute the real beginning of the Algerian insurrection against France… thanks to a largely quiescent media, the metropolitan French seemed to remain generally oblivious to the bloodbath carried out, in some measure, in their name. (Sartre, for example, doesn't seem to have mentioned it in print until… 1961.)"

"Although his peers may have failed to notice what had happened… Camus himself had just returned from Algeria, where he had spent more than two weeks travelling 1,500 miles around the country. The information he gathered on this journey, formulated in the context of the still unclear reports of the massacre and bloody reprisals, was then published as a series of articles in *Combat*, beginning on 13 May. In these articles… He speaks of economic, humanitarian and political crisis in Algeria, of the continued failure of the French to realize that "most Algerians are experiencing a famine"…"people are suffering from hunger and demanding justice. We cannot remain indifferent to their suffering", says Camus, alluding to the Nazi occupation, "because we have experienced it ourselves." Hence, says Camus, rather than respond "with condemnations, let us try to understand the reasons for their demands and invoke on their behalf the same democratic principles that we claim for ourselves." He speaks of the inherent injustice of a society that allocates more grain to the settler population than to the Arab population, and further that neglects to ensure that the Arab population even gets its allocated share. "To quell the cruelest of hungers and heal inflamed hearts: that is the task we face today. Hundreds of freighters filled with grain and two or three measures of strict equality: this is what millions of people are asking of us, and perhaps this will help to make it clear why we must try to understand them before we judge them." This economic and humanitarian crisis is exacerbated by the underlying political problem of an Algerian policy "distorted by prejudice and ignorance."

Foley proceeds, "In the concluding article in the series Camus laments the evanescence of French media interest in Algeria, a fact compounded by efforts to limit retrospectively the significance of the recent events... with suggestions that they had been exaggerated or that they could be blamed on a few "professional agitators." He insisted upon the need to recognize the fact of a political crisis in Algeria "to which it would be pointless and dangerous to close one's eyes", and repeated the same call he had made in his "Misère de la Kabylie" articles for *Algér republicain*: an appeal for the application of French justice in Algeria... .this... contradicts the view of... others, who accuse Camus of being unconsciously complicit in the creation of a fictionalized French Algeria; that is, an Algeria where French justice already existed. The clearest refutation of this assumption is to be found in Camus's unprecedented attack in 1947 on French policing and military tactics in Algeria and Madagascar. He reminds his readers of the use of "collective repression" in the wake of the riots... and the recent revelation regarding the existence of a "spontaneous confession chamber"... in Madagascar, and compares this to the Nazis' use of torture as a weapon against the French: "the facts are there, the clear and hideous truth: we are doing what we reproached the Germans for doing." He suggests that if the French react to this news with indifference it can only mean that they, like the Nazis, were "unconsciously certain" of their superiority to those victims of torture. Furthermore, he suggests that only when the French have "vanquished" that "racism" will they have earned the right "to denounce the spirit of tyranny and violence wherever it arises.""

"Repeatedly, in this... period, Camus intervened in the defense of North African nationalists... In 1951, he submitted an affidavit in defense of fifty-six Algerians being tried in connection with their... activism... In July 1953, in a letter to the editor of Le Monde, Camus protested against the killing by police of seven [nationalists] at a protest march in Paris, demanding an inquiry into who authorized the use of lethal force, and attributing the police violence "to a racism that dare not say its name." In April 1954 he personally appealed to President Coty on behalf of seven Tunisian nationalists who had been condemned to death (and whose testimonies were understood to have been extracted by torture). Shortly thereafter, he condemned outright "the profound infirmity of French colonialism", which "presents itself with the Declaration of the Rights of Man in one hand and the truncheon of repression in the other"... Camus contributed two articles... in July... he argued that necessary to the future of Algeria would be dialogue between European and Arabs in the political sphere... he argued for round table negotiations involving all sides in the conflict... and that in order for this to happen, the current Algerian Assembly (which was, he pointed out, the product of a rigged election) should be dissolved, and a fresh election held. A fair election could result, he suggested, in legitimate representatives of both Europeans and Muslims engaging in the creation of a new Algeria, no longer colonial possession but part of a French federation, with internal autonomy."

Foley tells us, "In November 1954 the FLN [Front de Libération Nationale] insurrection against French rule in Algeria began... in August 1955... the FLN massacred more than one hundred European Algerians and moderate Algerian nationalists... these attacks were followed by widespread, indiscriminate and disproportionate repression by the French military. This reflected a significant change in tactic for the FLN (which had not hitherto generally targeted civilians), and it also marked a significant change in France's attitude to the war, where voices demanding repression were fast drowning out calls for liberal reform and compromise… The events… prompted Camus's decision to intensify his journalistic efforts on behalf of a peaceful solution. He was anxious that the polarization of positions should not force all other voices into silence. In an open letter published in the first issue of *Communauté algérienne,* a newspaper set up by his friend Aziz Kessous… he expresses solidarity with Kessou's sentiment that European and Muslim Algerians "are condemned to live together", affirms his common cultural identity with Kessous, as an Algerian "brother", and asserts that although the existence of one million European Algerians cannot be ignored, neither is there any reason why "nine million Arabs should live on their land like forgotten men; the dream that the Arab masses can be cancelled out, silenced and subjugated is just as mad"…"you and I know that this war will not have any real victors and that, once it is over, we shall still have to go on living together forever on the same soil.""

Foley expounds, "Although Camus sought to create a space between warring factions where dialogue might take hold, it is not the case that he sought to keep this space unsullied by the presence of either of the warring factions. Given their targeting of civilians, Camus abhorrence for the FLN hardly needs explanation, but the tendency to assume he refused to have anything to do with them because they were "terrorists" is untenable… While Camus continued to press for round table negotiations involving all parties to the conflict… he also developed what was to be his most significant intervention in the conflict, the "*trêve civile*" or civilian truce. In an article in *L'Express* on the first anniversary of the FLN uprising, Camus suggested that all sides in the conflict agree, simultaneously, not to harm the civilian population, irrespective of the circumstances. This measure, were it to be adopted, would preclude both the FLN's targeted attacks on civilians and the French use of collective repression. This idea, developed in subsequent... articles, culminated in a piece... published on 10 January 1956. Here Camus calls for... a "truce until a solution is finally arrived at, a truce to the massacre of civilians, on both sides! As long as the accuser does not show an example, the accusations are vain... there is no other solution but that of which we speak. Beyond it, there is only death and destruction.""

"At the same time Camus was calling for reconciliation in Algeria, he was in regular contact with associates and friends in Algiers, in the hope of contributing to a more direct effort to the same end... these friends... both Europeans and Muslims... Concerned by the escalating violence in Algeria, the group agreed that an effort needed to be made to attempt some degree of compromise between the two communities. They decided that they would ask Camus to take a prominent role in the group "and to write its manifesto." As a result of their efforts the Comité pour une Trêve civile was formed, which comprised leading intellectuals from both the European and Muslim communities. This organization sought to forge an agreement between the two sides in the conflict whereby civilians on either side of the cultural and political divide would not be seen as legitimate targets. The group's efforts culminated in the "Call for a Civil Truce", a meeting in Algiers on 22 January 1956 at which Camus was the keynote speaker... Rather than jeering at him, right-wing *pieds-noirs* issued death threats against Camus, and attempted to hijack the meeting at which the idea of the truce was launched (by producing forged invitations), such was their implacable hostility to any policy even resembling negotiations with the FLN. In the end an angry crowd of about one thousand *pieds-noirs* did congregate outside the hall where the meeting was held, some shouting slogans such as "Camus to the Wall"... and making fascist salutes. This group was met by an even larger group of Muslims, "thousands... who had descended from the Kasbah to contain the opposition demonstrators" (the estimate of the correspondent for *Le Monde*)."

"Camus's speech echoes much of what he had been writing... in the previous six months. He dismisses the naive view that the conflict is Algeria is a question simply of a homogeneous Arab majority subjugated by a small but powerful alien French colonial minority... He asserts that as bleak as things look in Algeria, there is still hope of recovery from the seemingly endless cycle of reprisals: if each individual, "Arab or French, made an effort to think over his adversary's motives, at least the basis of a fruitful discussion would be clear." All Algerians, Arab, Berber and European, "must live together at the crossroads where history has put them." It is in this context that Camus situates his call for a civil truce. Although not sufficiently optimistic to believe that a general cessation of hostilities can be achieved in the midst of such a bloody conflict, Camus does suggest that it is at least possible "to have some impact on the most hateful aspect of the conflict: we can propose, without making any change in the present situation, that we refrain from what makes it most unforgivable—the murder of the innocent." The "civilian truce" would serve the dual function of reducing the number of non-combatants being killed in the war, and of creating a climate "for a healthy discussion that would not be spoiled by ridiculously uncompromising attitudes." If a civil truce were to hold, it would prepare "the ground for a fairer, subtler understanding of the Algerian problem.""

Foley goes on, saying, "... the FLN leader Saadi Yacef... promised... that if the French ceased executing imprisoned Algerian "patriots", the FLN would stop targeting civilians. Although the French initially showed interest, they continued to execute Algerian militants. The FLN, on the other hand, appear to have stopped their attacks on civilians, and did not resume until Yacef himself was arrested... In any event, the failure of Camus's truce appeal quickly resulted in his decision to withdraw from public discourse on Algeria: after making one final appeal in favour of the truce, he resigned from

L'Express. The polarization ... which he evidently blamed for the complete failure of the truce proposal, convinced Camus that he could no longer have any influence regarding the future of Algeria ... Camus went to Algeria hoping for an exchange between communities, and all he encountered were death threats. He did not refuse dialogue, as has been alleged, but instead found himself in a political context where dialogue was no longer possible ... It was only in a situation where dialogue was impossible that Camus reluctantly chose silence. He told friends ..."The repression by the French is without justification, without excuse ... it is necessary to say the same thing, if we are fighting for justice, about the methods of the FLN who see in every French individual living in Algeria a representative of French colonial oppression ... It is necessary to fight for the truce, for the end to the massacre of innocent individuals, in order to establish the political and moral conditions which will finally permit dialogue. And if we no longer have influence over either side, perhaps it is necessary to remain silent for a while ... When two of our brothers engage in a fight without mercy, it is criminal madness to excite one or the other of them. Between wisdom reduced to silence and madness which shouts itself hoarse, I prefer the virtues of silence. Yes, when speech manages to dispose without remorse of the existence of others, to remain silent is not a negative attitude.""

"In his Nobel Prize speech in 1957, Camus declared "The only really committed artist is he who, without refusing to take part in the combat, at least refuses to join the regular armies and remains a maverick"... At an informal question and answer session with a group of students at Stockholm University... Camus told his audience ..."I have been silent for a year and eight months now, though that does not mean that I have ceased to struggle. I have always been a partisan of a just Algeria, where the two peoples can live in peace and in equality. I have repeatedly called for justice to be done for the Algerian people, that they be granted a fully democratic regime ... I have always condemned the use of terror. And I must also condemn the use of terrorism which is exercised blindly, in the streets of Algiers for example, and which could one day strike my mother or my family. I believe in justice, but I will defend my mother before justice.""

Foley notes, "Even sympathetic critics... consider the claim to be regrettable and grounded on "poor logic." In fact, Camus made the same point on several occasions, and consequently we should avoid treating it as an unguarded comment... Indeed, the reference to his mother—far from unfortunate—pithily expressed the key philosophical concept of *limites* as it pertains to the legitimatization of political violence. The year 1957 had seen an escalation in the number of FLN attacks on civilians in Algeria (in June and July they bombed several tram stops and a casino). Such violence was only part of the endless cycle of bombings, tortures and executions, but it was nevertheless being committed in the name of justice. Camus certainly did not believe there was any justice to the French policy of brutal retaliation and *ratissage*, but the justice of the FLN's fight was frequently taken for granted... and it was this assumption that he sought to address... Camus's point was that an idea of justice that, in his estimation, licenses the indiscriminate killing of innocent civilians ("terrorism practiced blindly in the streets") is an idea of justice that he would never defend. The targeting of civilians is morally repugnant not because such attacks could conceivably kill Camus's mother, but because the victims of such an attack were inevitably like Camus's mother; that is, innocent civilians. This identification of civilians as legitimate targets was a practice Camus had addressed directly in his analysis of political violence in *The Just Assassins* and *The Rebel* and, of course, in his call for a civil truce."

Foley informs us, "Unsurprisingly, one of Camus's strongest critics on the subject of Algeria was Sartre, who considered his political differences with Camus to have been at their most significant during the Algerian war... In the November 1955 editorial in *Les Temps modernes,* titled "Algeria is not France", Sartre argued that indeed Algeria is not France and that only violence will succeed in achieving its liberation… Five days after Camus's speech in Algiers calling for a civilian truce, Sartre gave a speech in Paris at a rally "for peace in Algeria" (which began with the announcement of the FLN's benediction). Sartre speaks of the "infernal cycle of colonialism", and insists that "it is not true that there are some good *colons*, and others who are wicked. There are *colons*, and that is it", each of whom embodies "the very principles of the colonial system." Whereas Camus had insisted that the task that faced Muslim and European Algerians was to find a way to live together, and had called for immediate economic and political reforms, Sartre criticizes the "tender-hearted realist who suggested massive reforms to us, saying "The economy first!", and argues that, rather than radically overhauling the colonialism of French Algeria, the role of the French must be "to help it to die", concluding that the "neocolonialist is a fool who still believes that the colonial system can be overhauled—or a clever cynic who proposes reforms because he know that they are ineffective.""

Foley says, "Doubt about the feasibility of a peaceful solution to the Algerian conflict may have been at the source of Camus's public silence, but this silence did not mean that he had abandoned Franco-Algerian politics… it was in relation to the execution of Algerian militants that Camus hoped he could still effect some amelioration in the deteriorating situation in Algeria… As James Le Sueur observes, Camus perceived a "direct correlation between the escalation of terrorism against European civilians and the uncompromising use of the death penalty—the ultimate abuse of state power—against Algerian nationalists." Throughout this period he was actively involved in petitioning on behalf of Algerian militants condemned to death… Camus intervened in more than 150 such cases. Furthermore, beyond these direct political interventions, in 1957 Camus also published "Reflections on the Guillotine", which, as we have seen, called for the abolition of the death penalty, condemning the practice as "obviously no less repulsive than the crime" that it is designed to punish, and declaring that "this new murder, far from making amends for the harm done to the social body, adds a new blot to the first one." Nevertheless, Camus's support for the clemency for condemned militants was not given unconditionally, and he insisted that his petitions not be used as part of a public appeal."

Foley shares a quote from an anthology of Camus's writings on Algeria that Camus published in June 1958, which Foley says, "sought to delimit and explain his silence over events in Algeria, firmly attributing it to the polarization of opinion: "The truth, alas, is that a part of French opinion vaguely holds that the Arabs have in a way earned the right to slaughter and mutilate while another part is willing to justify in a way all excesses. To justify himself, each relies on the other's crime. But this is a casuistry of blood, and it strikes me that an intellectual cannot become involved in it, unless he takes up arms himself. When violence answers violence in a growing frenzy that makes the simple language of reason impossible, the role of the intellectual cannot be, as we read every day, to excuse from a distance one of the violences and condemn the other... . If they do not join the combatants themselves, their role... must be merely to strive to calm the situation so that reason will again have a chance... . We could have used moralists less joyfully resigned to their country's misfortune and patriots less ready to allow torturers to claim that they were acting in the name of France. It seems that metropolitan France was unable to think of any policies other than those which consisted in saying to the French in Algeria: "Go ahead and die; that's what you deserve" or else "kill them; that's what they deserve." That makes two different policies and a single abdication, for the question is not how to die separately but how to live together." In other words, Camus attributes his silence to the polarization of discourse in relation to Algeria. He explains his silence in the context of others' silence: on the one hand, the silence of the *pieds-noirs* in the face of the use of torture by the French, and, on the other hand, the silence of pro-FLN French in the wake of FLN massacres of *pieds-noirs*... and of Arab... supporters. He especially objected to the "lethal frivolity" with which the French Left adopted the FLN's cause, beating their *mea culpa* "on someone else's breast" (as Sartre would in 1961, in his Preface to Fanon's *The Wretched of the Earth*). As he had… in 1948, Camus condemns those intellectuals willing to "excuse" violence without themselves taking up arms.""

"Camus also includes in this volume a statement of what he believes to be legitimate and illegitimate in the demands of Algerian nationalists. He argues that they are right to denounce and reject "colonialism and its endemic abuses", "the perennial lie of constantly proposed but never realized assimilation" and "the obvious injustice of the agrarian [land] allocation and of the distribution of income." "Arab demands of all these points", Camus states, are "beyond doubt… thoroughly legitimate." However, he rejects the demand for complete Algerian independence, asserting that "as far as Algeria is concerned, national independence is an entirely emotive expression [*est une formule purement passionnelle*]. There has never yet been an Algerian nation. The Jews, the Turks, the Greeks, the Italians, the Berbers would have equal right to claim the direction of that virtual nation." This is… a statement of historical fact… far from being a general dismissal of Algerian demands as illegitimate… it is a direct riposte to the FLN's stated aim, the "*restoration* of the sovereign Algerian state." (According to their 1954 manifesto, the FLN sought "the restoration of the sovereign, democratic and social, Algerian state, within the framework of Islamic principles.")"

"In 1956, Camus [said] whereas there had been an Algerian state [*Etat*] and there was presently and Algerian homeland or country [*patrie*] "none of this has anything to do with the concept of a nation… Had I discovered the Algerian nation I would be a nationalist and I would not blush like I had committed a crime… I will not die for the Algerian nation because that nation does not exist. I have not found it. I have examined history, I have questioned the living and the dead, I visited cemeteries: no one spoke to me about it… Algeria is today a territory occupied by two peoples… each with an equal right to justice and to preserve their homeland." "At present the

Arabs do not alone make up all of Algeria… The Algerian French are likewise, and in the strongest meaning of the word, natives.""

Foley summarizes, "One may, of course, argue that even if there has never been, historically, an Algerian nation, and the territory had been ruled or occupied successively by Berbers, Phoenicians, Romans, Vandals, Arabs, Turks and Europeans, and settled in by peoples from every country in the Mediterranean region (in fact it is estimated that by 1917, only 20 per cent of European Algerians were of true French descent, and these included Alsatians and Corsicans) it was nevertheless the case that the vast majority of the people living in Algeria were Arabs and Barbers, and they no longer wanted to live under French rule. However, this takes no account of the 1.2 million European "natives", who in contrast to the popular image of "a million colons with riding crops and cigars, driving around in Cadillacs", were actually significantly less well-off than their metropolitan co-citizens. Neither does it make the FLN's aim to "restore" the sovereign Algerian state any less spurious. And it was precisely this claim that Camus was addressing."

"This point leads us to Camus's second objection to Algerian independence: the nature of Algerian nationalism. Democracy, Camus wrote in his *Carnets*, "is not the rule of the majority, but the protection of the minority." It is not possible, Camus appears to think, for France to countenance surrendering territory on which over one million of its citizens live to an authority deemed implacably hostile to it and its people. (In 1957… declared in the FLN's newspaper *El Moudjahid* that "every Frenchman currently in Algeria is an enemy combatant.") Camus, perhaps mistakenly, attributes this aspect of the FLN's demands to…"Arab imperialism", and he sees as its chief consequence "the systematic murder of French civilians and Arab civilians killed without discrimination and solely because they were French or friends of the French." He also warns that the USSR has used this rise in Arab nationalism to its own advantage, a claim that might now seem like scaremongering, although at the time there was a genuine anxiety in

Europe about the possibility of Soviet encirclement. Certainly, Camus was right to note that Soviet support for independence among colonies of the western powers contrasted starkly with its own imperialist acquisitions in Eastern Europe, not to mention its vicious repression of Muslim cultures in the Caucasus region of the USSR, in Dagestan, Chechnya and Azerbaijan, for example."

"This analysis leads Camus to conclude that he is left in a paradoxical position. Although he can approve of the "basic causes" of Algerian aspirations for independence, indeed, from the beginning of his career he had been calling on France to address Algerian grievances, he cannot accept the demand for independence itself. As Camus sees it, the aspects of the problem in Algeria can be summarized as follows: (1) the amends that must be made to eight million Arabs who have lived until now under a particular form of oppression; (2) the right of 1,200,000 autochthonous French people to exist, and to exist in their native land without ever again being subjected to the discretion of fanatical military leaders; (3) the strategic interests that determine the freedom of the West."

"In this light he suggests that France make a direct appeal to the Algerian Arabs (he notes that "since the beginning of hostilities no French Chief of State or any Governor has spoken directly to the Arab population"), proclaiming again that the era of colonialism is over, admitting to past and present mistakes and, while refusing to "yield to violence", offering "to make amends." Camus further proposes that France offer to the Algerian Arab population "a regime of free association in which every Arab, on the basis of the Lauriol Plan, will truly find the privileges of a free citizen." The Lauriol Plan envisaged a new French parliament made up of Metropolitan French, Muslim Algerian and *pied-noir* representatives, constituted strictly on the basis of proportionality, and therefore comprising approximately 600 Metropolitan, 100 Muslim Algerian and 15 French Algerian deputies. The parliament in full session, with all representatives, would have authority over everything concerning both France and Algeria (such as taxation and the budget) but, crucially, the Muslim deputies would have the right to legislate independently on all affairs concerning them alone. This arrangement would ultimately be the basis for a French commonwealth (incorporating, for example, an Algerian Assembly and a Federal Senate in which Algeria would be represented)."

"Although he freely admits that with such an offer of a federalized Algeria the difficulties only begin, Camus is quite convinced that the only equitable solution to the Algerian question, which "would do justice to all parts of the population", is some sort of federalism. The Lauriol Plan seemed to Camus "particularly adapted to Algerian realities and likely to satisfy the need for justice and freedom felt by all the communities." It respects what is particular about both communities yet brings them together "in the administration of their common interest." France, says Camus, has no choice but to accept such a federal plan and, further, if it fails to introduce it, "Algeria will be lost and the consequences will be dreadful for the Arabs and for the French. This is the last warning that a writer who for twenty years has been devoted to the service of Algeria feels he can voice before resuming his silence.""

"Camus's support for the Lauriol Plan is easy to criticize , but that criticism frequently overlooks the fact that ... it was not just the Arab that Camus expected to settle for less than absolute sovereignty... Furthermore, although it is not difficult to criticize Camus's ... rejection of the FLN in general—for being politically unrealistic, there are a number of reasons why this realist argument may not be as persuasive as it might at first seem ... the realist argument for supporting the FLN is "retrospectivist," in that it is informed by a retrospective viewpoint from which Algeria has achieved independence (an achievement that ... was, even as late as 1960, far from being a forgone conclusion). Secondly, it fails to address Camus's own objections to the realism on which it is firmly grounded. For example, in his speech in favour of a civilian truce, Camus claimed:

People are too readily resigned to fatality. They are too ready to believe that, after all, nothing but bloodshed makes history progress and that the stronger always progresses at the expense of the weaker. Such fatality exists perhaps. But man's task is not to accept it or to bow to its laws… . The task of men of culture and faith, in any case, is not to desert historical struggles nor to serve the cruel and inhuman elements in those struggles. It is rather to remain what they are, to help man against what is oppressing him, to favour freedom against the fatalities that close in upon it.

"That", says Camus, "is the condition under which history really progresses, innovates—in a word, creates. In everything else it repeats itself, like a bleeding mouth that merely vomits forth a wild stammering."

Foley concludes, "The policy of Arabization and Islamization introduced by the FLN on taking power in 1962 (to say nothing of the exodus of almost 1.5 million European and other refugees, and the FLN's thirty-year suspension of elections) constituted the conclusive destruction of Camus's long-dreamt-of-pluralist, communal "Mediterranean humanism" in Algeria and a powerful endorsement of his antipathy for the ideology and actions of the FLN. (One of the most controversial aspects of the period of decolonization was the treatment of the *Harkis,* Muslim Algerians who had fought with the French against the FLN. Some escaped to France; others remained in Algeria with their families, where as many as 150,000 were massacred.)… Noting this level of cultural imperialism in post-independence Algeria is intended only to highlight the extent to which the ideology and actions of the FLN were anathema to Camus's conception of Mediterranean humanism. Although Camus's proposed federal solution may not have been viable, it needs to be understood in the context of his rejection of political realism as well as the political disaster fomented by thirty years of FLN anti-democratic rule."

Camus would not live to see this. On 4 January 1960, he died, as a passenger in a car accident.

Rich

JEREMY K. BROWN

Joe was experiencing a run of bad luck. He'd lost his job, gambled away his savings, his car had been repossessed, and his wife had recently left him. Feeling depressed, he goes for a walk on the beach to rethink his life. As he's walking, he notices something tumbling over and lover in the waves. He looks closer and sees it's a magic lamp straight out of *Aladdin*. Figuring he has nothing to lose, he picks the lamp up and rubs it. "Poof" a genie comes out. He bows to Joe.

"Thank you for freeing me from the lamp, O great one," the genie says. "In exchange, I will grant you one wish."

That's easy!" says Joe, I want to be rich!"

The genie nods his head.

"Your wish has been granted," says the genie. "Pleasure to meet you, *Rich*."

When Raindrops Fell

SUSAN BRUMEL

In still of slumber, raindrops danced
Beneath a moonless sky
Reflecting light of distant stars,
My dreams within, waltzed by

One by one the raindrops fell,
Then splattered on the floor
Evaporating in the air—
And dreamt of never more

I often wonder where they've gone,
Perhaps forever sleeping—
Or do they dance among the stars,
My dreams within their keeping?

An Emptiness

SUSAN BRUMEL

In stagnant pond 'neath water's veil
My body lies
A statue carved of crumbling shale,
Yearnings denied

No longer rhythmic river flows,
Nor songbird sings
No longer fragile flower grows,
Nor love's light wings

Gone the music in my heart,
The sun's rise stilled
Dreams come to end before they start,
Left unfulfilled

Deception sits on canyon's ledge,
Falsehoods I've known
To be but truths I've yet to dredge,
Of life I've sown

In chambers of my heart I see,
An emptiness
In shadow of myself—just me,
No more, no less

Time passes slower by the hour,
I bide in wait...
From wrath of scepter rod I cower,
To know my fate

Imagine: Even the Elderly

LIN BRUMMELS

You may say I'm a dreamer
but I'm not the only one
I hope someday you'll join us
And the world will live as one

Imagine, by John Lennon

I dream of fixing the big three:
        a world free
from war and bondage,
no hostilities over property,

        better wells
and water systems designed
to pump so all have clean
water to drink,

        a world that does not
need guns for defense
or to make war.

Yet, I can hear the skeptics
raining disbelief
like a shower soaking me,

        telling their citizens
people can't be believed.
Rather than argue, focus

        on the right to vote.

In a good but not perfect democracy
every vote counts once
and poll workers believe voters,

        everyone can cast their ballot,
even the elderly like my mother-in-law,
age ninety-nine, who has no ID.

        If we can dream it, we can
make it happen!

Gateway to Golf
photograph by Cindy Goeller

Ash Trees Know

LIN BRUMMELS

But it seems that the wind is setting East,
and the withering of all woods may be drawing near.

—J.R.R. Tolkien

The Emerald Ash Borer
hitched a ride on cargo
from China. It is spreading
from nation to republic.

The borer has already killed
millions of Ash trees
and is expected to wipe out
all the Ash in North America.

Somehow, feeling the deaths
of distant kin, Ash trees
in my yard know the evil
beetle has arrived in Nebraska.

As if they don't want
to have a barrel of regrets,
trees produce extra seeds,
thousands every month.

Seedlings emerge in flower
beds, under the cabbages,
next to buildings and in
beans after sweet July rains.

Desperate to propagate
they seed, seed, seed,
open their branches in prayer,
ask Mother Nature for time.

"Words do not express thoughts very well. They always become a little different immediately after they are expressed, a little distorted, a little foolish."

HERMANN HESSE

Shoplifters

LIN BRUMMELS

Art washes away from the soul
the dust of everyday life.

—Pablo Picasso

Art thieves are not
your usual shoplifters.
They are often educated
art connoisseurs. Teams
of thieves' case museums
during open hours, eye
expensive but seldom viewed
masterpieces, bribe guards
or find disgruntled employees
like the assistant manager
at the British Museum
to help select the perfect
pieces stored for research
or currently not on display
and won't be missed
for months or years. Small
items like gold, precious
gems, and priceless jewelry
are easy to pocket. They
complete the heist slowly
over years. it's only when
these thieves get greedy,
start selling on e-bay
or to dodgy dealers, does

their artful shoplifting
come-to-light. Once fingered
no amount of art can wash
the dirt from their hands.

2
ink and watercolor by Richard Hanus

Four-Pickup Repair

LIN BRUMMELS

Everywhere you look in the world, the extremes have now
seemingly reached a new level. —Al Gore

Endeavoring to appreciate wind and solar
to replace fossil fuels, I try to hold charitable

thoughts about turbine even when sun rises
behind blades to create strobe effects, for weeks
near spring and fall equinoxes, hurting my head.

White pickups with solo windfarm workers
drive by every day. Drivers stare straight ahead,
unlike neighbors who wave or nod as they pass.

Turbine trouble's seriousness can be assessed
by the number of pickups parked near towers.
This repair is a four-pickup and one trailer fix.

Overhaul stops blade noise for days, provides
a welcome respite from strobe light invading
my windows, flashing shadows against trees.

The crew hoists a fearless guy in a basket
slowly along the side of each blade.

The repair noise, like sharpening a garden hoe,
is a whisper compared to the turbine's thumping
during a high wind—hard to stand, let alone accept.

Fingers crossed, hexes sent, this fix calms
turbine's usual bad temper, returns it to work
generating green power, but quieter this time.

Mary Had Another Little Iamb

MARY CAMPBELL

Do the English-speaking population of the planet
and descendants of the guys who colonized
the archipelago of Curious, the Cat Star—
couched among the first and least-dense embers
cooled, the early incubators of fertility,
where growing things analogous to trees
still thrive in colors never seen on Molokai—
require another metaphor of mine, a fresh
pathetic fallacy, with sonnets scattered
here and there for garnish? Are my
anapests and little iambs, rhymed or un-,
necessities in galaxies where volumes equaling
in heft the OED are written, polished, proofed,
and posted hourly?

If something harmless should emerge, however,
on my watch—and all the world has been assured
I don't darn socks, do auto-glass replacement,
oversee production crews for artificial kneecaps,
or approve (nor do I vilify) financial backing for
an enterprise that's innovated still another way
to package non-prescription drugs in plastic
bubbles—then perhaps I satisfy my mission,
my *raison d'être*, and my strategy for staying
out of trouble, as a poetry creator and
purveyor, pointing out, with artistry not
yet achieved by chance by chimpanzees

by banging frantically on Smith-Corona
typewriting machines, that truth is poetry
and poems are so many mangoes hanging
from not quite so many
mango trees.

I have to write, it seems. It is my contribution, my
amusement, and my destiny, which God and I
agreed upon prenatally and not a word
exchanged about utility. With inactivity
the brain begins to hum Stravinsky
or Saint-Saëns off-key and thumbs
do calisthenics so as not to stiffen
up mid-simile. And thus I keep on
doing as I wish and as I ought,
conjecturing with all the merry
liberty of infancy, *Has anybody*
ever had that thought?
Why not? So what?

Assisi, a Beautiful Place to Visit

MARY CHIRNSIDE

Assisi, Italy, a World Heritage Site, is one of my favorite places to visit. It is located in the central part of Umbria, north of Rome. The hilly landscape, dotted with olive orchards and mature well-manicured trees and hedges dividing the pastures and fields, is stunning to the eye. Crops are planted in a patchwork of soothing shades of green, brown and yellow. In the town proper, stone streets and walkways flow up and around the hilly terrain, many of which are too narrow and winding for vehicles to navigate, other than an occasional scooter. Touring is best done on foot in old, comfortable shoes. Rustic window boxes and clay pottery filled with lovely plants and bright flowers, adorn the antiquated stone buildings and paths. It is an organically beautiful site, devoid of recent manmade materials that would degrade the durability and appearance of the ancient streets and buildings. An aura of endurance permeates Assisi on both the spiritual and physical plane.

Umbria is the only landlocked region in Italy. Trains or cars are the means of accessing Assisi directly. I chose to take the train from Rome which was a pleasant experience with the gentle swaying of the train cars and the meditative rhythm of the wheels clacking on the tracks. The scenery and quaint, small towns I passed through were charming and peaceful; life just going about its ordinary daily business. Local residents were getting on and off the train, many carrying bags or baskets of produce and other goods, going from one village to the next.

St. Francis, Patron Saint of nature, animals and birds and the environment, was born in Assisi in 1182 and died in 1226. He grew up in wealth, but chose a life of poverty when he became a Catholic friar who founded the religious order of the Franciscans. His love of nature, believing it is a mirror of God, has inspired pilgrims from all over the world to walk or bike to Assisi on St. Francis' Way, sometimes wearing simple handmade garments and leather sandals.

Shortly before departing back to Rome, I observed a rather tall man, a pilgrim, barefoot and wearing a tunic made of coarse linen that was belted with a piece of rope, knotted on the ends. He carried a staff, a smooth straight branch or sapling stripped of bark, and was barely able to walk up the stone street toward the Basilica of St. Francis, as his lower legs and feet were badly swollen, callused, cracked and bleeding. It was painful to look at his feet and imagine how each step must have been pure torture. It is said that pain and discomfort are part of the pilgrim's experience, leading to greater introspection and self-awareness, thus becoming closer to God.

Assisi is visually and spiritually beautiful, a feast for the eye and the soul and a place I would love to spend time in again.

Introduction

MARY CHIRNSIDE

In 2010, the year my mother passed away, I never expected that less than a year later I would lose my son, Mark, age 29, to suicide. Even though I am an RN and was working in a prison medical setting where suicide is a constant possibility and probability, I was not prepared to face this horrific life changing event in my own life. Mark had a history of depression, but was in school in a program he loved and was excelling at it, so to say I was completely unprepared for his death was an understatement. It has now been 13 years since Mark took his life with a firearm. What I discovered was that Mark left his physical body here in a violent and final way, but he still exists "over there"! I receive signs from him as a form of comfort and love, which I am forever thankful for. More on that soon!

The word suicide is frightening. It is a word people tend to avoid any way they can. I'm convinced that we must not be afraid to confront the word or approach someone we suspect might be contemplating this final act by asking them kindly if they are ok, or are they thinking of harming themselves or of suicide.

The suicide statistics are mind boggling. The CDC data at CDC.gov/suicide/suicide-data-statistics show that suicide is one of the leading causes of death in the United States. In 2021 the final number of deaths reported was 48,183. There was 1 death every 11 minutes, 12.3 million adults seriously thought about suicide, 3.5 million adults made a plan and 1.7 million adults attempted suicide. Adult males make up approximately 50 percent of the population, but 80 percent of suicides. People over age 85 have the highest rate with people 75 to 84 close behind and ages 25 to 34 right behind that. 55 percent used firearms,

26 percent suffocation (hanging, etc), 12 percent poisoning (overdose, etc), 8 percent other methods (car crash, drowning, etc).

Sadly, this is all too common and many, many people are affected by the suicidal death of one person. I did not expect to be one of the survivors, but I am. I had the self-doubt, the questions about how as a nurse and mother I did not see this coming, what could I have done differently, but it was too much to process in the moment of realizing my son would not be back, would not come through the door, give me a hug, tease me and tell me he loved me anymore. The emptiness and heartache were gut wrenching and tears flowed endlessly.

I wrote this not to continue the sadness, but to share my experience that has become full of hope and love, which Mark gives me. I would have him back in a heartbeat if that were possible, but it is not. Those who have not experienced a loved one leave in such an unexpected and final way may not understand the happiness and joy that can come from a simple sign such as a heart on a sidewalk, a feather, a certain song, a fragrance or anything that prompts the feeling of the presence of the deceased loved one. I hope this brief look into my experience gives you a different perspective if you are not familiar with a loss of someone you love to suicide or a death of any kind for that matter, or if you are feeling that there is no hope and your loved one is gone forever.

ONLY LOVE IS REAL

After my son, Mark, took his life at age 29, my life took on a totally different meaning. I wanted answers. Was he still alive, just in a different form, was there proof, if so, what would that proof look like? From the minute I found his note to me in his room and read the part that said "only love is real," I knew there was more to us than just being here on the planet for whatever our lifetime is to be. This became part of an existential journey that had started when I was very young, living on the farm in Missouri. I had always wondered what happens next, why do people live, die, and if that's the end, why be here in the first place? Why, why, why? Mark and I would discuss and contemplate this question among others, in the garage where he would smoke and I would sit with him. Often, I would come back to the old Peggy Lee song, "Is That All There Is?"

About two weeks after Mark's funeral, I decided it was time to get back into life. I went back to the prison where I worked as an RN on the mental health unit. Prison nursing is difficult in general, but the mental health unit is different. It is very rewarding at its best, but frequently it's sad and full of despair, with frequent bouts of inmates acting out due to their mental illness. Perhaps to prolong being away from the dark feel of the facility, I decided to visit the site of Mark's last minutes on earth at the park that was his favorite, which was close to my job. I drove, thinking maybe I'd see a cigarette butt or some evidence of him, but he didn't go there to smoke, so there wasn't any. As I drove up the hill to the spot under the trees by the elk and bison area, I suddenly got a whiff of his cologne. He had not been in the car for over two weeks and usually had the window down to smoke, so that didn't explain it. The odor was sudden and strong and I knew immediately Mark was giving me a sign, my first one. I was stunned, happy, sad and bawling all at once. I knew it wasn't a hallucination, so after I checked the area for cigarette butts, I decided I'd go down the hill and circle back around to see if the fragrance came back. IT DID! I was overjoyed! As I left to go on to work, I felt I wouldn't get that particular sign again and I didn't. However, he sent many, many more!

Walking up the steps to the main entrance, through the sally port, down the long cold stairs and through the main corridor known as the spine, to my office on the D unit, I felt like a zombie, leaden feet, not much focus, tears constantly flowing, but I had a purpose and whether people like it or not, inmates need health care. Mark was always pleased that I could do this job without judgment and knew that it was a thankless job for the most part. I arrived at the nursing station, separate from my office on the unit, walked in and was met with heart breaking looks from my fellow nurses and the Nurse Practitioner. They were very supportive and kind, it was a welcome back that I needed, but wished that I didn't. I saw one nurse that was helping out from medical at another facility, and she caught my eye. I needed to tell someone about the whiff of Mark's cologne, but I knew everyone would not see it as a loving gesture from my son, but a broke-hearted attempt by his mother to bring him back. We went to a room in the back of the office and I told her what had just happened. Caroline said, "Mary, when you came in the door, I could see your aura, with Mark just above your shoulder"! I was ecstatic, but more tears poured as I wanted to see him too. Thankfully now I had someone I could confide in who understood, which was such a relief. Over the next few weeks I discovered a couple of other nurses that had similar experiences when loved ones that had passed sent them signs, so I was not alone. Knowing I was not by myself in this was a god send and being able to speak my feelings to another person that wasn't judging was what I needed more than anything at that time.

My friend and I walked in the park nearby on a daily basis after work and I would always look for another sign. Specifically, I looked for cardinals, as that is what many people see and recognize as a sign from their deceased loved ones. I saw no cardinals, but I kept anticipating that I would. I did, however, keep seeing red tailed hawks. Mark and I used to watch for hawks as we travelled from place to place. No cardinals showed up, just hawks, but I wasn't getting it. They were very close in many instances. They seemed too close, almost like they were giving me a message, but I was looking for what I thought I should get, not for what Mark was giving me. Then one night while lying in bed wondering why I wasn't seeing cardinals and feeling down about it, it occurred to me that he was sending me HAWKS! I sat straight up in bed and exclaimed "It's Hawks!" I was slow on the uptake! Signs are personal. Thanks for being patient, Mark!

All the while, I read every book I could get my hands on about "the other side." I read books by Mediums, books by people that had near death experiences (NDE), particularly by people in the medical field who had personal experiences, and books by other parents like me, who had lost a child by suicide. It was clear to me that when we pass over, it's not to become compost, it's to continue life in a different form and from what I could figure out, at this point, it sounded like a way better experience than planet Earth. I began to feel hopeful! Still broken, grieving, crying and with deep sadness beyond description, life continued on, but with a glimmer of hope. I began to get the feeling of "I know that I know." No evidence, just an unshakable sense that we do have a purpose and it continues on after death. Mark is close and it is he sending me signs, not my imagination. Tears of thankfulness flowed!

One afternoon a few weeks after Mark died, in late February or early March, I let Nina, our white German Shepherd with her missing left hind foot, outside before I went to the store with my daughter. When I attempted to bring Nina in, she would not budge from the chain link fence, because there was an eviscerated rabbit on the other side, just out of her reach. Grossed out, I got Randy, the neighbor next door and together we put the rabbit in a bag and put it in his garbage can. While we were doing that, I noticed a large, red tailed hawk on top of the power pole at the back of Randy's yard. The hawk was keeping a keen eye on the rabbit and us. I got a photo of the hawk, as he seemed very interested in the goings on! I left for an hour or so, came home and the hawk was still on the power pole watching. I had the distinct feeling that the rabbit was for Nina, who was a rescue dog that had been found in the countryside in Southeast Nebraska. With seven puppies, she was used to hunting to provide for her family and rabbit was no doubt a mainstay of her diet, as well as garbage can raids and possibly chickens. Mark had gotten Nina a few rabbits in the past and had wanted to get her one shortly before he died. I had said "No, she'll get tape worms and it'll be a hundred-dollar bill at the Vet!" Again I called my neighbor, explained that I believed this was a rabbit for Nina, from Mark, via the hawk, and that I wanted to get it out of the garbage can, which we did. With the hawk still watching from his post on the power pole, we gave the rabbit to Nina, who devoured it down to the little white cotton tail, in less than 15 minutes and only then did the hawk fly away! Yes, Nina did get tapeworms and yes, I had a hundred-dollar vet bill, but it was worth it! Mark was happy, Nina was happy, the hawk was satisfied with a job well done and I was thrilled to see how things work in coordination with the other side!

After Mark passed, I contacted his cell phone company and had the account cancelled, so no calls could be made or received and the billing was stopped. I could see the last text he sent me that said, "Please love me in death" which was incredibly heart breaking. I only looked at it a few times and each time I relived the first time I saw the text and could not bear to do that again and again. I did, however, keep the cell phone plugged in. I don't know why, other than removing the power cord seemed like accepting that he was gone and I was not ready for that. I still had a glimmer of hope that this was all a terrible dream and I would wake up from it. That did not happen. In his letter to me, he said to let his friends know and that their phone numbers were in his cell phone. I enlisted Dan, the next-door neighbor who is tech savvy, but we couldn't get to his address book. Mark was in school at Milford for Machine Tool Technology and had purchased a new computer. We decided to try accessing his computer to get the addresses, but it was also locked. Over the next couple of weeks after Dan got home from work, he managed to get into it. As soon as Dan said he was in, Mark's cell phone, with no active account, rang with a strange, abnormal ring tone. It was not a smooth ring, just kind of jagged, like it wasn't getting enough power. His flip phone was a smart phone type with a screen on the outside and when it rang, his photo popped up! There had been nothing on the screen previously! Dan said, "That's weird!" and I said "It's Mark telling us it's about time you cracked into the computer!" Mark and Dan were always ribbing each other and it seemed like just the thing Mark would say and do! I was overjoyed! There was no way the phone should have rung and to have his photo pop up put me over the moon! Apparently that kind of encounter is somewhat common with deceased people who are good with technology and electricity, which Mark was!

Approximately two months after Mark died, my friend and I went on a trip to Italy and Germany that had been planned for months. I was hesitant, but knew it would be good to do something different. I needed a change, a different perspective. We spent the first part of the trip in Rome and one of the things I noticed immediately was that there were skulls and crossbones everywhere! There was a cathedral and/or chapel on almost every block. Memorial plaques or Memento mori, which is Latin for "Remember your death", would be on the walls outside of the building or inside in a larger collection called an ossuary. Skulls and bones were definitely everywhere I looked and it occurred to me that the Italians did not seem to be afraid of death, perhaps because they saw these reminders all the time. They grew up with this as a part of their everyday life, their culture. Our culture, in the United States, is entirely different. This was a revelation to me and the more I looked and the more photos I took of skulls and crossbones, the more comfortable I began to feel about death. I didn't think about it at the time, but by inadvertently confronting what I feared, I was relieving some of my anxiety. All this increased my desire to connect with Mark if I possibly could. During the entire time in Europe, I felt like Mark was with me. I had a sense of his presence, but he wasn't there, at least not that I could see. I knew I would have to pursue finding a medium when we returned to Lincoln.

When I got back home, I asked my hairdresser if she knew of any mediums. She saw many people in a wide variety of professions, so I figured it might be worth a try. She did! She gave me Sandra Monroe's number and after a couple of weeks thinking about it, reading about what happens and how a session works, I gave her a call. I only gave my first name and set it up for a week or so later. In a few days I got cold feet. I called Sandra back to cancel that appointment, saying that I would call another time. This was a huge step for me, I had to think and read more about it. Several weeks went by till I took a deep breath one day, got the courage to call Sandra again and set up the appointment that I kept. When I arrived and we got started, the first thing that Mark came through with was "It took you long enough to get here!" He had been nudging me frequently after I returned from the trip to Europe. I laughed and cried as it was true, I took the long circuitous route to get to Sandra! I felt like the little kid, Billy, in the Family Circus cartoon that goes a mile out of the way to get from one room to another! But the session finally happened!

It was approximately four months after Mark passed, that I went to Sandra the first time and my journey in understanding the "other side" blossomed. What a blessing it is to get validations from Mark that he is nearby and watching. A validation is something very personal that no one but the sender and receiver would know. It could be something I was thinking about, a specific thought in regard to solving a problem perhaps, something that only I would know. During one session Mark said he saw me in the backyard working with the iris. I was puzzled and said that I don't have iris in the backyard, but I have tulips and other bulbs in the front yard. Sandra said he was adamant about the iris in the backyard and then suddenly I remembered that I DID have a clump of Japanese Iris which were not in bloom and I was working right beside them the day before! That was something very personal that only I would know and obviously Mark knew as well!

After years of attending churches in the Bible belt with the fear of hell fire and damnation, things were beginning to make more sense and hope had begun to replace that fear, which was allowing me to live a more peaceful life. It was wonderful to know that I would eventually be with him again, but until that time, "More signs, please!"

And more arrived! Mark smoked, though not in the house. Over the years, I have occasionally gotten a strong smell of cigarette smoke in the basement. There are no smokers living nearby, but I would always go outside and look around to be sure no one walking or working in close proximity was smoking. Always, no one was around, so it was Mark, missing our "smoke, talk breaks!" I'm overjoyed to get that sign from him!

A year after Mark passed, I had a dream that he was lying on an object that appeared to be a large rectangular stone with a thin, white gauze-like sheet covering him. His head was bandaged in gauze with a pink tinged area where the wound was and he was looking over his right shoulder at me. One large, surreal tear fell from his right eye, like you would see in a Salvador Dali painting. Then we were hugging and swirling upward together in a misty, cone shaped tunnel that seemed pastel in color and we were going toward a light. It was the most indescribable feeling of love, peace and joy I have ever had. Then suddenly it was over! I woke up and started crying, I didn't want it to stop. It was an out of body experience for me and a visitation from Mark and I knew it beyond a shadow of a doubt. It gave me conformation of life continuing on in a wonderful form, because I experienced it for a brief moment. Fear and anxiety were gone. It was intense, passionate, so real, but no words were spoken, just knowing within my being that we were together and it was a foretaste of the future. It was unlike any dream I have ever had and I can remember it vividly to this very day.

I called Mark's best friend, Rocky, in New Jersey, and told him about the dream. He was happy for me. A few weeks later I got an email and call from him telling me about his dream! Mark came to him and they had a joyful, but brief interaction. They hugged several times; Rocky said it was like hugging the sun, energy beyond comprehension, wonderful, loving, and indescribable. Rocky didn't want it to stop, just like my dream, but he said he couldn't understand why Mark said he had to go, because he was there with a *pilot. I whooped with excitement since Mark had always wanted to be a pilot when he was young, but priorities changed and apparently when they were friends, that subject never really came up. I said, "I understand! That was for me!" It was a validation that Rocky had a visitation from Mark. Rocky didn't understand the "pilot," but I sure did! Every time I see a jet high up with a beautiful contrail, I say "I love you Mark!" Our loved ones contact us in different ways and through various people, so keep your eyes and heart open!

The second December after Mark passed, I received my first heart. It was formed from water that ran out of the garden hose in early December as I was bringing the hose into the garage for storage. Later I went outside and discovered a lovely heart on the patio where most of the water had dried. I took a picture of it and immediately showed it to my neighbors next door. Dan asked, "How did you do that?" and Randy said, "Mark did it!" That was the beginning of my collection of hearts that Mark has been giving and continues to give to me! I receive them most often when I'm stressed or down and they will appear in the most unusual places! He has always had a gift for creativity. For example, I received a heart from sock lint the other morning after a restless night of unsettled dreams. Really! A sock lint heart was in the bed when I got up. It lifted my spirits like nothing else and prompted me to put this story together. It also brought tears to my eyes, which had not fallen for quite a long time. What a relief, the sign was so healing. Again, it was another prompt or push, from the other side! Mark is funny, bright, creative and a little bit mischievous! Personality comes through! That is even more evidence that it is our loved one contacting us!

Trust your gut and your heart. Your experience is yours and it's real. There will be people that don't believe you. They have probably not had a loss of the magnitude of the death of a child, death by suicide or death of anyone who is very close to them. When they do experience that kind of loss, then their search for answers and hope will begin. There is no need to argue; your experience is real. Their time will come, or not. That is their journey. Since I am not one to hold back in putting my experiences out there, I have seen many raised eyebrows, many looks that say "poor thing, she's just grasping at straws," or arguments that the Bible warns against this, and other words of disbelief. That is their prerogative. Embrace the love sent to you by your loved one and don't be afraid to ask for a sign! "Please send me a sign." Then watch with fresh eyes! You may have been getting signs and didn't see them, just like me! They love us and want us to be happy, not sad.

Walking outside in nature is therapeutic, especially in areas with open spaces and few people or other distractions. I walk at least a couple times a day, as that's where I work out things that are on my mind. For several years, I called the sidewalks around my neighborhood "the trail of tears," since I was frequently in tears at the beginning of the walk and would come to terms with whatever the issue was by the time I'd gone a couple of miles and was back home. That is also where I've seen lots of hearts on the sidewalks. Nature is healing, tears are cathartic.

I took a picture of a heart in a tree formed from the twisting of the main branches, at my cousin's house near Overland Park, Kansas. She had lived there 20 years and had never noticed that heart in her tree by the garage. I have photos of images of two white doves that had flown into the plexi-glass at the Overland Park Arboretum where my cousin Sarah and I were touring. When I walked into a small shed that had 360-degree visibility so people could watch the birds at the feeders, the doves' very lifelike impression was on the plexi-glass. It was made from the micro dust on their feathers which leaves a residue on the glass that they collide with. White doves are symbolic of peace, love and new beginning. I felt Mark was sending me a strong message!

I have no idea whether the hearts and other signs already exist and Mark prompts me to look and see them or whether some are nudged into place by him. I just know that the signs give me comfort and hope knowing that he is nearby and watching and I am thankful for these gifts he is giving me. Because of the signs and the connection I live a much happier, more peaceful life than I would without them. This continues to be a spiritual journey and I have found that listening to my feelings and inner self has been an opportunity for personal growth. The most important thing I've found is that Mark is right, "only love is real."

EPILOGUE

My story will not be complete till I have crossed over. Thirteen years have passed. I still get hearts and other signs from Mark, the raw feelings have diminished, however, the sense of loss has not. The first several years were full of tears and sadness, but also discovering new things about myself. What I've gotten from this process so far is there's more to us than we realize, much of what we won't know till we have passed to the other side. If we are open, if we keep persevering and living a purposeful life until our last breath, there is much to be discovered here and now. I believe we are here to learn. Lessons seem to be hard, but when we have moved through a difficult time and we reflect on it later, the value is great and we would not have gained that gift without the pain. I remember those terrible minutes when I read Mark's letter on the night he died. I remember being crumpled on the floor, sobbing and saying, "Your death will not be in vain. I will do my best to help others in similar circumstances." Mark has given me the gift of love, which is the greatest gift one can receive.

About two months after I finished my story, I was in the twilight consciousness just before waking up one morning. It suddenly occurred to me that my dad was a pilot and a smoker! I had completely forgotten about him having a single-engine Cessna. Before I was born, he would fly mining supplies into the area where he had a small strip mine and would land in flat-bottom dirt about a half mile away! I was a year old, when he sold the plane, so all I remember were a couple of stories about the plane and its canvas body, but we did still have the old wooden propeller.

Dad was asthmatic from youth, smoked non-filtered Camel cigarettes, and the "extra nail in the coffin" was deciding he wanted to use the heavy equipment that he successfully sold to Allis Chalmers for several years to strip mine coal. He died at age 57 of a severe case of COPD, but I was only 11 years old, then.

Mostly what I remember was that Daddy was always ill and always had a hard time breathing. Not only did Mark want to be a pilot, he was with my Dad, the pilot who smoked, when he visited Rocky! The part I left out was that Mark wanted to buy a couple of cigarettes from Rocky, because the pilot was out. When I woke up and had my morning coffee, I reflected on how I could forget about that important bit of information that Dad was a pilot and a heavy smoker. Because smoking is frowned upon, nowadays, I wonder if I left the part of the dream out because I didn't think it was relevant, or if I thought it was a sign of personal failure, even though in the '40s and '50s smoking was very much acceptable. I can't say that I thought much about it. However, every piece of a dream is relevant, and it came back to me to further flesh out Rocky's dream.

"If you're going through Hell, keep going!"

WINSTON CHURCHILL

wheelchair & dance

JENNIFER CHOI

yes,
it was closer to crying.
your feet,
& the voice of the black singer,
shook off tears like taking off shoes covered in dirt.
i'd never learned the steps,
but when i reached out to you sitting in the wheelchair,
you smiled like a seasoned captain.
with a *calm face,*
as if you'd faced every wave of the world,
the music began again,
& our feet spread across the floor, echoing.
like grass stitching the torn earth,
like the wind bringing together the split waves,
one movement led to the next.
every time our arms drew closer,
you returned from *hell,* your face soaked in sweat,
& every time our arms parted,
you smiled from a *far-off heaven.*
a small, round wheel
took the place of your feet, spinning.
the strange boat that carried us sailed far away.

yes,
it was closer to crying,
the steps you taught me.
when my body swayed, following the path of tears,
that day's memory became a dance.
on the other side of the sea,
are you still dancing?
today, which wave
reached out to you before the stage?

the surplus of voices

JENNIFER CHOI

sitting across from the person i love,
i consume *frightening emotions.*
in a room where *blood-red clouds* swell like dough,
i don't say what's scary,
i just eat, with a *gentle face.*
a four-legged chair,
crawls up with *soft eyes,*
and mildew quietly spreads on the wall,
with no tail to wipe it away.
the person i love is *delicious,* so delicious,
the table practices a *fresh,* sorrowful expression,
time outside is *soft,*
and the more i chew my words, the tougher they become.
the room is slowly filling with things falling apart,
things that can't stop being *alive,*
things overflowing with wanting to act.
outside the window, blurry faces gather,
the claws of clouds, breaking and snapping,
only grass that regrows when cut.
i want to become a *vegetarian,*
there's a city i don't want to visit even in *death.*
the *death* i want to pretend not to see,
the dirty way things wilt,
the gulping of *goldfish,*
the bent neck in the shadows,
the fading light in the eyes,
things like the *dreams* of the sick.
like a stone that stays safe without drinking water,
tomorrow i may leave the swamp and become a person,

but the body of the world is *hollow,*
it breaks easily with even the slightest emotion.
constantly winning & losing, lumps of victory and defeat,
when i lift the stem, mouths fall with a *crash.*
leaning on the back of a frightening person,
i spit out the softened scene.
i wait for *love* to break into small pieces,
becoming each other's new skin,
burying the eyes i swallowed.
on a safe sunday night, are they all closing their windows?
i don't pick up the word "*flower.*"

"To survive, you must tell stories."

UMBERTO ECO

Sunspot

JENNIFER CHOI

In your dizziness,
　　which you keep pushing away,
　　　　there's something, I think,
　　　　　　growing secretly
on an autumn evening,
　　at dusk—
　　　　the pituitary gland,
　　　　　　a single seed.
As the sunlight flickers,
　　shrinking with your narrowed vision,
　　　　like the corona of the sun,
　　　　　　contracted in its own density,
you drift off course,
lost in confusion,
forever.

The Man Playing Go

JENNIFER CHOI

At fifty-five, he was always a loser on the battlefield.
The last game of a middle-aged man, already defeated.
Standing at the end, with nowhere else to go.
Even if he won, there were no rewards to claim.
But his hollow eyes were filled with sparks,
like a gaze that still held a trace in this world.
When the final desperate move was left,
if he couldn't strike, he had to be struck.
And so, his trembling hands finished their journey.
He was found, still in his summer clothes, in the middle of winter.
The relics of the man who played Go, still alive,
was once a shining sword—his father.

the romantic spot

JENNIFER CHOI

he sits on the sofa
his long, beautiful legs crossed
i watch quietly
as i stand
is this the basement?
after sitting for so long,
he has become part of it
in the darkness, it feels warm
i once thought darkness had a round shape
to break it, you have to stand
i stand in the corner
can i touch the shape?
i stand in the air
stones fall from the round ear
i stand, dizzy
the force that holds up the basement
he keeps breaking his beautiful legs
sitting
he can't stand up
stones fall from his legs
he walked & then came back
at the last corner where he arrived, i was sitting
how far do i have to walk to meet him?
from his legs, thick mist rises
i stand on the soil he sprinkled
this place smells familiar, warm
for a moment, he sat, but it became a round, dark spot
i, dizzy, flow out like a stone
sitting on the sofa, he looks at the scattered debris
no matter how far you walk, there's no home to return to
without a homeland, we sacrifice everything

My Dad

ED CONNOLLY

"My Dad" is a song that was recorded in 1962 by Paul Petersen. He sang it on the *Donna Reed Show*. If you haven't heard it you might want to go out to You Tube and listen to it.

I first heard this song a year or two ago. We were in Hawaii and attended the funeral of a good friend's son. Her grandson got up to sing this song, but really struggled. His brother joined him, and they got through it together. It was a real heart-tugger for me. That experience prompted me to write this article. My son never met my dad, although my daughter did. Our grandkids never knew my dad nor did my wife, who has been my wife for almost 40 years. I felt that this was a way for them to get a glimpse of him.

My Dad was born in Oak, NE, as Edwin Forrest Connolly. I am Edmond Gene Connolly. I am not a Junior. He was called Ed, and I was Eddie to avoid any confusion.

My Dad was an over the road trucker. He usually left home sometime late Sunday afternoon and returned on Friday or Saturday. If he had a shorter trip, he might be home midweek for a day or so. He had an 8th grade education but could add and subtract in his mind faster than I could with paper and pencil.

Below are some thoughts not in any particular order that still tell the story about my dad. The next to last section was written at the 2018 *Fine Lines* Creative Writing Class.

Did he love us? I never heard my dad say I love you, not to me or any of my siblings. As a matter of fact, I never heard him say I love you to Mom. But did he love us? Unequivocally, yes. The way he treated each and every one of us tells you he loved us. A Dutch-rub or whisker rub from dad was welcome activity and was never an action to create discomfort or harm. To us, it was a measure of endearment. A hug was also a good sign that he loved us. Did he have a favorite kid? Of course, he did. You may try to love every child the same, but every child is different, and when you have 13 kids, it's even tougher.

I make sure I tell my kids and grandkids I love them. Every day, I tell my wife I love her. One day, I couldn't remember if I had told her I loved her, so I said it again. She said, "You already said that."

My response was, "That's for tomorrow, in case, I forget to say, 'I love you tomorrow.'"

In my view, Dad had a great sense of humor; sometimes, people think I have a twisted sense of humor. He also loved to play pranks on his kids. I think, he also did that to some of his friends. April Fool's Day was a big one for him. If he was home that day, some of the kids would play pranks on him, not me, of course.

He also liked to tease. Never in a harmful way. He would have loved to tease my wife, and she would have given it right back to him. He would have loved it. I probably take after him on this count?

My Dad wasn't home much during the week, so you would think that, maybe, he would just veg out on the weekend. I still remember going on fishing trips. No not to some big lake, but just down the road to Turkey Creek. Now, this was no small task, as there were so many kids, and we only had one car. It took several trips to get us all there. We had to share fishing poles, and they were supplied by a friend of dad's. Who baits the hooks? The girlie girls won't touch a worm. Who takes the fish off the hook? The girlie girls won't touch a squirmy fish. In fairness, a few of my sisters did bait the hook and help take a fish off of the hook. I caught the biggest fish. A carp is a fish isn't it?

Sunday afternoon at our house was centered around games at the dining room table. Sometimes, it was gin rummy, sometimes pitch, sometimes checkers, sometimes Monopoly, although Monopoly took too long for dad to play, as he usually left sometime Sunday afternoon, AND we always had popcorn, usually buttered. Sure, it got the cards all messy, but what fun.

If he was in town on a Saturday, he would go down to the local bar and play pitch. Always 4 point, play it out for game. If you needed/ wanted to get money from him, you would go to the bar. It was a small town and an easy walk. Now, you couldn't just burst in and ask for money. That would get you a firm rejection. You waited "patiently" for the proper moment. Keeping in mind that they played for money, and if you timed it just right, and he had just won a game, you could get rich. Okay, maybe not rich, but you get what I mean. The other players in the group would shame him into giving you a little more than you asked for. What a deal.

Dad was a heavy smoker, 2–3 packs per day. Camels, unfiltered. When you're a young boy and looking to "borrow" a few to show your friends how cool you are, non-filtered is not the way to go. That may be why I never smoked. Now, to be fair, much of that 2–3 packs per day was having a cigarette between his fingers, you know, what I mean? Most of the time, the cigarette would burn down with very few puffs. My Dad had several hernia operations. After one of these, Mom was at the hospital, and he wanted a cigarette. Mom lit it for him. Yes, in those days people smoked everywhere. My Dad took one big drag and pretty typical was the coughing after the first one. He ripped the stitches out. He threw away what he had left and never smoked again. Mom quit smoking shortly after that. Tough way to quit.

Going on a week-long trip in a big truck to places you've never been seemed like some fun, right? Not so fast. Sometimes, when Mom thought I had done something wrong, her favorite words were, "Wait until your dad comes home." That usually meant a trip in the truck with Dad, assuming that it was not during the school term. This was in the time when there was no air conditioning in the truck, no power steering, and the ride was really rough. Just riding in the truck for a long time was bad enough, but the rough ride and the hot air made it worse. If you were about to fall asleep, Dad would reach over and slap you on the thigh. "Hey, are you awake?" Who could sleep through that? We usually got to where we were headed sometime in the evening. We would grab a bite to eat and then go to sleep. Usually in the truck. The next morning we got to unload whatever it was that was being hauled. Usually 50 lb. bags of something or salt blocks. It was always hot, and the sweat just poured off of me.

One time, we were unloading salt at a cheese factory someplace in Iowa. We took a break and were walking through the facility. As we approached a large vat that was processing cheese, a couple of big chunks fell out on the floor. A worker used a scoop shovel to pick up the globs and tossed them back in the vat. I didn't eat cheese for a long time after that. Dad didn't seem phased by it, as he'd probably seen things like that before.

Dad would pick up a loaf of bread and a package of minced ham (we probably call that bologna now) that we would have for meals. Once in a while, we would go into a café, where he would let me order something, and he would usually just have coffee. I didn't understand that until later. We didn't have much money, and he made sure I ate.

I never really saw Dad angry. While Mom always said, "Wait until your Dad gets home," he didn't deliver what I thought was coming.

Onetime, Dad said, "Take out the trash."

I told him, "No." I was about 12.

His comment was, "Do you think you're big enough to take me?"

My comment was, "Yup."

Big mistake.

I picked myself up off the floor and took the trash out. He back handed me so quickly. I had no bruises, except my ego. At the time, I really thought I could take him. Stupid.

We didn't go on vacations. We didn't have any money and how do you take 13 kids on vacation? We did, periodically, take Sunday trips to another small town to visit Grandma and Grandpa Connolly. We would also see two aunts who lived in the same town. We liked this trip, because Grandpa always ate his dessert first. When we asked him why, he said he wanted to make sure he had room for dessert. We couldn't all go, so we took turns. One week, when it was my turn, I had a fingernail that was barely hanging on. Dad said I couldn't go to grandpa's unless I let him pull it off. I kept saying no' until they were ready to leave without me. I folded and away we went. The thought of it was worse than the actual pulling, as it was almost off, anyway.

My Dad loved 4th of July and Christmas. He would always make sure he was home on the 4th. In his travels, he would pick up big fireworks, as well as, sparklers and smaller stuff. I'm sure it put a crimp in the budget. Some of the big stuff may not have been legal in our state.

Christmas was also a big time. We each got a couple of gifts. One year, I got a boat that Dad made. I floated it in the ditch out front when it rained. It didn't dawn on me until later that this was just a piece of 2x4, painted, with a big nail in the middle to hold the sail made out of a handkerchief. I loved that boat.

Many of the small towns around us had what we called a Fireman's picnic. The volunteer firemen sponsored the event. It included a carnival, as well as, local booths for food, including watermelon, as well as a bingo stand. Dad and Mom would play Bingo, most of the evening. We would stop by periodically to get extra money for more rides. I don't think we realized that something else would be sacrificed, because we wanted more money.

I played baseball in the summer, and our games were typically on Sunday afternoon. If the game was a home game Dad would delay leaving on his trip long enough to watch me play. I was a pitcher who also played first base or the outfield, when I wasn't pitching.

One day, Dad was sitting in the bleachers right behind our dugout with a bunch of his buddies. I was in the on-deck circle, and he said, "If you hit it over that fence, I'll give you a dollar."

I don't think there was any way that I could hit it over the fence, as I was pretty small. Well, I hit the ball pretty well, but it was never going over the fence. The ball flew over the center fielder's head, as I raced around the bases. When I got back to the dugout, I turned around and asked for my dollar.

Dad said, "It didn't go over the fence."

I said, "It was still a home run wasn't it?

His buddies prodded him until he handed me a dollar.

I think he was proud of me.

When I was a senior in high school, we were playing in the finals of the District Basketball Tournament. Dad drove all night the night before and even had to drive his truck to the game to be there on time. With 43 seconds left, a teammate stole the ball and dribbled the length of the floor and missed the layup. I think he was fouled. I followed up and tried to tip it in and got fouled. I made both free throws, and we won the game. The next morning, when I got up, Dad was waiting for me. He said he was proud of me, and he added, "Remember, it wasn't just you who won the game. All of your teammates helped get you to that point in the game."

He's right of course.

It seems like when you're younger, you want to follow in your dad's footsteps. I was no different. Even though I knew being an over-the-road-trucker was a tough job, getting to see a lot of the country was a draw. My Dad squashed that thought by saying, "If you ever decide to drive a truck for a living, I will break both of your legs." There is no way, he would do that, and then, he followed that up with, "You can do a lot more with your life than I did."

My Uncle Frank (one of Dad's brothers) helped to build the Seattle Space Needle. When he died, his attorney contacted me and then sent two checks to me. One for My Dad and one for my Uncle Harry (another of My Dad's brothers). When I took the checks to them, they both cried. Neither of them had ever had that much money ($30,000 each) before. In less than a year, the money was all gone.

When I moved away from home and Dad would pass through the city, he would call me, and I'd meet up with him for coffee, lunch, etc. One of these times, he asked me if I'd be willing to be his partner in a pitch tournament. It was the town guys playing against the country guys. The losers had to pay for the food and beverages for the night.

Now I had played a lot of pitch, but most of it was against Dad not as his partner. I was surprised by the offer, and said, "Yes."

The tournament was on a Saturday and started at noon. We did pretty well for the most part. The last game, we were behind and really needed the bid. I bid four which is the maximum. I had the jack and the three. I led the jack (it had to stand as high or we would lose). The opponent played the queen. My Dad played the ace and followed up by leading the king. We took all four points and won the game. Dad yelled what kind of a stupid bid was that. I thought you were a better pitch player than that. Our opponents said what are you complaining about you guys won the match and the country guys have to pay. After a bit, My Dad said if we have another one of these will you be my partner again? I said yes.

One day I got a call from my parents' neighbor telling me that My Dad was in bad shape. I called one of my sisters and we headed out. When we got to my parents' apartment My Dad was straddling a kitchen chair. My mom said he had been there all night and couldn't get up.

My sister and I got him off the chair and into a lounge chair. He moaned most of the time as it pained him. I finally said to him that he should go to the hospital. He asked if that's what I wanted him to do.

I said, "Yes, I think it's best."

To my surprise he said, "Okay."

I ran over to the hospital, which was only a block away and got a wheelchair. My sister and I got him in the wheelchair and wheeled him to the hospital. After talking to the doctor, it was pretty obvious that My Dad was not going home.

My Uncle Harry and My Dad had not spoken for several years, and they lived in a small town. I went to find Harry and tell him it didn't look like his brother was going to make it very long.

Harry didn't seem to be concerned.

I went back to the hospital. Much of the family was there.

When talking to the doctor, he said that there was not much they could do except try to make him comfortable.

When Uncle Harry showed up at the hospital, I was pleasantly surprised. He took My Dad's hand and talked to him. I think he was trying to say he was sorry. Before Uncle Harry left, he said he could feel My Dad's hand squeeze his, so he knew it was okay.

I think we took turns holding his hand. When I was holding his hand, I felt his hand relax in mine, and I knew, I knew. I didn't know if I could be strong.

My Dad's nickname was "Admiral." He wasn't in the service, but I guess his buddies looked up to him like that. My nickname was "Little Admiral." My license plate on my car is "Lil Adml."

I love My Dad

Jang Soo Ho

TERRI DREISMEIER

Twenty-two years ago, born far away,
My spirit animal was strong, brave, bright,
My protector, my guiding light,
The Dragon.
She hid me from all,
Her womb became my petrifying walls,
I survived,
Only to still sense unwantedness.
I was her everything,
Then she and I were cast away,
Why?
What did I do?
She cried out for a beautiful life for me,
I was no longer in that place,
Across the horizon, a stranger took me,
July 19, 2001, Jang Soo Ho.
Eomma? Appa?[1]
Whispers of Adam,
Who was he?
Did I become him?

1 Korean language for Mommy and Daddy.

Identity Bares My Layers

TERRI DREISMEIER

My camouflaged disconnections
A mere glimpse might have softened the scars
To fuse my body, mind, and soul
Sprinkles of my heritage I had worn only to become numb
Lost between two worlds
My feet touched Buddha's homeland
Born in Korea, refined in America
I was student who earned As because of my work ethic; values infused
I was with my family who saw beyond race and ethnicity, plenty
of love and courage
My command of the English language most likely better than yours,
lessons were available
And I held a 2nd degree in Songahm Taekwondo; the journey I
    endured
And at times, kicked a little "real Korean" butt, I won at tournaments,
I placed at worlds
I was a pianist and violinist, a concert master; beautiful pieces practiced
for never-ending hours
Search YouTube and hark for yourself
I was known for my kind-hearted soul, a friend to all, yet I always
    searched for
inclusiveness, acceptance, belonging
I was not a model minority myth, but identified as a minority, a
    person of color,
a foreigner who was a Korean American

Written in loving memory of Adam Dreismeier (Jang Soo Ho), Korean adoptee who died from suicide April 12, 2023.

I LIVE IN THESE UNITED STATES

Harold Dwyer, WWI Veteran

Outside tonight, it's ten below,
And hand-in-hand with that is snow;
A swirling, sifting, drifting flour
Is piling deeper by the hour.
But here within, the Andiron Twins
Have kept a fire to toast my shins.
It both reflects, and radiates,
The life in these United States.

With unlocked door and undrawn blind,
I think my thoughts, and speak my mind.
My neighbor there across the way,
May also think, and have his say.
Each night, I lay me down to sleep
Without a fear. And then down deep
Within my soul I thank the Fates
I live in these United States.

In this free land we have no dread
Of knock at night, or heavy tread.
I know I'll not be led away
And disappear, for what I say.
I know I'll not be made a slave,
And at the last, dig my own grave.
To me, no man on earth dictates—
I live in these United States!

I need no dole—I ask no bread;
I'll take my liberty instead.

With it, I'll go where choice shall lead,
And get the bread—and every need.
I'll earn these things for me and mine
The while I'm serving thee and thine.
It works that way where each man rates—
I live in these United States!

I'll always thank my lucky stars
For this fair land of food, and cars,
And lights, and rights that ease the load
As we folks journey down the road.
And I thank my God for eyes to view
That Grand Old Red and White and Blue
That waves on high and guards the gates!
I live in these United States!

SCIENCE VS. SPIRITUALITY

For all those who still believe that spirituality and science are incompatible, here are some quotes from the most popular scientist.

"When you examine the lives of the most influential people who have ever walked among us, you discover one thread that winds through them all. They have been aligned first with their spiritual nature and only then with their physical selves."

"Concerning matter, we have been all wrong. What we have called matter is energy, whose vibration has been so lowered as to be perceptible to the senses. Matter is spirit reduced to point of visibility. There is no matter."

"Time does not exist—we invented it. Time is what the clock says. The distinction between the past, present and future is only a stubbornly persistent illusion."

"Time and space are not conditions in which we live, but modes by which we think. Physical concepts are free creations of the human mind, and are not, however it may seem, determined by the external world."

"The intellect has little to do on the road to discovery. There comes a leap in consciousness, call it intuition or what you will, the solution comes to you and you don't know how or why. I think 99 times and find nothing. I stop thinking, swim in silence, and the truth comes to me."

"When something vibrates, the electrons of the entire universe resonate with it. Everything is connected. The greatest tragedy of human existence is the illusion of separateness. Our separation from each other is an optical illusion."

"A human being experiences himself, his thoughts and feelings as something separated from the rest, a kind of optical delusion of consciousness. This delusion is a kind of prison for us, restricting us to our personal desires and to affection for a few persons nearest to us. Our task must be to free ourselves from this prison by widening our circle of compassion to embrace all living creatures and the whole of nature in its beauty."

"The true value of a human being can be found in the degree to which he has attained liberation from the personal self."

"The more I learn of physics, the more I am drawn to metaphysics."

"One thing I have learned in a long life: that all our science, measured against reality, is primitive and childlike. We still do not know one thousandth of one percent of what nature has revealed to us. It is entirely possible that behind the perception of our senses, worlds are hidden of which we are unaware."

"I'm not an atheist. The problem involved is too vast for our limited minds. We are in the position of a little child entering a huge library filled with books in many languages. The child knows someone must have written those books."

"The common idea that I am an atheist is based on a big mistake. Anyone who interprets my scientific theories this way, did not understand them."

"The ancients knew something, which we seem to have forgotten."

"Energy cannot be created or destroyed, it can only be changed from one form to another."

"Everything is energy and that is all there is to it. Match the frequency of the reality you want and you cannot help but get that reality. It can be no other way. This is not philosophy. This is physics."

—Albert Einstein

A Version of Bigfoot: The Hoaxer

ANNA FAKTOROVICH

I was born in 1918, the year the last riverboat docked in La Mancha, Washington. The riverboats had brought people who did not want to live in the loud and smelly streets up in Portland down the river to a quiet half-mile town overlooking the water. Craftsman were the builders of La Mancha, and its main residents in those days. The couple hundred houses that were built back then by our own tree-loggers, blacksmiths, tin-benders, wood-cutters, and manufacturers, and much of their hand-polished furnishings are what folks still use today out here. There were many "factories", but these were just two-story houses where craftsman serviced little orders for locals. My father took jobs at a few of these shops, before starting his own blacksmithing business in a wooden shed with a tin roof, and a stone oven, tools, and an anvil inside. He trained me in wood-carving, and metal-bending when I was a kid because he needed an extra hand to fill orders. La Mancha reached its peak population when I was ten at a bit over 500, gradually declining since. I think most have stayed because they had arrived in a riverboat, but there were no more riverboats. Having built up a town out of a forest in four decades, the builders could keep fixing up their houses, while living off the land by fishing and other survivalist tricks. Those little early factories either closed or became rebranded: a distillery became an illegal home-distillation unit making moonshine.

As I finished school, I continued taking on little jobs here-and-there. While our school was basically a one-room house, our art teacher was a professional artist who had sold some paintings and sculptures in Portland, before deciding to retire to the quiet life. He taught us tricks of different arts—from clay sculpture, to paper mâché, to fine painting—and instilled an ambition in me that I could become a great artist. I always had top marks. Our one-room library had continuously displayed my pen-and-ink drawings.

These successes had made me believe that my biography was going to be like Thomas Moran's: I'd travel to some big city, and would get a wood-engraving apprenticeship, before turning to illustration for my firm, and onwards to stardom. Or like Asher Durand's: I'd apprentice to an engraver, and then my earliest commission might be engraving something fame-making like some new *Declaration of Independence*. But I learned that in the 20th century, most artists were like Roy Lichtenstein: get a college degree in art in New York City, serve in the Army doing propaganda art, then teach and do art as a hobby.

I had no money even for a trip to Portland to apply for jobs there. And there were no free-board apprenticeships available for anybody without a snotty education, who just wanted to do the hard work of manual artistic construction. To afford renting a back-room in town, I had to take on available jobs. I took a gig as a lumberjack for a timber company. I was given a felling axe, pointed to the forest, and asked to meet the daily quota. There was a dozen of us working together: all in unwashed. ragged overalls, jeans, shirts, and hats with bushy mustaches, and long-boots. We'd come through a section, and it'd look like a tornado hit it, with bits of unused wood, and trampled shrubbery. I knew one of those boys from my art classes. I started realizing that my dreams of an art career were a fantasy. The reality was I might lumberjack until somebody figured a way to do it with machinery, cutting human toil out of it.

I had not yet given up though, as I kept telling the boys, and anybody who'd listen in town about my skills, and asking for commissions to do little projects for them. My fellow lumberjacks laughed because they hardly had the money for a simple chair for their places. I tried pitching lowering my price to what they could afford, but they just didn't understand the point of having some artsy chair, or a painting of themselves looking like a dandy hoodlum on the wall. I did make some sales. The forester or lugging-company-boss heard that I was soliciting, and asked what I was pitching. He agreed with me that original wood-carved furniture had great utility in advertising the frontier spirit. He ordered a table, a couple of chairs, and closet for his office in town. I added special, matching floral designs to this set, and painted it with wood-adjacent colors. The forester reported that seeing these in the office convinced a few skilled people from the city to move to La Mancha to work, or to buy a house from that lugging company's subsidiary that sold houses. But that set was all he needed to maximize profits, so that lead dried up. I kept lugging, while in my free time trying to sell a wide range of experiments in art: traditional, commercial, furniture, abstract, and absurd. Even our general-store did not allow me to sell my projects in their aisles. Without sales, the cost of materials that I could not scavenge grew to be too burdensome. I was still making some art-for-art's-sake, but my passion for these creations was dwindling as I was starting to see them from the perspective of those who kept saying "no" to buying them.

The year after the last riverboard drifted away from our harbor, a new cheese processing plant opened, and the Great La Manchan Cheese Festival began. The factory needed to advertise their cheese, and their marketer rightly decided some folk music, free samples, and cooking competitions were the sort of sales-pitches locals could stomach. The next major change in my lifetime was when a neighboring count installed a single-landing-strip airport in 1940.

This airport had come at the perfect time. If the builder had delayed laying it, they would have struggled to find the metal and concrete for it during the shift to war-industries in WWII. With the airport in place, our cheese-processing plant happened to have the machinery, cheap labor, and access to export to win a major contract from the Pentagon in March 1942. Soon as I heard about this contract, I applied for the dozen new jobs they had suddenly listed in our town's paper. I was hired as a pasteurizing machinery operator. I did that pretty good, before pitching my artistic skills to the boss. He looked over my portfolio, and since he lacked other options asked me to design their marketing materials (selling our cheeses to generals, or whoever decided what food would be sent), and packaging for the different cheeses. As I designed these materials, I learned about the business. The Defense Department was grasping for any suitable contractors to bring food to the troops that could withstand damp, hot, cold, and otherwise miserable conditions. Our plant began churning massive volumes of hard cheeses: cougar, cheddar, and Colby-Jack. We shortened their traditional year-long aging schedules to a couple of months to maximize output. The cheese would be loaded on agricultural aircraft, flown to the closest army airport, and finally shipped to troops in Asia, or elsewhere. It is a protein source that does not easily spoil.

I was delighted to be doing commercial art for the war-effort: I was walking in Roy Lichtenstein's footsteps. But printing new designs was costly, so I mostly did other jobs for the plant once the essential artistry had been completed. I did not dare sending my "designs" to serious marketing firms to convince them to give me a next-level job in artistic design. One of the more elaborate designs had a few rectangles radiating from a central company-name, and tagline, another had wiggly shapes. The plant-owner requested the simplest possible design because it had to be a two-color print, with few fine elements that would have been distorted in our cardboard printer.

I saw the positive side of this: I had been paid for some art; I could afford my room and food; and I did not have to enlist because I was in a war-essential industry. I might have been content to work for that plant until I retired. Then, our cheese-contract was suddenly terminated right after the war ended in 1945. The boys that worked at the plant went down to the bar to drown out our terror of losing our jobs. While we were singing, and drinking, the plant-owner came in and quietly asked me to join him for a chat outside. I figured I was about to be first to be fired, but could not figure why it was happening in the middle of the night.

"I have a special art project for you," the boss said, lifting his voice, as if he was introducing the next act at a ballad convention.

"Art project? Did you find a new contract?"

"No. I'm afraid the government won't be buying any more of our cheese, and our cheese is too plain for city-folk."

"So, what's this art project about?"

"I need you to do a spectacular—arson," he said with a straight face.

"A what?" My mouth dropped. I had trouble beginning to understand what he was suggesting, or why he thought I would be interested.

"It's just like organizing a fireworks display. There's artistry involved. You must plan it just-so, or it might not fully consume the structure."

"I've never seen no fireworks in La Mancha. Maybe some firecrackers."

"No, I don't need you to set fireworks. I am trying to ask you to burn down my cheese factory," the plant-owner decided to ask me directly to avoid a misunderstanding.

"It's still in a good shape. I can do some better flyers. Maybe I can go down to Portland, and shop our cheeses around."

"I've got just enough insurance on it to start a new appliance-building plant closer to a major city. The orders we have for the coming months do not cover the water bill. I'd have to close either way. This way, I'd give you a bit of money for all your help before I go."

The way he pitched it, I figured this was a demolition job. I had demolished houses and businesses before. The old is knocked down, to clear the land for new construction.

The plant had a barrel of oil for the different things that needed oiling. I inspected the rooms of the plant from what was most and least flammable, and then layered the oil just right for the whole thing to burn once the match was lit. I took out some of the priciest equipment, and papers that the boss had some use for. We did not really have a police department in those days. Even the sheriff enlisted in the war. I had no fear of some fancy investigation finding out I had done an arson. Afterwards, the insurance agency sent an adjuster; he looked at the ambers, and spent the rest of his stay at the bar before submitting his standard loss-report. The boss gave me a pittance for my troubles, and was packed and off to start his new enterprise shortly after the adjuster.

There was now a burn-pit in the middle of town, but at least I was careful enough not to set the whole town ablaze. I should have been applying to be a smith's assistant, or a furniture polisher. But Guilt was sitting on my chest, and I felt a deep depression over contributing to scarring the town. Through this stupor, I still knew I needed some income source.

It happened to be November: the season of the Great La Manchan Cheese Festival. The organization of this event had passed from the departed cheese-factory-boss to our grand open-sewer-ditch-digger, Charles Hill. Most houses had outhouses unconnected to the waterway. Some snuck out and used the river directly to do their business. But the factories needed channels to discard their industrial waste, and their workers' sewage. Charles was digging and reinforcing with wood these ditches that connected to the river. I think most houses in La Mancha started having indoor plumbing in the 1980s. Either way, Charles was dumbfounded at being thrust into this powerful position, and terrified that the Festival would fail on his watch and go the way of the cheese-factory.

"Just how are we even going to be affording buying cheese without a factory sponsoring free samples?" Charles asked me during a planning meeting that was also attended by a few of craftsman and musicians, who were hoping to participate.

"I can design some flyers for it. We can send some to the big cities nearby with anybody heading out of town? Maybe have them sell tickets?" I tried to suggest.

We brainstormed other ideas, and came up with just enough solutions to know the Festival was going to happen, but not enough to believe anybody would attend, or it would ever happen afterwards.

After the others left, Charles came up to me as I was shifting the furniture to return the chairs to their positions before we arrived. There might have been a juju lingering on me from the arson that Charles saw because he winked: "Hey, we gotta think out of the container on this one. We need a scheme—"

"Oh, no! What scheme?" I exclaimed, terrified of what ungodly solution Charles would pitch.

"We need to get tourists to come out here. Can't you design some giant sculpture, or some other roadside attraction that would make them stop?"

"Why don't I draw a giant poster advertising the festival on the main road?"

Paved roads had been built to connect La Mancha to surrounding towns by 1923.

"Maybe. But it would be on a material that wouldn't be damaged by rain, or snow. Come to think of that, we need something like Mount Saint Helens out here."

"A volcano? That's not a probable crafts project at the scale that would interest tourists."

"The volcano is less than a hundred miles away. Tourists drive by our town on-the-regular heading for it. We just need to have something here in La Mancha that would stop, and attract them."

"What supernatural trick can I concoct that stops tourists?"

"What about a river-monster?"

"What?"

"I read about this hoax somebody pulled. They constructed a giant wooden dragon-fish-like creature, and then maneuvered it over a lake with a pulley system. They got tourists going to that lake to see this thing, and nobody caught on. They were just happy to be amazed," Charles pitched majestically, as if trying to mesmerize me.

"The current is too strong on a river. The 'creature' would get swept up in the current. So it would be a one-time outing," I deflated his enthusiasm.

"Another idea: I have a fantastic dog. He does tricks—"

"How is this relevant?"

"We can say in a news article at a Portland paper that this dog had been parachuted into enemy lines dozens of times, and had rescued American soldiers during WWII. We can say that this dog will be on-display at our Festival, and doing tricks with human-sized puppets to show how it dragged servicemen to safety."

"This is so elaborate that it might be treasonous. If you publish it, and then actually try displaying your dog as a war-hero; you'll be caught before the fest is over."

"Alright. What if we send stories in to papers that we have a championship-winning football team in La Mancha, and they'll be playing a game during the Festival?"

"Nope. We have no football team."

"That's why it's funny."

"Who'd come to a small town just to see high-school football? Anybody who'd be interested would know enough about this region's football teams to know somebody else won whatever medal you'd claim we won."

"What about this: you make a little buoy with a giant thing on top that looks like a guided missile with Soviet markings on it and we float it down the river to convince people that a Soviet K-1000 battleship has come up the river from the ocean down to La Mancha and is scoping us out while deciding if this is a good place to launch an attack."

"Yea, that sounds familiar. I heard something about those K-1000 battleships. What if they are real, and the USSR sends a real missile our way for false-advertising?"

"How about you mold giant fake bones of like a new dinosaur species, or some pre-human ape ancestor. We stage an 'expedition', and 'discover' these in some dirt, publish articles in papers about it, and put these on-display in a little museum during the fest?"

"If I could make believable fake dinosaur bones; why would I still be out here planning a cheese-festival with you, and not on display at the big museums in New York?"

"So, you are not interested in making an Indian temple, or little drawings in stone to suggest it's an ancient Cowlitz Indian burial site?"

"Why don't I just make a clay tablet with the Ten Commandments in Hebrew, and you can claim that Moses came off a mountain out here in Washington, and the Bible has been wrong about its location?"

"Yeah, perfect. Do that."

"No."

"I think you are underestimating your abilities. Why don't you try crafting something that inspires you? If you come up with something profitable; I'll give you a share of our takings. It doesn't even have to be a hoax. You can just design like a statue we can put at the side of the road with an arrow and the words 'Cheese Festival' on it. Just a bit of marketing."

"Alright, I'll try to make something," I agreed, since I had no better plans. Putting one of my sculptures in a public place would be great advertising to help me sell my art. I couldn't put one of my pieces by the road myself without somebody taking it down as a nuisance.

My father had left his antique blacksmith shop to me when died. Its equipment was at around the Bronze Age level. But I did use it whenever I needed to bend metal, or do large art projects. I found a tree that had fallen in a recent storm, and decided to begin this experiment by stripping the bark off, and slowly shopping pieces off until the wood revealed what it was meant to be. It was a long Red Alder with few branches to chop off the trunk. As I was scraping off the crustose white and black lines of lichens over its gray-brown bark, I sensed that it was like the parts of a human form: a skin, with muscle, and bone under it. I kept thinking about my refusal to attempt to make realistic bones or monster because I doubted I had the necessary skills. How difficult was it to turn wood into realistic Giant's feet?

I took of my shoes and socks, placing a sheet of cardboard under my naked feet because the floor of that shop was filthy. I kept looking down at my feet and trying to magnify their features in this wood. It was difficult even to replicate the outline of the foot, as it kept getting crooked. I finally took a pencil and sketched around the edges of my foot into the side of the drunk, and then made an approximately twice larger outline around this sketch. This worked reasonably well, so I did the same for the other foot. It took several hours just to hack off wood around this outline, and to slowly start shaving the wood into the sketched shape. Then, I realized I had to give the foot an arch, and had to cut out the individual toes. There are so many bones in the foot: it is an architectural marvel. Replicating it turned out to be a task that would have taken over a week of sketching, and slow polishing. I had started work at dawn, and it had been dark for some hours. I had been working under candle-light. My fingers were bleeding from the sand-paper. I had a couple of splinters that were too tiny to take out without getting under better light with a needle. I dropped my chisel and looked over the simple shapes I had managed to form in this extremely long stretch of time. I had been dizzy with hunger earlier, but I could not move away from these objects before making progress. And now the day was over. I had to blow out the candle, and go home to watch nightmares about this giant failure. The only way to stop torturing myself by recycling the horror of acknowledging I was a failed artist was to put a period on this project. It was impossible for me to craft a giant's feet, or a monster, or a descent displayable sculpture. Years ago, I might have had the patience to find books, and find teachers, and keep carving for weeks, but I was done. I decided I had to head to Portland, and find some good factory job there with room to move up, then use a steady income to start a family, accepting that I was a laborer, and not an originator. I stumbled down a short path between the blacksmith barn and my back-room, fell on my bed, and instantly fell asleep, undisturbed by hopes of greatness.

When I woke up it was late in the day. I grabbed a snack and a coffee from the baker, who was near-closing. As I sipped, I recalled how abruptly my work ended the night before. I pictured having left a lit candle, and that barn burning down. Or that I had forgotten to close the door with a latch, and somebody seeing its antique metal equipment from the street, and going in there to steal it. So, I went down to check on things. I learned I had closed the latch. The place was not on fire. But, as I veered with trepidation to see the monstrosity I had carved, I realized my two giant feet had been chopped off with a clean axe-mark. The rest of the trunk was still there. But the feet were gone.

"Did I burn them before going to sleep?" I asked myself aloud. Without any alcohol in my system, I could not imagine forgetting cutting and burning my woodworking project. I sat on a stool and considered alternative theories. One: I had left the door open. Somebody was walking by, saw the feet, decided they wanted them, and took them. No: unlikely. Two: There were giants in this part of Washington, and one of them got so offended by me trying to stage a prank making fun of him that he magically disappeared the insulting feet. No.

I returned to my first theory, and exclaimed: "Charles!" Obviously, he had come to check on my progress that morning, and finding my chisel tossed, and other signs I had decided to quit, and had taken what I had finished to proceed with the hoax without needing to debate the matter with me.

The ideas he had been pitching were so extreme that I grew horrified at just what Charles might end up doing with me as his now-unwilling accomplice. I chopped off the remaining part of the trunk that had been somewhat carved, and burned it to get rid of evidence I had been wood-carving. Then, I went to different shops in town asking for work in part to have alibis, and in part because I needed work to save money to move to a city. One thing that kept me somewhat calm was that the feet were just absurd, clunky shapes, and certainly could not fool a toddler or a bear into believing they were authentic.

Next morning, I woke early on hearing the rooster calling. I went to the grocer and bought a copy of the paper. On page five, I alerted to the headline: "Giant Ape-Like Footprints Found by Huckleberry Pickers in the National Forest." These huckleberry pickers had found strange prints near their truck, and at first ignored them. But as they kept leaving their truck to work the next batch, new prints kept appearing that seemed to be stalking them through the woods. They partly started paying attention because prints were getting more defined, or deeper-sunk as they were heading into muddier ground closer to the river. The newly returned from the war sheriff had been called to check if there was some giant-animal out there after huckleberry pickers. He measured the prints to be 19.2 inches, or longer than any recorded human's feet. "I read giant ancient ground sloths had 20-inch footprints, but they have three giant claws on their feet. These prints look more like a primate's. Maybe some missing link between humans and apes. I hear scientists have been looking for those."

I marched down to Charles' house. I could hear him laughing even before I knocked on the door. He opened it with the paper in his hand.

"What did you do!" I shouted. "There's a sheriff already on this case? Is he in-on-it? Why is he making up stories about missing-links?"

"I didn't plant that story. The sheriff just let his imagination fill in the blanks."

"You have to confess to planting those prints before he figures it out on his own, and charges you for making him look like an idiot!"

"No, what we have to do is lean into this, and we'll get on the front-page of regional papers," Charles corrected my panic with gleeful composure.

I tried to convince him to stop, but Charles was too ecstatic about this project for me to manage to find the nerve it would have taken to insist on crushing his insistence.

The first time he left the prints he had been careful to keep his own feet off the mud or sinkable earth, so they did not leave their own impressions. To avoid this problem, I added a compartment for human feet to fit at the top with straps to hold them in place. Now, Charles could walk in these, like in stilts. With this flexibility, Charles went down to a campsite loggers were using as their base for a logging project. And as they slept, he left these giant prints all over the site. He rummaged, tossed out and stole some of the exposed food to make it look more like a natural beast had been looking for a meal that night. I assumed this would be the end of this scheme because the sheriff would notice the space between prints was too small for foot-strides that had to be twice-larger than an average human's. But as Charles predicted, the loggers made another report to the sheriff, and he turned over his findings this time to the paper at the big neighboring county. Because there were miles between the two sites, the sheriff now questioned if there might have been two or more of these giant-primates roaming our forests. He recommended avoiding staying in the forest at night, and locking up anything that smelled like food. This county reporter coined the name "Bigfoot" to avoid repeatedly referring to the "human-ape-like-creature" or the "giant-ape."

This nickname was so catchy that big-city papers reprinted it. They even sent their own reporter to "investigate." This he questioned loggers, and fruit-pickers in our region, they all wanted to get their name in those big-city papers, so a few of them "remembered" new details about spotting a giant oil barrel having been moved by some creature in the night, or giant scratches appearing in tree bark that were larger than any they had seen before.

Every story mentioned La Mancha, and a few specified that La Mancha was best-known for its cheese-festival. So, we had a spectacular turn out for the Festival. I carved little wooden feet and sold dozens to delighted tourists, who ventured into our forests to find this Bigfoot, instead of heeding the sheriff's advice. Some philanthropists came by, and donated huge sums to the community-organization behind our festival. Charles paid me a fair share for my work.

The festival kept seeing growing numbers as they years passed, and Charles left a few refresher footprints to keep the story alive. Once he stole apples from an old woman's backyard orchard, knowing that she kept track of them, and would complain if she saw footprints that proved a trespass had indeed happened.

Though Charles eventually went too far when he decided to prank gold prospectors in a forest closer to the St. Helens volcano. Those gold-diggers are an easily-aggrieved group. They carry rifles for bears, or for thieves coming for their gold alike. With earlier winnings, I had used a black bear's hide to create a costume of Bigfoot that Charles could wear to add stronger evidence than mere footprints to our building myth.

When he departed, Charles was unsure if he would just leave prints, or would try to be sighted in his costume. Either way, he wanted to be in a costume, so that if the prospectors happened to spot him, he would not be outed as a hoaxer, but rather would be taken for a bear, or as proof of Bigfoot having been there. Once there, Charles began tossing stuff the prospectors had left outside their tents around, as he left prints. He learned the prospectors were light sleepers, as a couple of them rushed out of their tent, and immediately aimed their rifles at the bear-like figure that was in the process of tossing their sifter down a gorge. Thankfully both of their shots missed. They were probably warning shots to scare the apparent bear away. It did indeed scare it.

Charles started trying to run away, but those stilts were barely maneuverable at a slow walk. Terrified he was about to be shot, Charles picked up another sifter and tossed it at the closest tent, making its fabric collapse down at a few more now wide-awake prospectors. As a final maneuver Charles raised his fur-covered hands and gesticulated and took a couple of steps towards the prospectors. The unnatural sight of a black bear standing straight-upright, and making such awkward slow steps towards them, without any concern for the sound of gunfire frightened even the prospectors, who fled the scene, giving Charles just enough time to free his feet from those stilts, shove them under his arms and to run to his truck that was parked behind shrubbery at the side of a road.

That was the last time Charles volunteered to stage a Bigfoot sighting. Over a decade later, I resold that costume to a prankster from California, and I hear he made some famous film with it. The popularity of this Bigfoot project gave me renewed trust in myself as an artist. I made a brief experiment in creating the footprints of a giant three-towed penguin, and leaving these on beaches at low-tide, to be washed away just after they were spotted by observers. Without prints left for the next day, this hoax was not as believable. I tried making a human-sized penguin costume to convince cryptozoologists there was indeed a new species of giant penguins in Washington. Birds were just not as exciting to newswriters as ape-adjacent-humans, so I abandoned this experiment.

I decided to show my wooden Bigfoot feet to wealthy potential patrons to convince them to purchase sculptures or other art projects from me. While I was worried about outing myself at first, I learned that they either did not believe me, or had heard about the hoax and were excited to discover who was behind it. Apparently, wealthy people enjoy spending money to make poor people scared, as regular commissions started coming in. I cannot even confess about some of the artistic pranks I pulled for them because I signed NDAs.

I saved up money to build an outdoor studio with a large stove to cook enormous sheets of metal in for giant statues. Age has been catching up to me, so I hired some assistants from those fancy city art-schools, who helped polish my artistry with skills I was never taught. I erected several of my abstract metal sculptures by the highway of La Mancha, completing my initial plan of advertising my artistry somewhere it could stop traffic due to an excess of gawkers.

On May 18, 1980, Mt. St. Helens volcano erupted and covered La Mancha in volcanic ash. Despite the smell, I put on a hat, and walked around the town. It was as if God had turned my town into stone: everything was blackish-gray. People had fled, fearing being buried like the folks at Pompey.

"If only I could spray this whole town with varnish, freezing it into a giant sculpture. This is God's prank on us mortals. This is what a truly great hoax looks like!"

A Lone Chick
charcoal by Isaak Olson

Bloom

WENDY FETTERS

I am certain I have bloomed, been uprooted, and replanted more times than most of my female peers. While some would wilt under stressful circumstances, my resilience prevailed. On some days the clouds would cast a gloomy shadow, yet I thrived. With the help from rain and the grand yellow star, the joy-filled days outnumbered days of stifled growth.

My first memory of a flowerbed was one tended lovingly by my mother. She created a safe and secure home for the bulbs in the fall, and with confident anticipation we waited. Next season the prolific green leaves poked through the rich, dark earth. Such hope for new beginnings. She said flowers are like people: different sizes, shapes, colors. Yet, they all invariably elicit joy.

I would tend many gardens throughout my lifetime. I would become imbedded in other gardeners' gardens. It seems with attention and essential nourishment I blossomed in each garden. My beauty and vitality thrived. Until I didn't.

As Oprah commanded, I have turned "pain into purpose." Blooming is exhilarating. Being uprooted can be traumatic. Change can be volatile, bereft of certainty and comfort. Each time I was replanted, the sun's light filled me with hope. I refused to give in to seeds of pain.

My life's cycle has been interrupted by much pain and tragedy. It wasn't the path I envisioned for myself in my tender youth. Yet, I continued to grow. I didn't harbor regret, hatred, or anger. Planting those seeds is certain death where growth is concerned. That's not what I wanted to model to my little offshoots. I may be considered a late bloomer, a euphemism for naive, but I wanted to raise grateful sprouts. Joy is what I have embraced for my dash. You know, the time between birth and death.

As I reflect on the times I deviated from my self-prescribed perfect path, I could very well be overly bitter, jaded, and apathetic. I wanted to bloom with renewed grace. I could have withered away as I perceived haughty judgement from others who have no clue what I have endured. Who among them has ever had to call the police for domestic violence? Who among them has ever had a stalker who tried to commit suicide when he was rejected? Every single time, I steeled myself to survive. Bracing myself for the storm was the driving force. I always found my way back to the circle and came back to life where I was planted.

Eventually the trowel, God's loving mercy, would appear, uproot me, carry me to fresh soil, plant me, nourish my soul, and wait for me to bloom. My flower was renewed, my strength was replenished and hope returned.

But, with time the nourishment from the new gardener faded, and the elements proved harmful once again. When the essential components for thriving disappeared, I knew the trowel would eventually appear and transport me to a peaceful sanctuary void of damaging storms.

Over the years, my garden contained some weeds. Some noxious and toxic in an insidious way. These weeds were intent on strangling my essence, my inner beauty. Intent on stunting my growth; insisting I flower according to their landscape.

Giving me minimal nourishment doled out at their discretion. Only enough to keep me hanging on. Sometimes I was too limp to care.

My purpose is to enable other flowers to thrive. My desire is for them to proudly peek through their flowerbed, grow, and perpetuate the cycle of survival. When a warm breeze carries off their seeds of positivity into the great wilderness, may they find joy in knowing their offshoots will continue spreading strength as they rotate through their lives.

Many would argue that I did the same thing over and over and over while each time expecting a different outcome. This could be considered insanity. But, for me, the surest indication of sanity is the ability to change one's mind, intentionally choosing a healthier, happier new path. If we accept that change is constant, we need not fear the unknown. Life WILL change. So my advice is to bloom wherever you are planted. Adjust. Trim the old roots, shake off the dirt, find the sunniest spot, and make new friends in the flower bed while you blossom and flourish!

Don't put your trust in another gardener for your survival. Only you know what you require to thrive. Find those like-minded blooms to fill your soul. To nourish you and read your label. Do you need full sun or part shade? Do you need to dry out between waterings? Are you compatible with weeds? Or are some more toxic than others for your variety? Do you need protection from animals who find you tasty? You must know your own label before you can make your desires known. Be your own gardener.

Leaving a Legacy

KRISTI FITZGERALD

Many of us, the older we get, begin to feel the need to leave behind some kind of legacy. We spend our lives trying to do good for others: volunteering for non-profit organizations or events, fundraising and making donations for charities, buying gifts and necessities for local programs, or even donating food to food banks. These kinds of things can help us feel like we are doing something meaningful while we are still alive, with the possibility of the stories of our self-sacrifice and generosity outliving us. It just doesn't always feel like it will leave a lasting impact for generations to come. Some people are able to expand their charitable reach through using their talents and skills to create visual pieces of their lives to donate, pass on, or leave behind. They do it through art, craft work, music, photos, fashion, written work, film, and audio recordings just to name a few. These representations of our innermost thoughts, feelings, and dreams, are made to hopefully leave an impression created by our hands, to be held in someone else's, long after ours have been laid to rest.

For me, I have spent most of my life doing charitable work as much and as often as I can. I have often struggled financially to support myself and even with two college degrees, a teaching certificate, graduate school experience, and many, many jobs, I have found myself with only a few dollars to my name on several occasions and bankrupt on one. But even during those hard times, I would still donate what little money I had, and donate gifts, necessities, handmade items, and volunteer time to organizations and events or programs that captured my heart. I have tipped generously, having worked in food service, given small gift cards to our vet, nurses, and other service workers, having worked in retail, and left out snacks and drinks for delivery workers. I have painted faces, manned information and merchandise booths, and cleaned up at festivals and fundraisers. I have taken my dogs to assisted living and memory care centers, bought stuff off wish lists for animal shelters, donated proceeds from book sales to organizations like my state Alzheimer's association, or a special animal rescue where we got one of our dogs, and filled stockings or dropped off toys for kids in need. There is nothing better than helping someone else in need, even just a little, as every little bit helps.

Because I am creative, I have also donated things I've handmade to charities, organizations, and programs as well. I have been sewing, crafting, drawing, painting, taking pictures, and writing, since I was a kid. I have always loved giving homemade items as gifts or donating them to charity. But I also love knowing that things I create will outlive me and hopefully make someone, or many someone's, happy for years to come. Certain things like pictures, arts, crafts, fabrics, could grow old and break down eventually or be destroyed by age or elements. But others can survive and thrive by being passed on or passed down. We now live in a digital age where, even if original works disappear or are destroyed, if they have been scanned or posted online, they can spread out in the world. I have donated and sold things that are in homes from Washington to Massachusetts. I have found stories I have written listed in libraries around the world and a college student in Australia quoted one of them in her paper. Writing, actually anything creative, for me, is beautiful and personal. I pick out fabrics that speak to me, usually nature and wildlife themed, and put them together in patterns to showcase them in my quilts. I recreate images of my favorite characters, like Arwen from Lord of the Rings in pencil or watercolor, I scrapbook my life with my husband, I design and create elaborate and colorful Renaissance costumes, and I write stories, poems, and essays about my life and experiences that I send out into the world in the hopes that they move or inspire someone or at least give them a break from whatever unpleasant reality they may be facing, to lose themselves in a story, if just for a few moments.

Creating or crafting things can be therapeutic, but writing especially can be cathartic. The process, whether it be world or story building for fiction writers or connecting the dots in a rewarding way for non-fiction, getting those stories out to readers is like taking a piece of ourselves and putting it on paper and hoping readers will take good care of it. It can be scary, but the reward is when we get positive, loving feedback for any of our works, art or crafts, and our written words. That, and being part of a community with like-minded folks who share their own abilities while openly commiserating over the process is like finding another family.

I love to write. But I also love to sew, scrapbook, draw, paint, sing, take pictures and make cards, do needlework, and so on, and so on. I also love making things for the people I care about as a way of showing them how much I care. And donating handmade goods for auctions or to benefit an animal shelter or a battered women's shelter or any other local program that protects wildlife or the area or at-risk youth, etc., makes me feel like the things I make now have a higher purpose, while going to someone who really wants it. In the end, the things I have created, all these little pieces of my soul, will leave a legacy of love that will outlast me in the best possible way.

I BEFORE E

I before e
except when either your weird feisty neighbor or his eight
foreign heirs forfeit their beige heifers and seize freight

I before e
unless you leisurely deceive eight overweight
heirs to forfeit their sovereign conceits

I before e
except when your foreign neighbor receives eight counterfeit
beige sleighs from feisty caffeinated weightlifters

I before e
except if eight beige reindeer leisurely seize an overweight
freight of neighbors in their sleigh and begin to neigh

If You Could Change Time

KRISTI FITZGERALD

If you could change time, would you?
If you were given the keys to a time machine,
would you take them?
Would you open it up to the endless
possibilities that could change your reality?
If you were given instructions
on how to use a time machine,
would you use them?
would you follow the steps
To create an alternative, epic adventure?
If you could teleport through time,
would you go?
Would you fly through the stars
to a magical new destination?
If you could go back in time
and change one event, one decision, one moment,
would you do it?
Would you be the ripple in time of butterfly wings
creating future chaos?
If you could change time and be someone else
would you do it?
Would you erase who you are
for the chance to find unattainable knowledge?
If you could change time, would you?

Economics of Love

MARCIA CALHOUN FORECKI

Two silent diners stared out the window beside their booth. Once a month, Milt treated Sophie at Smalley's Diner out on Highway 36, the only extravagance Sophie allowed.

"Roy Rogers," the counter worker called out. He was too young to recognize the joke when Milt gave that name for the order. Sophie giggled into her hand. Milt half-smiled, the left side of his face still partially paralyzed from Bell's Palsy.

Milt returned with the food. Sophie whispered, "Did you get extra ketchup packs?"

"I'm having a fish filet sandwich. No one eats ketchup on fish," Milt argued.

"Those kids up at the counter don't remember what you ordered."

"Why do you want more ketchup? There is a bowl full of packets in your kitchen already," said Milt.

"I'm thinking about making a meatloaf for supper and I need ketchup for the top. You always say you love my meat loaf."

"Nevertheless, it's practically stealing."

"It is stealing. I haven't bought a bottle of ketchup since 1992," Sophie said with surprising pride.

Milt walked back to the counter. He pointed over his shoulder towards Sophie. The young man shrugged and filled both of Milt's palms with ketchup packets. When he returned to the booth, Milt deposited the packets in Sophie's open purse on the bench beside her.

After the meal, Milt cleaned up the sandwich wrappers and refilled their coffee cups. They sipped the sweet, milky coffee and conversed in short, clipped sentences. They knew each other's histories so well that few words were needed. No new information was exchanged.

They were verifying their experiences and observations from recent and far away times. As new customers arrived, Milt and Sophie took their measure and compared their conclusions.

As she rose to leave, Sophie reached across the table and straightened Milt's collar.

"I wish you'd let me have a go at your shirts with an iron, at least on the collars and front plackets. They would lay down so much smoother."

Milt whispered, "Hey, no messing with my clothes until we're married."

"Keep looking like a slob, you'll stay single."

"Should I ask you to marry me again, for the umpteenth time?"

"Maybe later," said Sophie, struggling to close her purse.

"Maybe later you'll marry me?" Milt asked.

"Maybe later ask me again. How much ice cream do we have left?" Sophie asked.

"Enough for tonight."

"Let's pick up a carton on the way. Save some gas."

Sophie absently counted on her fingers. It was an old habit, justifying every expenditure. Milt understood. She and her husband had raised a big family together. Sophie still took the smallest portion or did without. Milt loved Sophie and longed to free her from having to count every cent. He could take care of her and give her a more comfortable life.

They met while in line waiting to vote. As they inched forward, Milt began talking. That night, when the election returns were announced, Milt called Sophie.

"Congratulations," he said.

"On what? Who is this? Do you know what time it is?" Sophie said before hanging up with a bang.

Milt called again the next morning. "Hello. It's Milt, from the election line. Just called to say 'Congratulations.' Looks like it's four more years of your nitwit Governor."

Sophie recognized the voice this time. "I think you mean 'our' nitwit governor." she corrected.

Thus, began weekly meetings over coffee at McDonalds. Sophie learned about Milt's wife, gone now five years. Months passed before Sophie told Milt that she had been married twice. Her first husband died in combat during World War II only weeks after their marriage. After T.J., her second husband, died, she was eligible for a Navy widow's benefit. "I couldn't live without it," she said.

Soon, Milt was spending more time with Sofie at her house than his own. Sometimes they took naps together; always on top of the bed covers.

Sophie made meatloaf with the purloined ketchup packs. It was a mess opening and squeezing so many little packets, but worth it. She and Milt ended the evening, as always, watching the ten o'clock news and eating ice cream, one generous scoop each.

"If we have one more half-scoop each we empty the container," said Milt.

"I already had a scoop. I don't think I can eat any more tonight."

"Just a couple of teaspoons each, and we'll finish off this French vanilla."

"You finish it. I'm ice-creamed out, tonight." said Sophie.

"All right. I'll finish it up myself. I'll probably have to stop on the way home to pee, but this finishing the carton is worth it, I guess."

"You're hinting to spend the night with me, I suppose."

"I never hint. I'll say outright. Why don't we live together, Sophie? It makes no sense for me to drive all the way to my house every night. Alone."

"You know I'll lose the pension from the Navy if I remarry. That's $527 every month rain or shine. It's my money and it keeps me from being dependent on a man."

Milt did not argue that being dependent on a man's death benefit was close to the same thing.

"Sophie, why do you hurt me so?"

Milt followed Sophie into the kitchen with the ice cream bowls. He scraped the last bits from the carton and offered the spoon to Sophie. She took the ice cream and made a playful shimmy-shiver. "That's so good it's practically sinful,"

Milt proposed marriage to Sophie regularly. She always refused, afraid to lose what independence se had because of the Navy pension. Sophie reasoned that no man was worth $527.00 every month, although she did not explain it that way to Milt.

Sophie ran hot water in the empty plastic ice cream carton and added a drop of Dawn. She scrubbed the corners and rinsed the carton. Milt dried the cardboard carton before throwing it in the trash.

"They discovered a new kind of dinosaur," he said.

"Who is they?"

"Whoever discovers such things. I read about it in a *Smithsonian* at the V.A."

"My oldest daughter says people and dinosaurs lived at the same time," Sofie said, applying a lavender scented hand cream Milt gave her.

"Ridiculous. Dinosaurs would have eaten all the people and we wouldn't be having this conversation."

"She also thinks that you should not move in with me."

"She gets a say?"

"I make my own decisions," Sophie said.

"But, you're thinking about it?"

"I always feel a little hollow space in my chest when you pull out of my driveway."

"It would save money for both of us, and we could go on some trips, maybe go to Branson for a weekend," Milt said. He took Sophie's hands, still slick with hand cream

"I could only do it for love," Sophie whispered. She rubbed Milt's hands, sharing the lavender scent between them.

Sophie lifted the dish towel from the counter, refolded it, and turned to hang it on the drying rack. With her back to Milt, she said softly, "I guess you could stay tonight."

"Speak up, honey," Milt said. "If you mean it, say it to my face."

Sophie turned around and kissed Milt. Maybe it was the lavender scent that surrounded them. When the kiss ended, Sophie said right to Milt's face, "I wouldn't mind if you stayed the night."

"Aren't you afraid of what your daughter might say?"

"Yes, but I'm more afraid of you stopping at a gas station to pee on the way home and getting mugged or picking up some germ in the public toilet."

Milt hugged Sophie and whispered close to her ear, "Oh baby, you say the sweetest things," he whispered.

"If my doctor told me I had only six minutes to live, I wouldn't brood. I'd type a little faster."

ISAAC ASIMOV

I Understand

NANCY GENEVIEVE

I'm using the Now
to focus on what I call Daily Miracles,
those tiny blessings just waiting to be seen and felt,
the returned smiles in a grocery store,
the Thank You nods when letting someone in front of me
(or me in front of them) in traffic,
buying food for our Food Pantry
for those who should never be hungry,
getting rid of the un-needed clutter I've moved
more times than I can count (and my children don't want),
noticing the animal tracks in the snow,
hearing the owl calls as I drift off to sleep,
writing letters to distant friends.
My list grows, as I notice more,
thanking those of you who make
the world a better place by inviting
us to be a part of your world.

Flake

NANCY GENEVIEVE

Flake-by-flake

clatter and roars

hush   listen
to the healing white silence.

Almost There
photograph by John Palmer

Grow Up without a Father and This Is What Happens

JOHN GREY

Only my mother's voice truly exists.
It's indelibly in my head these days.
'Dinner's ready!" "Have you done your homework!"

"Behave yourself!" 'Turn that down!" "Go to bed!"
Her voice is in charge of the cluttered kitchen.
It gives warning to the spill on the floor.

There is no countermanding, "Wanna go fishing?"
or "Let's play ball." From my earliest memories,
the male voice is conspicuously absent.

So I head to dinner and not the fishing hole.
I stick with my studies and don't toss a ball around.
I behave myself, turn the volume down and slip into bed.

My mother's death has proved to be
no impediment to her continued survival.
Meanwhile, my father lies buried in a silent grave.

My City

JOHN GREY

On my side
is the Point Street Bridge
and the drugstore.
I can't go into battle without them.

And then there's tooth paste,
trash barrels and the gun
that's pointed at somebody else.
Those are my boys.

They're a regular posse—
just throw in a fast food restaurant,
a tattered copy of "On The Road",
an empty office building, a carpark
and a discarded pizza box.

If it was just myself,
I'd be so easily defeated.
A stray sheet of newspaper
would take me on and win.

But not when I've got
the power house to back me up.
And the real estate office.
And asthma.
And the homeless.

I live in this world.
I'm not here on a brief visit.
I breathe the air.

I stand on the ground.
I'm on equal footing.
with other guys
who can say the same.

We all have each other's back.
Each other's weather forecast.
Each other's facial tics.

Vultures

JOHN GREY

The words, seeking vineyards
find nothing but stone.
It's the page's fault.
It's the ink's doing.
Where's the wild plum?
Where are the hazel bushes?
This is all regiment—the military—
a revolt.

The words found barren caves.
Nothing in the nests.
Grass low and brown
that concealed nothing.
Crevices but no honey.
Bones but no song.

Write of a drought
and I may as well
wrap pebbles in paper,
break my toe on a boulder,
sniff dust like a drug.
The sky is equally
hard up for living things.
Nothing soars.
Only vultures have wings.

A FEW FOR THE ROAD

Q: Why was the chef a tough boss?
A: He'd always beat the eggs.

Q: Why were sodium chloride and sulphuric acid in jail?
A: For a salt and battery

Q: Did you hear about the new movie *The Elevator*?
A: It works on so many levels.

Q: I heard Arnold Schwarzenegger won't be playing the *Terminator* anymore.
A: I guess he's an ex-*Terminator*.

Q: What's the best way to have a good day at work?
A: Go home.

Q: Why can't you be too sad on Sunday?
A: Because the day before is always a sadder-day.

Before I Had the Chance to Leave

UMA IQBAL

The last time I saw you, a scorching heatwave gripped the city, yet the apartment felt strangely cold. Once alive with routines, a past and a present, a witness of imperfection and our guts and pain, was now empty. The remnants of your life lay scattered amidst boxes piling up at the core of the living area.

You put off packing until the eleventh hour. Our friendship had soured, so I hid my belongings and pretended I had plans to leave. Amidst the chaos, you hurriedly gathered your belongings, slowly coming to terms with the reality that this place no longer felt like home.

To make things worse, I hid the Wi-Fi router, and my phone died. Desperate to escape, I searched for the router, but all that was left was a lone mattress and a worn, ashen-colored couch. No television with a different story, no music to drown out the silence.

I offered to help, but you responded with a gentle smile, assuring me that everything was under control. I hesitated, pressing softly and hoping you might reconsider. Instead, you nodded and suggested it would be better if I went to bed—so I could wake up to find you already gone.

I went into your room where the lone mattress lay and slipped beneath the covers, but the blanket fell short. I abandon my upper body, concealed my feet and tried and tried to disappear into sleep. Instead, I lay there listening to the shuffling of boxes and the screeching of scotch tape, and the sound of your footsteps patting the wooden floor of the apartment.

Scattered Leaf

ZAN V. JOHNS

My number one issue at this moment is that I'm preoccupied with the not-yet future, i.e. upcoming events, travel, visitors, etc. Our enticing Colorado weather is demanding my full attention. Fall wants me to come out and play. I want to play. I want to plan. I want to *just be.* I am a maple leaf, absorbing sunrays and crisp air. I'm changing hues, pleasing to those who watch. Gayly tossed and turned, I refuse to fall. When and wherever I land, it will be of my own choosing... on my own terms. That is how I live. As shorter days become longer nights, I yield to a deliberately measured pace. I won't succumb to outdoor or indoor pressures. Winter is coming with snow in tow, yikes! Winter changes my attitude and behavior. I retreat inside, literally and figuratively. I cuddle. Of course, as a maple leaf, I will eventually be blown away into someone's open space—mind open, heart open, pen in hand. Write on!

David's pearl: Use the weather to write about where you are in life. My phrases about fall: rather than describe fall, borrow these to describe my current situation...

One of my most important memories is when I moved from Louisiana to Colorado. Young and innocent, the world at my disposal. My parents trusted my brother to look out for me. They trusted me to follow his lead. I was happy as a lark, still am. In June 2025, I will celebrate fifty years of living in Colorado.

WHY I WANTED TO WRITE, IN 100 WORDS OR LESS:

Writing for me is an involuntary attraction between my thoughts and the universe. I sense a gravitational pull to share my feelings, my truth, with the universe. I write to process emotions in response to my life's experiences. Once I discovered my voice and gift, writing became a force to be reckoned with. I feel empowered when I write. I feel obligated to write—for myself and for humanity. Spiritually, I have to let my light shine before others so they may see my good works, bringing them closer to God. I take that seriously.

Abundance

ZAN V. JOHNS

In Celebration of my birthday 2024

Abundant grace, another trip around the sun
Abundant health, mental and physical stamina
Abundant fruit, offspring... books... light
Abundant prospects, open doors and hearts

Abundant adventure, destination Santa Fe, New Mexico
Abundant enchantment, arts... culture... cuisine
Abundant privilege, never taken for granted
Abundant relationships, unforgettable

Abundant bliss, outpouring of global love
Abundant reflection, unforeseen tributes
Abundant sunshine, warmth... light... energy
Abundant rain, Mother Earth rejoices with me

Abundant spirit, soft whispers from my ancestors
Abundant memories, good times rolled
Abundant sounds, jazz... rhythm... blues
Abundant delight, dances of my heart

Abundant purpose, burning flames of passion
Abundant acclaim, widespread admiration
Abundant laughter, welcomed daily medicine
Abundant gifts, material covets fulfilled

Abundant appreciation, deep within my soul
Abundant wishes, for an abundance of time

Why I Write

ZAN V. JOHNS

I watched Nikki Giovanni trip over her ego
I witnessed the phenomenal Maya Angelou rise
How could I not be totally mesmerized!

Countless strong women preceded me
        surrounded me
        nurtured me
I honor them as I nudge the next wave
of strong women to
write
        trip
        rise.

My pen—my weapon—my best friend
Mouthpiece for my muse
It remembers what Nikki said
It remembers what Maya said
It remembers what my parents said
It shares my truth as it repeats what God says.

I write to spread love
I write to heal, help, and honor
I write to leave a footprint—my literary mark.

I want my great great great grandchildren
to know that I was here
I want them to know how and what I felt
I want them to speak their truth
I want them to know what matters.
This is why I write.

The Beauty of Spring

KAREN KADER

Who can deny the beauty of spring?
Where flowers bloom, so does hope.
Time spent alone reflecting, revising and learning
is never wasted. It is necessary for growth and
finding inner peace.

Be grateful & be humble. For that's more important
than how perfect or powerful you are. If you're true
to oneself, you know who you are & people will see
you for who you are. A wonderful human being. We're
all in this together, let's build others up, not ourselves

You learn to appreciate the little things when you lose everything.
You learn forgiveness when you love.
You learn to be tolerant by experiencing intolerance.
You learn kindness from unkindness.
I sit & wonder do you think of me as I do you?

Time doesn't wait, use it wisely.
Time is priceless, yet can be spent.
Time is a precious gift to share,
especially with someone who needs it.

When we're so busy with life, work and responsibilities,
we sometimes forget to pause & rest. We can be more
successful in our endeavors if we could slow down more often.
Give yourself permission to pause, regroup & breathe.
A calm mind is essential to take on your challenges.

A Letter to My Daughters

JILL SHARON KIMMELMAN

In a large house with hidden closets aplenty
my precious children once played
I watched you turn yourselves invisible
cracked apart your little fingers to peek
during a jolly round of hide and seek

In closets like ours
mingled cedar with dainty perfumes
you were Hansel and Gretel
hiding for imaginary reasons
behind each door stood boxes atop boxes
shoes tagged for each outfit
jewelry, color, heel height and seasons

You never knew how close you came
to all I secured in great secrecy with care
excitement, nostalgia, perhaps a bright tear
a passionate celebration of what you would find
all of it simply awaiting you there

Two little girls joyous
making games so very merry
seeking refuge from that tall skinny witch
in black shoes, black hose, tall black hat
from a fairytale that promised no good fairies

That is where you shall find them
thousands upon thousands of my words
penned and locked away
my legacy

a bit lofty a name for what they are
nothing more after all
than notes from a mum you can barely recall

Written so long ago
your brother was but a babe at my breast
you girls were my dearest of treasures
young swans dancing, silken braids, matching ribbons
all remembered pleasures
a moment of grace giving thanks for God's best

Each crisp cream linen page
with splashes of Schiaparelli and Renoir
to honor the imagination
that has always soared within

It mattered not a whit if skies
were dark and gray
where pears drooped on branches
heavy with fruit
those violet blossoms crystallized
trapped in amber like butterflies

With each slim volume, before I began to write
I chose a color, a reason, a mood, a season

Springs must come first!

When that glorious season permeated my being
I reached with both hands for pinks
pencils, charcoal sticks, paints and pens

Pinks
Peonies, lilacs, champagne, blankets, roses,
so very much more
pinks for the daughters
I shall forever adore

Oh I so hope it will turn out
that way for you
brave, brilliant, bold, the palest blush
a palette of pinks in every possible hue

For your very own daughters,
the little girls you named for me
who could imagine such a joy
a thing a heart can almost touch
but still can never see.

"I am irritated by my own writing. I am like a violinist whose ear is true, but whose fingers refuse to reproduce precisely the sound he hears within."

GUSTAVE FLAUBERT

Until We Meet Again

JILL SHARON KIMMELMAN

I see you when I close my eyes
the way that you appeared in our bedroom
on our last night of shared pleasure
a celebration of our hearts and bodies
entwined a final time

You stood before me fully naked
resembling a warrior devoid of brilliant body paint
fierce in your wanting me
some tiny part of your spirit gentled by my touches

Parallel emotions were revealed in your eyes;
there exists the whole of a poem in those eyes,
a magnificent poem I know I will never write.

My mirror has changed, not entirely the result of
a horrific haircut
I could click my heels three times,
still it would remain that tell-tale "chemo cut."

Purple shadows have appeared beneath my eyes,
bruises and angry eruptions splatter across my back,
my belly, scarred limbs, and upon my breasts

Announcing the undeniable, a weakening of
my immune system

Often my eyes simply fill up with tears
they slip free barely noticed, rarely acknowledged

You have been my world, my best friend
lover, husband, and forever muse

Drizzling the warm oil of a muse's magic into my
waiting palms
releasing the manna of my words, fitting themselves
round each other forming sonnets and stanzas of
love and adoration

Once more before you go my beloved husband
lean in closer
celebrate this unexpected gift with me
press your lips to mine, warm and softly-supple

Amidst the morphine drip, hospice paraphernalia,
and roses, in our final hour, we have been given a magical gift
to see one another as once we appeared
at first blush, in the splendor and magnificence
of our earliest days.

No need for messy farewells, we rejoice in the knowledge
this is not an ending, simply another beginning,
the first step of a different journey,
only a passage of time apart.

I will meet you there soon enough,
when I have readied our new home,
our forever home.

MAIL

Dear *Fine Lines,*

So good to hear from you, and I am hoping to have something to submit soon. Going to produce a concert of my choreography this year, too. Hope all is well with you.

Dance on,
Julian Adair, Omaha, NE

Dear *Fine Lines,*

This is a great 2024 winter issue. I have been meaning to get ahold of you and submit some writing. This is fine work you're doing.

Thank you so much!

Lucy Adkins, Lincoln, NE

Dear *Fine Lines,*

Thank you. I have a printed version on the way now!

This quarter's *Fine Lines* workshop was: the most important, interesting, and scary class or workshop I've attended in YEARS!

David Barnes, Ashville, NC

Dear *Fine Lines,*

The 2024 winter issue was a very impressive selection.

Thank you,
Roberta Batorsky, Omaha, NE

Dear *Fine Lines,*

Thank you! My heart is full of gratitude and appreciation that you published my writing in your winter issue. I am looking forward to the January 2025 Zoom creative writing webinar and meeting fellow writers! Thank you so much for inviting me into the *Fine Lines* Community. It brings such an immense feeling of comfort and confidence to be among peer writers.

My next course has started so my workload is a bit heavy. However, I am hoping to write a poem about writing: I am finding I am feeling alive once again for I died when my son died. My goal is to have this accomplished for the spring edition of *Fine Lines.*

Have a great day and looking forward to staying in touch!

Sincerely,
Terri Dreismeier, Omaha, NE

Hi Chanah,

I wanted to congratulate you again on the Henry Winkler interview. I can't wait to read it. Your presentation today was outstanding. In the simplest way, you showed us how to score a touchdown! That's what I call my wins, and I'm sure David would appreciate that analogy, lol. One of my biggest takeaways was that it requires thoughtful planning and work. I love how you passionately pursued your dream AND focused on the potential impact that your interview would have on your readers. Sharing your experience was a perfect way to emphasize the benefits of journaling. Thank you for walking us through the exercises. You are a great teacher.

Zan

Dear Lisa Tomey, *Fine-Lines,* and Kristen Martin,

Wow! That conference was amazing, and I am so glad that I was able to attend. There were some new faces, and I enjoyed hearing their thoughts and ideas!

Kaelen Felix's illustrations just blew me away! Her attention to detail and her use of color make me think that her career as an artist will take her far. I definitely want to buy a copy of her book, when it comes out!

Kristen, thank you for your words of encouragement. It really helped put things in perspective, like "... eating an elephant one bite at a time," not that I would ever want to! I realized that I am nowhere near ready to publish a book. The only essays, poems, and narratives that are in my computer are the ones that have been published in *Fine Lines*! Egad! Everything else is in journals, notebooks, sticky notes, scratch paper, and on the backs of envelopes! Guess I need to get to work on putting what I have into my computer.

I also appreciate the words of support from the other participants on Zoom. Apparently, I had a "deer-in-the-headlights" expression on my face! Charles de Flanders sent me a nice email with a couple of good ideas.

Thank you all for making this a really successful conference on "Publishing Your Writing."

Have a great week!

Love,
Kathie Haskins

Dear *Fine Lines,*

Seeing Kyla Cooper's art in the 2024 winter issue is a proud grandmother moment. Thank you kindly! I look forward to reading more after scanning the contents and reading a few poems. One story caught my eye and wouldn't let go: "An Unforgettable Soul's Brokenness" by TERRI DREISMEIER, wow!

Good night.

Zan V. Johns

Dear *Fine Lines,*

I have written another story I didn't intend to write or know I would be writing. I wrote it just this week in two days and have made a detailed plan on how to turn this draft into a suitable submission. I don't know where this stuff comes from, but I'm glad it popped up.

I will be submitting the fully edited story by April 1 and, probably, before that date.

Do not worry about a spring deadline. If accepted, I suggest publishing this in the winter *Fine Lines* issue. My reasoning for recommending the winter edition is contained in the story's title: "The Boy Who Loved Winter."

It's partly a Christmas story, but instead of Dickensonian redemption, it's about the gift of healing.

I don't know if you're interested in this or not, but I am making a journal of taking this first draft and turning it into a submission. I have made a specific enumerated plan for how to put this writing into its final form. The plan includes taking a two-week vacation (beginning now) from it to let it settle into what it is, and then work weekly, one day each week to let it become what it was always going to be.

I have been writing almost every day since the end of October. I grab my coffee with one hand, when I come downstairs, and grab my pen with my other hand. I spend the next hour and a half or so writing with very little thought given about what to write. That's how this latest story happened. I had no idea I'd be writing a story this week.

Marc Lund, Omaha, NE

Dear *Fine Lines,*

Thank you for sending the latest issue of *Fine Lines*. It is my lifeboat.

Kathy Maloney, Omaha, NE

Dear *Fine Lines,*

Thank you so much, sir. You cannot imagine how grateful I feel, when I find my pen in your 2024 PDF winter issue. Honestly speaking, I cannot afford to buy the book. I'll send more work for your consideration.

Thank you very much, again.

Munmun Samanta, India

Dear *Fine Lines,*

Thank you. The *Fine Lines* 2024 winter cover is smashing!

The issue is great!

Kim Sosin, Omaha, NE

Dear *Fine Lines,*

Thanks, David. As it happens, I just ordered the 2024 winter issue print copy, as well, and yesterday, Santa sent me a present! First time in about 70 years, and of course, he mailed it, since even his sleigh can only hold so much.

It's very interesting to see the evolution of *Fine Lines* over the past 20 years, from a chapbook-like magazine of 60 pages [with ads!] to a soft-cover beauty of well over 200 pages. You should be proud. Very few get to say their life's work affected others in heart, mind, and soul.

I'm attaching some poems in 2 files, but please check that none have been sent before. It really is a mystery how I am more creative in my 8th decade than the previous 7 decades combined, yet I worry all the time about losing my wallet/car keys/cell phone, etc.

Nolo Segundo, Moorestown, NJ

Tony B.

KATHY MALONEY

The shadow of your smile when you are gone
will color all my dreams and light the dawn

—Johnny Mandel and Paul Webster

His open-hearted smile
for those whose faces
he looked into…

His refined art created
from a spirit having
more to give than just
sublime music…

His remarkable voice
for everyone who ever listened,
jazzy when he chose to be…

Silver-haired hip cat for the ages,
and there were many ages
that loved him at 96…

And even at the end,
when he could not remember,
all those who knew
the shadow of his smile
will remember him.

Wild Lullaby

KATHY MALONEY

On a wintry November night,
while I drowse
beneath warm blankets...

from the silent dark outside,
perched in some leafless tree
a great horned owl
lulls quietly with his velvet call...
inviting sleep.

Kristen Martin in Iceland

Iceland, 25-Year Wedding Anniversary – June 2024

KRISTEN AND BRADLEY MARTIN

Kristen and I spent our 25th anniversary exploring Iceland for a couple weeks. The past several years we've planned travel and expeditions around kids. Now it was time to return to our dirtbag roots and explore the island of fire and ice in a minimalist way, carrying only what we needed with us into the land of the midnight sun.

Reykjavik ("Smokey Bay") is believed to be the first permanent settlement in Iceland in the Viking Age, 874 AD. Iceland has no prehistory, but there is a healthy influence of Viking pride, similar to that of Norway.

Iceland was under Danish rule until 1786. It is now among the cleanest, greenest and safest cities in the world. It has a rich artistic scene, unique architecture and pumping nightlife. We spent a few nights acclimatizing here before setting off into the mountains.

From Reykjavik, we traveled east into the Rhyolite mountains, heralded by *National Geographic* as one of the most scenic and wild places on earth. Our route took us near Hekla, Iceland's most active volcano, with its last eruption in 2000.

Highland roads in Iceland are rough, unpaved gravel roads leading to the inner parts of Iceland. They require 4x4 vehicles and often involve river crossings. Many of these vehicles have super-wide tires which are run with low pressure to better gain traction on the wet, soft sand. We rode up in one of these vehicles, fording many streams pulsing with milky glacial till.

We arrived in the heart of the southern highlands, specifically part of the Fjallabak Nature Reserve, north of Mýrdalsjökull glacier. Before heading out on foot, we stopped for a soak dip in a mountain creek fed by several hot geothermal springs. The act of bathing necessitated finding the right mix of hot and cold-water currents flowing around us.

We grabbed our packs and headed up into the lava fields. All the geography consisted of volcanic activity, including a canyon painted with all colors of the rainbow. The green, red, yellow, pink and blue kaleidoscope of colors were created by the different minerals in the rhyolite. The iron (red) and sulfur (orange) and copper (green) were visually stunning.

After several miles, we stumbled upon a series of scalding hot, bubbling air vents releasing plumes of steam along the base of the hillside. The discovery revealed a mountain scape in its geologic infancy. The vents and springs were boiling and too hot to soak in. However, we were able to make a round of hot drinks in a matter of minutes by placing a cup of water directly on a small steaming vent hole in the ground.

Another thousand feet of climbing snowfields brought us through black rock piles of obsidian skerry and to our snowy campsite for the night. We set up our tent with a stunning view of Hrafntinnusker, a small volcano in the Torfajökull caldera with a small glacier on top. Plumes of geothermal steam drifted from nearby Storihver thermal vents.

The following day we began by navigating snow-covered hills into rugged gullies formed by more geothermal activity. We kept the peak of Jokultunger in view, as we descended into the Fjallabak area. Soon we had a river crossing to do. So, we swapped our hiking boots for river shoes and crossed. It was refreshing and a much-needed wash.

We arrived at Lake Alftavatn (Swan Lake), part of the River Sog, created from retreating glaciers. It is the 19 km long discharge of Lake Thingvallavatn and is surrounded by stunning mountains. We cooked a hot lunch here and continued on, crossing two more rivers. We made our way towards Maelifellssandur, passing by the Storasula and Hattafell volcanoes. We made camp in black sand and filled our water bottles with cold water from a nearby melting snow field.

The next morning we slept in, having traveled over 14 miles the day previous. Our snowfield had frozen during the cold night, so we packed up and headed across the vast, open lava fields in search of water.

Blasts of strong wind whipped up curtains of sand at our faces, stinging any areas of exposed skin, as we made our way through the flat, rocky moonscape. Red dirt devils swirled around our boots. We found a small creek and filled our bottles, careful to face away from the dust storm as we traveled towards Emstrur.

We continued through petrified lava fields and snow-dashed peaks, along gurgling rivers that smell of sulfur, and over tussock meadows interspersed with ancient rock formations. Around halfway through our route, we descended to the valley of Thórsmörk (Þórsmörk—Valley of Thor). This was a change for us, as Thórsmörk has road access, trailheads and concessions. It had been several days, since we saw other people and the human activity was in stark contrast to what we were used to. Here, we were able to check weather forecasts, re-supply, and sample local carbonated beverages.

We continued on, crossing Thórsmörk Valley. Another afternoon of climbing took us to a high plateau. This ascent is one of the most amazing routes in Iceland with unforgettable views. It was 10:00 PM and still light, but we needed rest. We bivouacked on a ledge over-looking the snowy mountains in the distance.

The following day, we continued climbing up steeper snowfields. The wind had picked up during the night and was now blowing a gale. Soon, we navigated between the glaciers of Eyjafjallajökull and Mýrdalsjökull. We worked our way up through some snowy mountain passes with very high winds with fog. We came to a mountain hut, Fimmvörðuháls, but opted to keep going. We found a nice camp tucked away in the rocks, where we could see and plan tomorrow's descent.

We descended down through rocky slabs and black sand. This final day offered some of the most dramatic scenery Iceland has, from a series of canyon waterfalls and grass tundra. We began to see the coastline and ocean in the distance, and it became larger as we descended.

As we neared the end of our journey, we began to see day tourists hiking up from our ending point. Again, it had been many days since we had seen people. Some of these day-hikers looked at us extra-long, making up their own stories of where we had been and where we had come from.

As we descended the final mile of our route, we came to the top of the famous Skogafoss waterfall. It is 82 feet high and one of the largest waterfalls in the country. Skogafoss is at a cliff marking the former coastline. After the coastline receded (three miles), the former sea cliffs remained parallel to the coast over hundreds of kilometers, creating a clear border between the coastal lowlands and highlands of Iceland.

All counted, we traveled just under 70 miles, climbed over 11,000 feet, and crossed two glacier passes. Our remaining days in Iceland consisted of being tourists in Reykjavik. Also, we had to sample more soaking pools and hot springs to rest some weary muscles.

I Am a Poem

DAVID MARTIN

David

Quiet, adventurous, books, journals, and dogs

Brother of John, Bob, and Rick

Lover of Yolie-Bradley-Ashley-Erin, and the Milky Way

Who feels at peace, mystical, and writing is a gift

Who needs lots of time, laughter, purpose, and passion

Who gives quiet spaces, compassion, and hugs

Who fears repeating mistakes and not doing my best

Who would like to see people healthy, families happy, and writing
good

Resident of Earth and Rockbrook Road

Martin

Vision

DAVID MARTIN

Philosophers, the antennae of our
times, look beyond the horizon.
We are what we do, and
if we change what we do,
we change who we are.

Some believe the world is still flat,
the holocaust never happened, astronauts
have not been to the moon, Elvis never died,
censors have the right to tell us what to read,
and public schools should be teaching religion.

Columbus pushed the barriers back, broke the limits
of geographical knowledge, and achieved the unexpected
without a formal education. From the Canary Islands,
he sailed due west for three weeks, the longest time
anyone ever was known to do this.

On 10.10.1492—his crew was ready to mutiny,
but they agreed to sail for three more days
and then turn back. On 10.12 at 2:00 AM, San Salvador
in the Bahamas was sighted by moonlight.
While we breathe, let us hope.

More than 90% of Earth's animals have no backbones,
and written on the Bachelor of Science Diploma given to
Louis Pasteur was the word "mediocre."
Say the profound simply,
"Philosophy is perception."

What goes into history remains.
What goes into work lives.
Dream now. See today.
We must build our philosophy,
and create our vision.

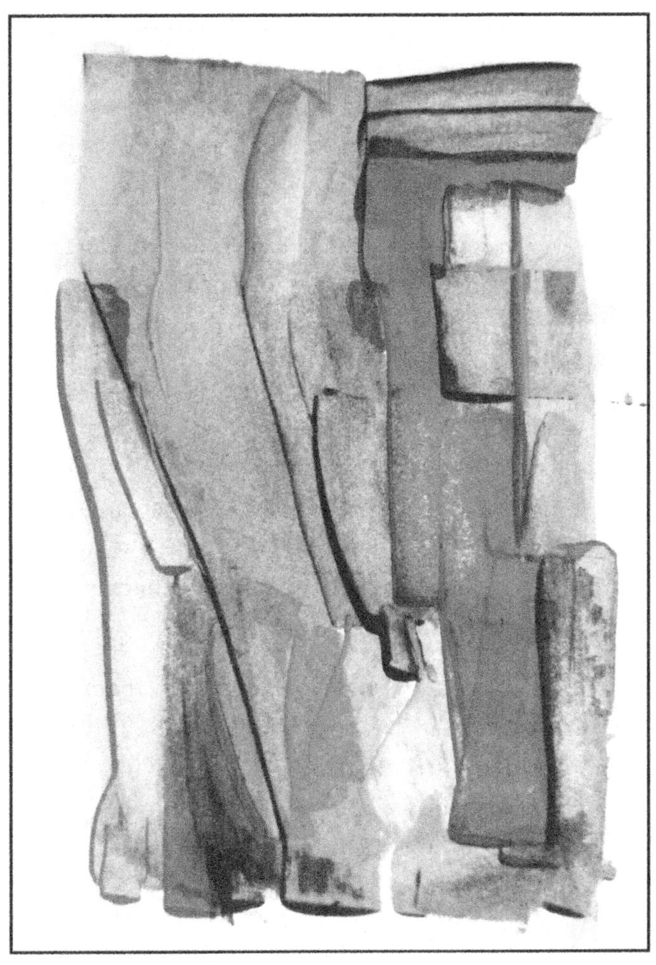

Neaten
Michael Moreth

Sum ergo, cogito. (I am; therefore, I think.)

DAVID MARTIN

There are many ways to exist and relate to situations.
What is crucial to people determines their consciousness.
Individual experiences show what is important and how
the world reveals itself. In the midst of our lives,
we establish the rules for how things work.

To create meaning in a cosmos, which is devoid of objective meaning, is difficult. Educating ourselves, as we grow older, is a process of creating ourselves. With age, we learn to not depend on precedent or others, when deciding what is the best for us. Our lives become individual classrooms. This independence is an ominous responsibility for every act taken.

A person is an abstraction, a category, an essence,
as Aristotle said a "rational animal," a part of a system—
"thought objectified," a statistic with an IQ score, a social class,
an age group, a uniqueness, and a specialness. If there is a meaning
to the universe, there is a meaning for mankind.

People who do not choose, who let life choose for them,
who only want a comfortable, complacent, and conforming
life avoid their own uniqueness. These bland individuals become
automatic stereotypes, hollow beings indifferent to life's choices.
No suffering also means no rejoicing.

Faith, for some, is important. For others, atheists and agnostics,
a world of no absolutes presents a nothingness outside of life
that accentuates a world of no guarantees. The challenge of being
responsible for one's own destiny becomes paramount. Existentialists
use reason, intuition, and liberty to create their own meaning.

We Survived

DAVID MARTIN

Dear Jess,

We survived the wedding, reception,
8″ of snow, ice, bad drivers, and a late
flower delivery to the church.

The mother-in-law was ill. The father-in-law looked like
he could bench press 300 pounds, and our two daughters
are still as different as night and day.

Leona prayed in the car non-stop that the blizzard
would not hurt us, and we would arrive safely.
Evie was tense. Jesse was silent, and Yolie was exhausted.

Brad and Kristen flew into Lincoln through Denver.
An hour after they left, the airport closed. One of my
three brothers made it, but Mother did not.

Now, my oldest daughter is a "Roskilly," but she will
still be my little "rascal." Her husband, our son-in-law,
has unique qualities, and he can imitate Mick Jagger.

I danced every dance to the music I understood.
It was a happy day, a beautiful time for the family,
and your check was appreciated very much.

David

Dear Bubba

DAVID MARTIN

I enjoy writing to you, my personal journal. Sometimes, we meet daily. Other times, we converse weekly. Today, I need a listener.

Complexity in writing muddies the water, obscures the purpose, and boggles the reader's mind. Most truths are best stated simply, the farmers and cowboys talk to each other. These blank pages in front of me invite the accuracy of vision. Like a blue ski on a cloudless day.

As topics appear from left to right. I compose for you and me. This name that I now give to you, Bubba, like a father gives to his son, is one of raw and sincere simplicity. It has a country connotation that I respect, and this daily journal will be unadorned and unaffected, just like the clothes you wear. Writing every day, this year, my New Year's resolution promises to be creative, real, and sincere.

When this concept first shook me awake, I loathed the idea. Writing something original on a daily basis sounds a lot like unpleasant work. Just the idea of you was a thorn in my side and consistently gave me headaches. When I decided you wanted to grow to be 365 pages or more in one year, I cringed. At first, you scared the heck out of me. How was I ever going to feed you enough ideas so you would gain that much weight in twelve months? At the beginning, just completing an entry every day for a week exhausted me. I didn't like you one single bit. For a while I ignored you, hoping you would go away, but the more I neglected you, the more demanding you became. You began to roar for food, like a starving lion. Still, I refused to feed you.

After a while, I realized that if you weren't fed, you wouldn't grow. I looked at you, as you lay there on the shelf, a skinny spectacle. You were so thin that your three binding rings showed through like skinny ribs with a few paltry scraps of flesh attached. Four weeks later, you were a little better, and some color returned to your face, but you were anemic and begging for more. In four more weeks, you were larger, and I knew I could neglect you no longer. You didn't go away, as I hoped. In front of me, you loomed like a sickly, pale apparition too tough to die. What kind of parent would I be, if I did not nourish my child? We had a pact, and I must carry out my end of the bargain.

I started feeding you a couple of pages a day and soon realized that this wasn't going to be enough to guarantee your health, so I increased your rations. I started to feel more like a concerned parent. You weren't getting a prime rib dinner at each meal, but at least you were not starving. The most interesting development in this process was that the more I fed you, the more you gave back to me.

When I heard you talking to me in the middle of the night, I was surprised. There you were on the top of the shelf, and your little notebook covers opened. The voice that came out of you was soft and weak: "Feed me. Feed me."

I stayed in bed, not knowing if I was dreaming, but when I heard you say the same thing one more time, I forced my legs over the side of the bed and stood up. I picked you up, and we went to the front-room table. I turned on one light, picked up a pen, and wrote for three hours, until the sun peeked through the window.

When I put you on the shelf, I heard you sigh, like people do, when they complete a filling meal. Just before you went to sleep and I went to work, you said: "That was really good. Let's do that again, soon."

Secretly, there is something I must tell you. I'm growing fond of you. I've taken a liking to you, I guess. Perhaps, this change in my attitude toward writing has come a little late in my life, but I don't mind. You have allowed me to discover things about myself that I never knew, and you have opened many doors to let in some much-needed fresh air.

Since this relationship began and every time we meet, you always teach me more about myself. You are a window through which I look, when I want to glimpse what is inside me. You are a place where I can be alone. When I am hurting, I can cry with you. When I have a problem, you are the friend I confide in and share how I feel. I only wish that I met you, when I was younger. Oh, the memories, the emotions, the pains, and the dreams. There are so many things to say. There is no sense in worrying about the past. All I can do is start now, and make each day better than the last. You made a lousy first impression, but I don't know what I would do without you, now.

Bubba, you are helping guide me through life's expedition. Writing on your pages is becoming a journey of self-discovery. Together, we are going down roads I have not seen before to new, exciting places. You are showing me insights that I did not know existed, helping me write to enlightenment, allowing me to heal from previous wounds, and find answers to questions that I previously avoided.

I propose these guidelines for our daily travels. Poetry may count, but good prose is what we will emphasize. Artwork counts, if we explain it. If we react to their messages, quotes by others. Practicing good grammar and standard English weigh heavily. Words matter. Originality, quantity, and pride in the writing will become routine. Ten weekly pages of concerned, honest writing is our minimum goal.

Bubba, have you noticed that writers, who feel good about themselves, enjoy the experience and power of self-expression? When we get together, let's sit down in front of the computer or pick up a pad and pen in a positive frame of mind. Let's not be afraid to express ourselves. We are not writing for a grade. We are writing to learn. We cannot fear the writing process. We must embrace it. Let's make writing fun and rewarding.

"Learning to employ the mechanics of grammar automatically makes one a good writer" is an old myth. There is no more truth to this than the idea that I can build a house, because I know what a hammer and nail are.

"Good writers use long sentences and show off their extensive vocabulary every time they write" is another myth. Many good writers are masters of simplicity. Writing is not always difficult, and consistent writers place ink on paper, when they are at the top of their bio-rhythmic cycle, not when they are tired and hungry. The secret to enjoyable writing is to always have a topic one cares about.

"Only a few can write well" is a lie of large proportion. People write well, if they take the time and acquire the discipline to formulate their thoughts and string them together into efficient sentences. Consistent authors write, regardless of how they feel. Some writers do their best work, when they hit bottom, emotionally, or are not at the top of their craft.

"Good writing only comes when inspired" is a falsehood. Writing well is accomplished by anyone who cares, uses patience, practices, receives encouragement, and is willing to rewrite and revise.

When they emphasize content and self-expression rather than political correctness, journals allow writers to develop faster. We will have complete freedom in choosing our topics throughout the year, because we will write much better with an ownership of the discussion or write because we feel committed to the specific issue.

Struggle. Celebrate. Challenge. Enjoy. Create.

According to L.M. Boyd, who wrote a syndicated newspaper trivia column, "Casper Eberhard came up with the notion to put erasers on pencils. He did this 1765 in Germany. However, the Germans didn't think much of the idea. They and other Europeans said it would make children careless, and they held this attitude for many generations. Pencils with erasers caught on in the United states long before any Europeans accepted them."

Great inventions take a long time to catch on, sometimes, just like the pencil eraser. Don't give up, Bubba. I will not give up on you. Journals work, and do not forget Casper Eberhard.

Bubba, we will have fun with sentences, learn to play while creating poems, stories, essays, and discover corners of our minds that we did not know existed. Metaphorically, we will take our journals under shade trees and talk about issues that matter. We will swim around important "buoys" on our writing treks. We will row boats to lighthouses that show us our own paths through the fog. We will take our minds for jogs to libraries. We will learn to compose more, faster, and better. Most importantly, we will create time to dream about our ideas, applaud the power and beauty of words, and celebrate our language.

> *Simplicity is the ultimate sophistication.*
>
> —Leonardo da Vinci

Write on,
David Martin

Opportunity in Chaos

DAVID MARTIN

Second team players, who might be a little shorter, a little slower, and weigh less, often,
are the ones with as much enthusiasm in the fourth quarter, as they held in the first.
Give me those with uncommon hustle to replace a lack of athletic technique.
Those are the players, who know if they beat their opponents on every five-yard play
will not have to worry about running down the opposing prima-donnas on their one
90-yard spectacular effort in the game.
Give me the wannabe starters on second team, who know every down might be their last,
who love competition, who get simple hugs from their girl-friends at the end of the games,
win or lose, even though they can barely walk to the bus from the locker room.
Give me the players, who hear their coaches say, "Boys, that was the best game I ever saw
you play. I am proud of you and want you all to start in next week's game. I don't care
what the first team players say. They lost their starting jobs, tonight."
I told head coach Brown my players on second team are going home to get some rest and
take their vitamins. They won't stay out late. They will get sleep, and on Saturday morning,
they will tell their parents how much they love them.
On Monday, they will come to school and walk inside, like they are first team players.

They will smile at every teacher and thank them for teaching students so much. Every day,
my players will ask at least one question about something they don't understand.
The players I want on my team are just like you, the ones who realize there is opportunity in chaos.
If they remain calm, work together from one outstretched hand to the other, and learn to control their
space in this world, they will become winners in the game of life.

May I Be Wrong

VINCE McANDREW

But are we heading for an exit ramp?
There is more than one exit off our evolutionary path,

more than one way to land in the cosmic ditch,
surprised, broken, and fatally injured.

We seem determined to crash and burn as a species.
Not that Earth would mind or care.

Comedian George Carlin gave us the analogy
of a dog shaking off a pesky flea before returning to his day.

Ironic to use that analogy in view of the fact that dogs,
for canine lovers,

are here to show us
what unconditional love looks like,

the one force powerful enough to save us from ourselves.
Hubris, myopia, maybe both,

propels us to our undoing.
Can't count out religious fundamentalism

or excessive consumerism either
as fatal dynamics in our demise.

Our home planet teeters in a hot wind,
wobbling enough to send us flying off, as it were,

returning us to space as star dust
whence we came

before Life birthed us as a species conscious of ourselves,
conscious of the cosmos,

conscious enough to choose living in harmony with Earth
or not,

with power enough to be our own undoing.
As said, may I be wrong.

*"I went for years not finishing anything.
Because, of course, when you finish
something you can be judged."*

ERICA JONG

Both/And?

VINCE McANDREW

How do we get out of our own way
as we each, in our own way,
journey toward a lightness of being?

Do we travel back in our mind to how our species
came about, evolved from stardust born in a cataclysmic light show?

Are we not tangible, momentary iterations of this light,
this energy, this dust evolved so intricately?

Yet in understanding our distant origins,
how to factor in dark matter that comprises
by far most of our (barely) known universe.

Dark because it emits no light,
like the love of an absent beloved,
real but invisible.

Do we not originate as much from dark matter
as from light?

Both/and comes to mind as we think of ourselves,
our origins and our present configuration
of flesh and blood, body, mind, and spirit.

Simply put, are we children of the dark
as well as children of the light?

We know, don't we, that a lightness of being
necessarily means letting go of pettiness and the
encumbrance of unnecessary things.

Can we release our ego untethered
    into the space/time continuum that is Reality
    freeing our essential selves to seek the
    Essential Self
    in the unfolding mystery that is Life?

ALS Journal, Monday, December 2, 2024

VINCE AND KAY McANDREW

Dear Family and Friends,

Journaling for this past 12 months since 'D Day,' diagnosis day, has been helpful for me and, when shared, for Kay, and, it seems, for others as well. Writing clarifies, helps us keep perspective, helps us see the forest while amid the trees, to see the mountain itself as we climb along our unfolding life-path, sometimes with head down lest we stumble and fall. Step by step, day by day, we, like you, live one day at a time, sometimes one long night at a time. Though our days often seem so similar to each other, each one is precious. We are grateful for each one, knowing every breath, however labored as it often is for Kay, is a gift, as it is for all of us.

Cuing up a Creighton women's basketball game we watched yesterday on ESPN, there was short video of the last paragraph of the moving speech then retired BB Coach Jimmy Valvano gave on March 4, 1993, on the occasion of his accepting the ESPY Arthur Ashe Award, given to someone who shows exemplary courage in the face of adversity. The excerpt went as follows: *"I know, I know, I gotta go; and one last thing, and I said it before and I'm gonna say it again. Cancer can take away all my physical abilities. It cannot touch my mind. It cannot touch my heart and it cannot touch my soul. And those three things are going to carry on forever… . I thank you and God bless you all."*

I replayed this short clip three times yesterday for Kay and myself. I've seen and heard the entire speech before. It has new meaning for us now. As I've said to Kay more than once during our year of coping with ALS, "You are still here." The essential you, the essential bright and loving, generous and caring Kay Evans McAndrew is still here, regardless of continued loss of mobility and speech. "You are still here."

So this Christmas greeting is one of affirmation of what is most important for each of us as we celebrate the astounding miracle of Love made incarnate in the child, in the man Jesus, yes, but in each of us as well. We too are flesh-and-blood instances of divinity because that's how Life, Holy Mystery, continues to evolve. In this way Christmas is a celebration of our shared incarnations of God who is Love, the Endless Energy of All That Is.

An important go-to theologian for me is a German Dominican priest, philosopher, and mystic, Meister Eckhart (1260–1328) who said, *"You may call God love, you may call God goodness. But the best name for God is compassion."*

Kay and I, perhaps more than anything this past year have taken this reality to heart. Isms, dogmas, beliefs mean little when living life close to the bone. Compassionate outreach to each other, given to us by family and friends, means everything, transforming our minds, our hearts, our souls through grace each time we make love tangible through service to one another.

We very much appreciate your love and concern for us; you are a presence in our day to day life. May you be well in every way as you joyfully celebrate and honor the incarnation of Love in life, in all of us.

ALS Journal, Tuesday, February 11, 2025

VINCE MCANDREW

When asked how I am doing, as Kay's home, healthcare worker, care-taker spouse, I tell family and friends, "Generally, I am doing okay." I often am more specific, and I try to stay active, that I walk about our three acres, now and then, that I exercise in our living room using my mini elliptical machine and light weights, that I read, reflect, write in this journal, write longer texts and emails, cards, and letters. Phone calls help, too. Engaging with reading that connects me to the how and why Life works and why Life happens at all helps keep me grounded, as well.

My go-to author/theologian for the past many weeks is a 69-year-old Franciscan nun, Ilia Delio, scientist-turned-nun-turned theologian. Her synthesis of the insights of psychotherapist Carl Jung (1875–1961) and Pierre Teilhard de Chardin (1881–1955) explores their views of life against the backdrop of quantum theory and the fundamental driving force of evolution.

This reading helps me stay tethered to the fact that Kay and I are more than flesh and blood, that as temporary configurations of matter conscious of itself, of the cosmos, we are "Christic" (her word), that is, embodiments of the entanglements of human and divine. We are embodiments of God who is Love, who is the energy that enlivens and propels the always unfolding cosmos.

Kay and I, therefore, as all humans, are essentially spiritual beings having a human experience as Teilhard wrote. So, while living out the privileged role of caring for Katherine Evans McAndrew, I remind myself my task is sacred, caretaker of our 57 years together, as soul mates, parents and grandparents, retired educators still filled with gratitude for friends and family, for continuing to live in the wonder of Wa Con Da, Holy Mystery.

We will continue to care for Kay here for as long as feasible. We will have her live out her final days at the Josie Harper Hospice House in Omaha after that. If we can manage her care here to her final breath, so much the better.

Springtime at the Bridge
photograph by Cindy Goeller

Sleeping in Her Chair

VINCE McANDREW

Death speeds towards us
on glacial feet,
yet it comes,
silent, day by day,
night by night
inexorably.

A Northern Cardinal appears,
just now, beyond our east window,
a bright red against our gray winter sky.

Labored breath by labored breath
she sleeps
birthing not daughters
but loss and gain,
immeasurable tears,
exhausted relief
fixing indefatigable
love in slow orbit
around my heart.

This Fire

IVY MOON

(Lyrics, verse 1)
In this crazy world
You do what you can to survive
Doing what I can to keep the fire alive.
You thought you could keep me down
But not for too long
I'll never give up cause
I'll be fighting strong

(Chorus)
Cause this fire
is burning inside of me
Its giving me the will to succeed.
This fire
Will never fade away
I'll keep it burning every day.
I've got a message that
I'm sending to the nation
Never give up or back down
Within you lies a spark of determination.

(Set it free)
(Chorus repeats)

Feel this fire!

The American Museum of Lawn Care

RIC NUDELL

Grandma only came to Serenity Farm twice. The first time she and Frank rode the California Zephyr seven hours from Chicago to Osceola where they'd expected Grandpa would pick them up. Instead he'd left a message, which was relayed by Station Master along with directions for the bus to Mason City. So Frank and Grandma stepped like dazed pilgrims into the suckling heat of the Iowa dusk with Frank carrying his suitcase and dragging Grandma's by two of the truculent wheels. Before they'd managed a single block, Frank was dripping sweat and swearing, and Grandma was mince-stepping a few steps behind, fanning her neck and pretending not to hear. Luckily, just then the Station Master's car rolled to a stop beside them and she offered a ride. In the air-conditioned car, Frank's sweat soaked shirt stiffened against his skin and he began to shiver. Returning to the heat at the bus station was an unexpected relief.

Frank and Grandma had also expected to stop for dinner with Grandpa, with Grandma even speculating about the restaurants in Osceola or Pere Foyse, guessing at early closing times, and specials that included meat loaf or Salisbury steak with mashed potatoes and green beans. Instead, they bought Baby Ruths and sodas from a vending machine, and the silence between them while they ate was as suffocating as the heat. They were tired and talked out and now newly guarded, with Frank hesitant to voice what he was thinking about Grandpa and worried that whatever Grandma would say would be far worse.

It was after 10 when the bus dropped them at the Mason City airport, and they were met not by Grandpa, but by Ed, Grandpa's hired man. Ed was round-faced and stubbled, with a barrel-chest, almost nothing for a neck and a truncated body. He wore a sneaker on one foot and a lace-up boot on the other that he dragged behind with a limp that left him listing heavily to the side. A sweat stain the color of a cowpat showed under his arm when he lifted his bucket hat to greet Grandma, "Pleased to meet you, Mrs. Karth." He smiled and shook Frank's hand, "You must be Frank." Ed's voice was expressionless and his fingers were rough and dry as bark.

Ed loaded their suitcases into a station wagon so long that Frank imagined it extended the dozen years back to when it was new. Inside, the car smelled of ammonia and animal-bedding and Grandma cracked open her window. The whistle of air through the window and the rattle of the air conditioner fan made it difficult for Frank to follow anything but the bones of Ed's monologue as they drove—the lack of rain and depressed commodity prices, and then a farm they were passing in the dark that Grandpa had bid on unsuccessfully before purchasing Serenity Farm.

Ed pulled in at the farm and cut the car lights and the darkness was encompassing, swallowing sound along with sight. Ed and Grandma were talking as he guided her to the steps, but all Frank could hear was a sound like the spray of wind against wooden siding. Frank needed extra time to wrestle the suitcases into the house and by the time he stepped into the kitchen, Grandma and Grandpa had said all they had to say to each other and Grandma had disappeared into a bedroom.

"Good of you to come, Frank," Grandpa shook Frank's hand. "Are you hungry?"

"I'm famished."

"Help yourself to whatever you can find, I'm going out to help Ed. Shopping is on Tuesday if there's something you'd like that you don't see."

Frank knocked on Grandma's door. "Grandma? I brought your suitcase." He opened the door, "Do you want dinner?"

Grandma had spread a sheet over the duvet on the bed and she was sitting on the sheet. "Tomorrow I'm going home," she said. She told Frank to leave the suitcase and close the door.

"How was it seeing Grandpa?" Frank asked.

"Make sure the door is latched," Grandma repeated and she reached and turned off the lamp.

Their return trip to Chicago was a test of Frank's endurance. They caught an early bus from Mason City to Rochester, then waited two hours for a bus to take them from Rochester to Madison and on to Chicago. Grandma said little the whole way. She sat with her hands in her lap and watched the fields and towns unfold out the window. She and Frank shared a package of licorice in Rochester and another of cookies in Madison, but they didn't eat a full meal until they arrived in Chicago. Their travel time was hours longer than if they'd returned to Osceola and taken the train, but the goal seemed to be to put as many miles as quickly as possible between Grandma and Pere Foyse.

Frank stayed the next month in Chicago then went back to Serenity Farm, this time without Grandma. The idea of farming intrigued him, and he felt he wanted to do something about the disconnect between his grandparents although he wasn't sure what. Also Frank was concerned about what Ed said when Frank joked about the labels on the drawers and cabinets—DISHES, CUPS, TOWELS, CLEANING—and Ed motioned him into the hall and explained, "Your Grandpa doesn't remember as well as he did." Ed's whisper was as dry and brittle as the concern that broke inside of Frank at that.

There was no reason Frank couldn't go back to Serenity Farm. After high school he'd enlisted in the Army, attracted by the promise of training and money for college. He'd been trained as a welder, and when he dropped out of Community College after one semester, he was still able to bounce from one good-paying job to the next, all the while feeding his constant need to be traveling somewhere else.

That need was still strong, but not as strong as the tug of family. And the economics of Serenity Farm were so constantly a single wobbly step from ruin that Frank didn't feel comfortable abandoning Grandpa and Ed. Also Ed was so effusively thankful that someone from the family had stepped up to help with Grandpa. So Frank stayed on.

Early on he realized that when Grandpa would say he was going out to help Ed, it was more a refrain than a performance. Grandpa would sit and kibitz while Ed worked, then wander away to fiddle with the levers on a harrow or start up a mower, or fill the water bowls for the barn cats and narrate the comings and goings of the swifts that nested in the rafters.

One of the things Frank took over from Ed was driving Grandpa. On Tuesdays, Frank and Grandpa would eat lunch at the Pere Foyse diner then shop for groceries and pick up whatever Ed had ordered at the feed store. Evenings after supper, Grandpa would ask for a ride back to Pere Foyse, and he and Frank would join Aynor DeSilets and Cornrow Thompson at the bar. Frank found their conversation dull, repetitive and mostly inscrutable, the minutia of seed varieties and commodity prices, the mystery of indicators in the seemingly unchanging tableau of the weather, and the encroachment of corporate farms. Most nights there was a long cadenza about acreage being worth multiples more in house lots than in crops, with Aynor and Cornrow supplying the rhythm and backbone of the conversation, and Grandpa punctuating their complaining with stories. A few beers in, and Grandpa's stories would slump from narrative to episodic fragments, and whenever he'd pause for a swallow of beer, Aynor or Cornrow would repeat whatever he'd said last and nod, then resume their separate conversation. Relieved of accompanying Grandpa in the evenings, Ed would clean up after supper and watch television then go to bed before Frank and Grandpa returned.

Before he came to Pere Foyse, Grandpa had worked in business. He started as a salesman for Chicago Candy, with a route that extended from Vermillion to Indianapolis to Kansas City to Chicago. Snacks and cigarettes were good business, and Grandpa loved the people and the travel, and especially Pere Foyse. Even after he was promoted to territory manager and then vice-president, and even after he bought Chicago Candy from the Patersons, when they retired, Grandpa continued to drive his original route each fall, renewing old friendships and developing new ones.

Grandma was never convinced it was just the scenery and memories that drew Grandpa, imagining something more specifically human and less honorable. But she was content with her life in Chicago. She had her friends and engagements, and she and Grandpa would travel on vacation to Europe and South America and Asia. So if Grandpa still drove out from Chicago each August, to Springfield then Lincoln and Sioux Falls, with a postcard home from each and a week in Pere Foyse, that was just the way it was between them.

When Grandpa retired and sold Chicago Candy, some of the money went to a build a new house in Burr Ridge and some went to buy Serenity Farm. For the next few years, Grandma and Grandpa continued the life they'd been living. They were Gold Council Members of the Chicago Opera Theater, and Grandma chaired the Donations Committee of the DAR. They continued to travel, and now when Grandpa took his yearly tour, the week he spent in Pere Foyse he stayed at Serenity Farm. And even though Farm Journal magazine began arriving each month just like Forbes and Newsweek, Grandma was still gob-smacked when Grandpa announced he was moving to Pere Foyse to take up farming. But she never wavered, her response was unconditional and clear, she had no intention of joining him.

The first summer after Grandpa moved was when Grandma and Frank took their trip, and on the bus ride back to Chicago, Frank remembered thinking that no matter how frosty the aftermath of his parents' fights had felt, he had no words for the sub-zero emotions running then between Grandma and Grandpa.

Over time, those emotions softened. When Frank and Grandpa would go back to Chicago, for Thanksgiving and Christmas, for the President's Council Opera Banquet and the DAR Fundraising Dinner, Grandpa and Grandma were unfailingly cordial and outwardly loving with each other. The trips were enjoyable. Frank would reconnect with high school friends, and Grandpa's failing memory was always more functional in Chicago where years of routine and familiarity had imprinted. When it was time to say goodbye, Grandma always seemed to be of mixed minds. She was clearly relieved, but also wistful, and consistently and absolutely resolute that she had no intention of ever leaving Chicago for Pere Foyse.

Frank settled into the routines at Serenity Farm. In January he and Ed would develop a budget for the year and create a farming plan—chickens, a few cows and a kitchen garden for themselves, 15 acres of hay as a hedge, and corn and soybeans for the rest. The farm's finances never seemed to improve, but they weren't getting worse any faster. Which meant Serenity Farm would need to be sold at some point, an acknowledgment that was as solid and true as needing air to breathe and food to eat, and discussed just as infrequently. But when it did come up, it always framed with the hope that it wouldn't happen until Grandpa was gone.

Frank made friends in the community of characters who called Pere Foyse home. There was Rebecca, a third-grade teacher who became his girlfriend and Sarnie and Ruth, the lesbian couple who ran Roots and Shoots Nursery, and Doug who owned Puff Works, a company that made organic cheese puffs and corn chips.

Frank had met Ruth at the Feed Store when he snickered at the t-shirt she was wearing which was emblazoned with the nursery logo and the words: *Proudly (Not) Fucking the Man Since 1978*. "They don't sell at all here, but the mail order is good," Ruth explained. That afternoon, Frank drove to the nursery and bought one.

His third January at Serenity Farm, Frank told Ed that he wanted to plant some marijuana plants in the garden. "Why not hemp?" Ed said. "It's legal ok and it grows just the same." But Frank insisted on marijuana, "For personal use."

That fall after he harvested, Sarnie told Frank she could connect him with buyers if he had enough marijuana to sell. She, Frank and Doug were sharing a joint and Sarnie had just finished a rambling explanation about how she and Ruth, the lesbians that Pere Foyse knew, were fine, but that other, outside lesbians were definitely a threat.

"Absolutely! Our lesbians are champs, solid, upright, church-going entrepreneurs. But a gay school teacher or a gay scout master?" Doug exhaled, "Uh-uh." Frank had stopped listening when he heard the marijuana price Sarnie had named, the potential dollars were staggering. That night Frank told Ed that the wanted to plant an eighth of an acre in marijuana the following year.

"That amount, you will get caught and you will lose the farm."

"We're losing it anyway," Frank said. He repeated the price Sarnie had quoted. "We'd make money for the first time since I've been here."

The argument continued for several weeks before Ed finally gave in. As a condition of agreeing, he insisted the plants be separated and not edge-planted, and camouflaged by corn, pole beans and trellised vegetables and flowers. He also swore if he heard a single word about the marijuana all summer, or if anyone, gawkers, partners, buyers, *anyone*, came to see the plants, he'd pack a suitcase and be gone.

Frank took extra care preparing the soil in the spring and built a distribution tap with fixed hoses for watering. The weather in April and May was perfect and the season got off to a great start.

In July, Grandpa sliced through the hoses and chopped up the kitchen garden with the ride-on-mower. Half the marijuana was lost and Frank elected to not replace the hoses, worried the purchase would invite questions and scrutiny. Looking over the devastation from Frank's bedroom window, Rebecca said it looked like Jackson Pollock had designed a crop circle.

"Who?" Frank asked. He felt as tired as he'd ever felt in his life.

In September, Frank and Grandpa came back from town to find Ed on the porch with his suitcase. "They know," Ed said to Frank. He pressed his hat onto his head and clumped down the stairs. "I'll take a ride to the bus now," He said.

"Wait! Hold on. *Ed!* What are you saying?"

"Aynor's selling his farm. The county agent and the assessors were out and a realtor whose sister-in-law works for the Sheriff. The realtor said they know about your marijuana."

"I don't see how."

"How doesn't matter."

"Ed! Wait! This farm doesn't work without you. There's no way."

"It's not work with me either and it's nothing worth getting arrested for."

"I'll pull the marijuana, I'll burn it. Today. It'll be gone by dark."

"All of it?"

Frank hesitated and Ed slid his suitcase onto the back seat of the car. "*Alright*! Alright, all of it," Frank said.

After he finished burning the marijuana, Frank stood under the shower spray for a long time. He'd scrubbed with pumice soap and then paint soap but there was still resin on his hands and a smell that hovered wherever he went.

They was unusually quiet at supper, food passed with careful *pleases and thank yous,* punctuated only by the clinking of silverware. After supper Frank asked Ed to drive Grandpa to Pere Foyse so he could have the night off.

"I'm glad you burned it," Rebecca said. She and Frank were drying the dishes, "Even though you stink right now."

"Why?"

"You know."

"No, tell me?"

"Pere Foyse is a small town, and I'm a school teacher. People talk about things like that."

"But you never said anything before."

"I know. You were so hopeful, and you made it sound so important."

"We would have been in the black for the first time, since I've been here."

"And there's nothing else? No different crops? Or techniques? Maybe, you should talk with Aynor, while you can, and see what he thinks."

"Aynor decided to sell. That's what he thinks."

"But still. Maybe there's something you're doing that isn't the best way."

Frank shook his head, "Ed knows whatever Aynor knows."

"Or not. Maybe there are things that Ed doesn't know, it can't hurt to ask."

"Sure," Frank didn't sound persuaded.

Rebecca brought it up again when they were in bed. Frank was stroking her hair and his stroking had slowed as he tipped out of waking. The canvas behind his eyelids had filled with the color of her hair, a chestnut bronze, the color that the oaks turned in the fall. "I'm glad you burned it," she said.

"Uh huh," Frank murmured.

"I can go with you to Aynor's if you want."

"Sure," Frank said and then his breathing lengthened and he began to snore.

The following weekend they drove to Aynor's. Cornrow was with Aynor in the barn and they were arguing, but they stopped when the door opened and they turned to face Frank and Rebecca. Each was holding a beer.

"Beer in the cooler," Aynor gestured. He seemed mildly annoyed.

"How are you doing?" Frank asked.

"Stupid is how he's doing," Cornrow grumbled. "He shouldn't be selling."

"Not selling is what's stupid," Aynor said. "Get kicked and squeezed for another year and never get as much tomorrow as you will today. You'll be asking if I have room for you in Florida soon enough."

"Florida?" Frank asked.

"He's not going to Florida."

"You'll see."

"Hey, what's this thing? It looks pre-historic," Rebecca was pointing at a piece of equipment.

"The Toro? First powered mower we ever bought, the first mower I ever mowed with," Aynor said.

"You had a Toro? We had that Jacobsen and that was one *dangerous sonnabitch.* My god I was glad to see it gone. It's probably still in the barn somewhere."

"What happens to the equipment?" Frank asked.

"Auction," Aynor said. "You and Ed want something, come over now and I'll give you a price."

"What about me?" Cornrow asked.

"Price is double for the lunkheads who'll just be selling it again before I have my curtains up in Fort Pierce."

"Ed said he doesn't know what he'd do if Grandpa sold Serenity Farm, farming is what he knows." Rebecca said.

"He's good too, but good doesn't matter like it used to. And he's slower since his accident."

"He was plenty slow before that, that's probably why it happened," Cornrow said.

"You," Aynor shook his head and pointed. He turned to Frank, "Pay attention to him and you'll end up worse than you are. You and Ed take whatever you can for help."

Frank forced a smile. "We're trying."

Aynor grimaced, "What I heard, but not the stupid help. Remember to tell Ed to stop by soon, they'll start tagging for the auction this week."

On the drive home Rebecca was still talking about the Toro mower. "That belongs in a farming museum, what a weird rusty cyclops looking thing. And those stories too, on one of those phone things that you pick up and there's Aynor talking."

"Except it's not really farming, it's more like lawn care."

"Okay, a lawn care museum. Put Aynor's mower in and Cornrow's too."

Frank repeated the mower conversation to Ed as part of relaying Aynor's invitation to look over his equipment. Ed's response was as close to a laugh as Frank had ever heard from him, "A Jacobsen and a Toro? You know your Grandpa still has a Hills reel-mower in the barn?"

That wasn't the precise moment that the American Museum of Lawn Care took form, but Frank did collect Aynor's mower, and Cornrow's, and locate the reel mower. That winter, as part of his off-season maintenance of equipment at Serenity Farm, Frank welded repair parts and cleaned and painted the mowers. He left them in an empty barn stall and he saw them every day as he worked, but the idea of starting a museum didn't take hold until after the spring planting and cultivating.

Frank was eating lunch with Grandpa at the diner and he was looking at the ads printed on the placemats. He thought if Serenity Farm had a lawn care museum, they could place an ad for it there. When he repeated the idea to Rebecca she laughed, "I said you could come up with something."

So they opened the American Museum of Lawn Care with the three mowers, and a scythe that Ruth and Sarnie had donated. Rebecca hand-lettered signs for the mowers and a large museum sign for the end of the driveway. Frank bought an ad in the Pere Foyse Trader and contracted for one to be printed on the next run of placemats. For the Grand Opening he arranged a mowing demonstration and Doug agreed to demonstrate scything in return for storage space for Puff Works in the barn.

Ed thought the museum was a waste of time, and he was proved correct when opening day came and went without a single visitor except for Sarnie and Ruth. "We'll call it your soft opening," Sarnie consoled Frank. "And we'll plan a real grand opening for later in the summer."

"Or call it a dumb-ass distraction. Farming is hard enough without distractions," Ed said.

"Count me out," Doug said. "My arms are killing me, that was brutal. I could use a joint."

"Time to bulk up, Chip Boy. It's going to be long summer if we can get this puppy launched."

The second Grand Opening went a little better. Sarnie and Ruth set up a display of jams and tinctures and gave away samples of flavored spreads they were testing. Doug donated chip. Frank hired a band and arranged for refreshments. The mowing and scything demonstrations went off perfectly and about thirty people attended over the course of the afternoon.

"A thirty-fold increase," Rebecca laughed.

"Just ten more grand openings and we nail it," Ruth said.

"No more grand openings. Ed's right," Frank said.

"You can't just give up," Rebecca said.

"Why not?" Frank flipped a table on its side to break it down.

"We lost money for the first four years we were in business," Sarnie said.

"You did?" Frank stopped.

"Three for me," Doug said.

"Making this a success will take time," Rebecca said.

Frank decided the museum would only be open on weekends. Sarnie and Ruth donated products to sell and Doug did the same. Doug also agreed to a scything demonstration every Saturday. The biggest change was the donations. When people heard Frank would take unwanted mowers and lawn equipment, they started to call, or just drop things off. The barn was filled with rusty discards. Then the Pere Foyse trader ran a story about the museum and the story was picked up and featured in the Des Moines Register things to see and do.

Frank reorganized the museum by chronology. *The first intentional lawn care was done by sheep or servants wielding scythes.* Frank split the initial exhibit between a sheep pen and Doug's scything area. Sarnie and Ruth created an interactive display of sod types with a dozen squares of different grasses and Rebecca sewed a servant's outfit for Doug to wear when he demonstrated.

The second exhibit featured a picture of a Buddings mower and explanatory text, and the Hills mower. Next came a power mower exhibit with a picture of a Beazley mower and the Jacobsen and Toro mowers. The final exhibit included a fleet of ride-on-mowers and a fence festooned with clippers, shears, string trimmers and leaf blowers.

The last Saturday before the museum would close for the season, Frank threw a party to celebrate their first year. As the day was winding down and they started to clean up, a handful of people were still milling the grounds including a mother with two children, one of whom was complaining, "You said there was a petting zoo but the sign says *Don't Pet the Sheep*."

"I thought they had a petting zoo. Let me ask."

"Sheep don't really like to be petted, they can be skittish and it's not safe," Frank said.

"*Frank*," Rebecca rolled her eyes. "Come on you guys, you can come with me," She held out her hands for the kids and gestured for the mother to follow.

"It's not really much of a museum," The woman standing next to Frank was dressed in a blouse, slacks and a sun-hat. She had a sweater knotted by the arms around her neck and she was wearing sunglasses. Her hair was gray.

"It's our first year," Frank said.

"I know. I was here in June just after you opened."

"And you came back," Frank smiled.

"To see if you'd made anything of it. The answer is not really. I'd expect you'd be happy to take what you can get and sell out."

Frank smiled. "Sell the museum? Why would I do that?"

"For five hundred free and clear?"

"Five hundred thousand dollars?!"

"*Please*," She made a face. "Five hundred dollars, and that's just for the name. Everything else here is junk." She handed Frank a business card that read Joan Groschens, Broker.

"The museum's not for sale," Frank repeated.

"I told them that's what you'd say. But hang onto my card anyway. You might change your mind." Her mouth thinned into the whisper of a smile and she walked away.

Any thought of selling the museum would have ended there, except that Grandpa died the following February. Over New Year's he seemed fine, but after he got sick, he went downhill quickly and a month later, he was gone. Outside, the February landscape was windswept and gray, with snow dervishes that spun into the heavy press of sky.

Frank called Joan Groschens and left a message about his grandfather. He told her he would take her offer of $500 for the museum.

"I'm sorry to hear about your Grandfather," she said when she called him back. "They said I could go as high as $5000 for the museum, I'll tell them you negotiated me to seven." It was only after the paperwork was signed and the check was deposited that Frank learned he'd sold the name and rights to the American Museum of Lawn Care to John Deere for $7,000.

Frank went back to Chicago to help plan Grandpa's funeral and memorial. When he asked Grandma what she was thinking about Serenity Farm, she said she'd be meeting with her financial advisor, but for the upcoming year, Frank and Ed should proceed as always. She told Frank she wanted to hold a memorial for Grandpa at Serenity Farm because that's what he would have wanted.

So in May, Frank and Grandma rode the California Zephyr again to Osceola and Ed picked them up. They stopped for dinner in Mason City then drove to Serenity Farm. Rebecca had lettered a new sign for the driveway that read "Serenity Farm, First Home of the American Museum of Lawn Care." In the area where Doug had done his scything demonstrations, Sarnie, Ruth and Rebecca had decorated with flowers and set up easels with pictures of Grandpa, Frank and Ed, the museum and Serenity Farm.

On the day of the memorial people came from Pere Foyse and the surrounding towns. A minister spoke, then Ed, and then Aynor and Cornrow, and then Frank got up to speak.

Grandma was dabbing her eyes with a tissue and Rebecca was holding her hand. In Grandma's lap was a model tractor that she'd brought from Chicago. In the cab she'd placed a lock of Grandpa's hair and his pocket watch, and she planned to leave the tractor at Serenity Farm. It was yellow and green, a John Deere, and Frank knew he'd need to change that, to sand off the colors and repaint it orange like a Kubota, or red like a Massey Ferguson or Yanmar, or blue like a Sonalika. Only the people who knew what Ed, Aynor and Cornrow knew would be able to tell what he'd done.

Frank looked at the assembled faces and then at Grandma, and then he began to tell the story of Serenity Farm, how Grandpa and Ed had farmed it, and Frank had joined them, and then Rebecca and the museum. He ended by wishing Grandpa Godspeed on his new and unknown journey, but before he did, Frank explained how they planned to continue what Grandpa had started. Sarnie and Ruth would be leasing acreage from Serenity Farm for Roots and Shoots and Doug would be doing the same for Puff Works. Frank and Ed would farm the acreage was left, but only until Rebecca and Frank had time to put their heads together to come up with another fabulous idea, one that was even more spectacular than the American Museum of Lawn Care.

The Breadwinner

ITTO AND MEKIYA OUTINI

"Be grateful." Shoveling heaps of toast onto his plate, Atiq laid into Hatim. "Think of what you have."

But he *was* thinking of what he had.

"A friend who's always there for you. Who keeps his freezer full."

The night before, Hatim had thawed his last eleven loaves, eaten whatever would fit down his gullet, then swept the rest into the garbage, telling himself that it would be all right, that he'd swing by the store for more bread on his way home the following evening. He hadn't, of course. Too exhausted. Instead, he'd come here.

"A roof above your head. A place to sleep."

Two places, really: Marie's musty futon, a hand-me-down on which she thrashed about as if possessed, releasing barbeque-scented farts until his eyes rolled in their sockets and he had to stagger to the living room and slump on the sofa; and Atiq's inflatable mattress—but what is a place to sleep, really? The first horizontal surface you happen upon before collapsing.

"A steady job."

The telecom center had hired him for one reason, one reason only: twelve Arabs already worked there, and they'd taken him for one of their own. He now spent his days refilling the Keurig in the breakroom and striving to pacify customers who talked too fast while the officers assigned to their cases were in the restroom. They'd even created a job for Marie, inexplicably deeming her one of their own, too, and now she occupied the cubicle across from his, battling her way through endless rounds of Clash of Clans, so that his eyes ached day and night.

"Insulin. All the insulin you need."

What he didn't spend on bread, he spent on medicine.

"A name these people can pronounce. At least no one's calling you Attic. Or Basement."

At that, Hatim snorted. "You're right, brother." He hunched over his plate, shredding his toast into small pieces fit for waterfowl. "But it's been fourteen years."

The anniversary of his arrival in the States had come hit harder than usual this year. Or maybe it always hit this hard. Maybe he'd mastered the art of forgetting, just as mothers forget the agony of childbearing, carrying on despite not knowing why he carried on, persisting out of sheer amnesia. He'd come with high hopes, lured by assurances of wealth from Marie, who'd turned out to be Marie's brother lurking behind Marie's profile picture, eager to slough off legal guardianship of his mentally unstable sister onto the first poor sop who took the bait. No hope of corporate sponsorship for someone like him, who used Google Translate to cobble together the simplest sweet nothings, and he'd already applied for the lottery three years running, all to no avail. Marriage to a citizen had seemed a surer thing, a straighter path to paradise. Not so—but how could he have known?

"Be grateful," Atiq repeated, taking a seat across from him and squirting ketchup on his toast. "Or have you changed your mind? Don't want this anymore? Just give the word. Don't wait for ICE; they've got their hands full. I'll book you a seat on the next flight to Casa. One less thing for me to deal with. One less thing." He took a drag on his dab pen, dug in.

"Isn't it a bit early?"

"I've got a stand-up. 8:00 AM. The bitch insisted."

"Can they make you do that?"

"What do you think?" Atiq tore wolfishly into his toast. Hatim eyed the clock behind him—6:39—and the window framing four neat squares of gloaming sky.

"I think I'll be finding my own way to work."

"Shit." Crumbs sprayed from Atiq's mouth across the table. "Let me call an Uber."

"Don't forget Marie."

They embraced in the doorway, the perfunctory hug of two men in the trenches together, Atiq's once-muscled frame deftly cradling Hatim's ever-plush one, and then Hatim slipped out into the hall. A one-two punch pummeled his nose: first asbestos, then musty dry rot from the stairs. Outside in the parking lot, beneath flickering lights, he stood wheezing, gazing around for the car that would whisk him away from this crude refuge, stocked with ciabatta and sourdough, pita and naan, toward the breadless latitudes where he would labor, spilling sweat from his brow and bitter coffee down his shirt, not to rouse himself from dull and stupid slumber, but to sink ever deeper into this zombifying American Dream.

The Uber driver, as it turned out, was a fellow slumberer: a rickety, sour-faced South Asian man engulfed in a button-down, wrinkled, too large. He steered with a single claw-like hand while the other scrabbled keenly at the radio dial. "You know this thing they are talking?" he wanted to know. "You think China is happy?"

"I don't know anything about it, brother." Hatim cranked his seat back, closed his eyes, but this turned out to be the wrong tack.

"You don't know." The driver gunned the engine through a red light at an empty intersection. "*I* know. My uncle, he is on the security council. He tells me things, all these things, what they are talking. He tells me, get ready. The whole world, all the countries, they are wanting America to fall, see? China is not happy, Iran is not happy, even my country, Pakistan, is not happy. So, they are working together. You see how they are working together?"

"Yes, that's true. No one is happy."

Marie was waiting for them in the gravel driveway at the far end of the cul-de-sac, decked out in a red and white kimono, a brown dishtowel wrapped around her head, a can of diet Dr. Pepper in her hand, looking for all the world like a frog stuck halfway through her transformation back to princess. Behind her, their dilapidated prefab slouched atop the hill, her only contribution to their marriage, melting at a steady rate of several centimeters every year downhill into the hollow where they grilled each summer, a concave wasteland of crabgrass, candy wrappers, empty propane cans, and bones.

"Where the hell you been?" she demanded, squeezing into the seat behind Hatim.

"With the planes, they are doing it," the driver was muttering. "With the planes, they are spreading it all over. All over. But now the Americans, they are shutting down the airports. They are saying no more planes." He locked eyes with Hatim, daring him to mount a contradiction. "Isn't that right?"

"That's right. You're right, brother."

"Knock, knock!" Marie rapped on the back of his skull. "Where you been, I said?"

Eyes shut, Hatim concentrated on the center of his forehead, the electric fizz that came into his mind when called, a sensation not externally imposed, a self-created thing—the only thing that answered to him in this world.

"What am I, shit-face?" Marie barked in his ear. "Fucking invisible?"

"With the planes," the driver was chanting, a low and threadbare incantation, a sultry, smoldering melody. "That only is how they are doing this. With the planes."

Every peace was fleeting. Too soon, timeworn thoughts rushed in: if he'd only finished school. Even just high school. That had been his father's dream: to see his son rise in the world. If his father hadn't vanished when Hatim was twelve—into a jail cell, he'd learned later, much later, though his mother still said that he'd gone to his grave—then maybe he would've amounted to something, acquired skills sought after in this country, or even in his own. If only his English were stronger. If only he could put his foot down, boss the underlings around. If only he could code.

The first to clock in at the telecom center, they found the salesfloor empty, screen savers chugging steadily away in every cubicle, gray desks bathed in harsh and endless glare. Power coursed through the walls, its ragged chur exaggerated by the silence, amplified a millionfold. His teeth hurt. His eyes burned. His guts groaned and gurgled, rearranged themselves. His eyes darted high and low, expecting to find something waiting to pounce as he slipped into his cubicle, but there was nothing there, nothing with vicious teeth, nothing with claws; but there, on his desk, atop his keyboard—

Was he seeing things?

He did a double take.

It was still there.

Resting like a curled cat upon his keyboard—was it real?—there sat a loaf.

A loaf of sourdough.

"Lay off the carbs," the doctor had ordered the last time he'd seen him, back when he still had his documents, health insurance, a proper job, well over a decade ago. "Eat a salad."

But no salad could remind him that he was Moroccan, still Moroccan, however far from home, and so he'd compromised, resolving to swallow bread only from sunset to sunrise, chewing wads of spearmint gum rapaciously by day to fill the void. Religion had conditioned his digestive tract to these diurnal fasts, had perhaps even seeded the notion, felt more than consciously believed, that nothing eaten under cover of darkness could appreciably alter his blood sugar levels. Always dizzy, always weary to the bone, but these afflictions might well owe to other factors—stress, anxiety, existential shame—and here he was, all these years later, and still going strong.

But now this apparition.

Now this flagrant mockery—or was it a mirage?

Which of his colleagues knew enough to engineer this taunt? He kept his secrets close, never spoke of bread around the office, gave a wide berth to the Wonder loaves in the breakroom cupboard, through which Marie pawed with marsupial cunning, constructing her famous peanut butter and Cool Whip sandwiches.

But of course. Marie.

It must've been Marie.

Perhaps she'd been spilling his secrets for weeks, whispering to their colleagues when his back was turned, exposing his nocturnal appetites, his weaknesses. One of them, aiming to prank him, must've swung by some bakery that morning, someplace of which he'd never heard, which turned out fresh loaves as full-bodied and frank as his own mother's khobz, a hidden gem nestled in the heart of this colorless, middle-American city, and picked out this gorgeous specimen—perhaps to get under his skin, perhaps simply to see if the rumors were true. The culprit must be in the building somewhere, staked out beneath some desk, behind some door, watching to gauge his next move. Would he tear into this manna, sating his appetite but also handing social leverage to the layer of the trap? Or would he feign indifference and casually lob the loaf into the trash, even as thoughts of an empty freezer burned behind his eyes?

He couldn't bring himself to drop the sourdough into the trashcan, even if it was the clever thing to do—not this shapely dome of carbohydrates, this exquisite, yeasty temple, this golden-crusted beacon of the night to come—but neither could he leave it sitting on his desk all day. He would not have the will to steel himself against its siren song.

Gingerly, barely brushing the loaf with the tips of his fingers, he lifted it from his keyboard and lowered it into his desk's waiting drawer.

But the loaf was too leavened. The drawer would not close.

He placed a palm atop its dome and tried, as gently as he could, to press it down, but it resisted. Its crust was too resilient, its sponge too firm.

If forced shut, the drawer would tear through it the way only teeth should tear through it. He couldn't desecrate this beauty, couldn't violate the sheer perfection of its form.

Flushed with shame, he glanced around once more, anticipating faces peering into his cubicle. No one was there. He and Marie were alone in the building.

He put his face close to the loaf and breathed, as eager as Atiq with his dab pen, a long, luxurious inhalation. No trace of his spouse's flatulence penetrated the microclimate millimeters above its crust. Its scent was unearthly, too divine to be believed, the sort of smell he hadn't reveled in for over fourteen years. His lips quivered with pleasure. Tears sprang to his eyes. After a decade and a half of sweeping processed breads from supermarket shelves with all the bright-eyed and bushy-tailed verve of a veteran fentanyl user, ignoring their bleached white artificiality, telling himself that he could neither taste nor smell their stabilizers and emulsifiers, finally, at long last, real bread, *true* bread, would grace his tongue.

The paranoia that had gripped him moments earlier unraveled, releasing him into the sweet embrace of unadulterated joy. Maybe this wasn't a prank after all. Perhaps no human hands had left this offering. He wasn't a believer anymore, hadn't been for many years, but what could a nonbeliever do when brought face to face with a miracle? Might this be a sign that he'd finally endured enough? That the time for him to break his fast had come? That he might once more openly, in daylight, savor memories of home?

He barely registered the motion of his hands, frantically unknotting the twist tie, entering the bag, until the spongy stuff was at his lips. Synapses sparked. Endorphins flooded through his veins. The pleasure nearly made him swoon.

His phone began to ring.

"Hallo?" he exclaimed, spraying crumbs.

"Hatim?"

For a moment, he couldn't place the voice, out of context on the landline that only Marie and his boss ever used.

Then he knew.

"Atiq? Is this you?"

"Can't believe it," Atiq was saying. "Can't believe it."

"Can't believe what? What's wrong?"

"Laid off. Let go. Fired."

"Who's been fired?"

"That bitch," Atiq snarled, "got me on a conference call at 8:00 AM to fire me. To fucking fire me. I'm fucking fired."

Be grateful, brother. He almost said it, almost let his pent-up irritation loose, almost fired off a pithy quip distilled from God-only-knew-how-many narcissistic rants to which he'd been subjected, but he checked himself. He knew that now was not the time.

Then it hit him: why this news mattered. Why *he* was receiving this call.

"I've done as much as I can," Atiq went on, "but you should know, brother, that I've got nothing in savings. As a matter of fact, there's three thousand pending on my credit card. What I'm trying to tell you is, you're the one working."

The soggy bolus Hatim had just swallowed lodged in his esophagus, as heavy as stone.

In the restroom, he jammed a finger down his throat and let his bile flood the toilet bowl, an autumnal emulsion that gushed and dripped and gushed again. At the sink, he met his own reflection: wide mouth, flat nose, expressive eyebrows, deep-set, red-rimmed, soulful eyes. Jabba, they'd called him at his first job in the States, stocking shelves at Walgreens, back when his green card application was still pending. Denied. Denied. No explanation. At a certain point, he'd stopped applying, let his work permit expire, started working under the table. These days, he labored for the promise of $7.25 an hour, three months in and still not paid—but Atiq, who'd covered every drink, every ride, every meal, every break from the monotony for years, who could be self-centered and insufferable indeed, yet whom he arguably owed, was no longer making anything at all.

It was 9:15 by the time Hatim went slinking shamefacedly back toward his cubicle—9:15, but the salesfloor was still empty. Some of the computer screens were open now, suggesting that his colleagues had come and gone. Coffee burbled in the kitchen. Muffled voices reached him from the conference room.

Gathered around the conference table, they looked like oarsmen on a craft that was taking on water—all except Marie, who sat at one end of the long table, gnawing a Snicker's bar. At the opposite end from her sat Abdurrahman, the general manager, bearded, gaunt, and neatly dressed in a dark blue suit, an eggshell skullcap, and a periwinkle tie. He glanced up when Hatim peered around the door.

"Have a seat, brother."

Could this be the next stage of his punishment? Hatim wondered, taking the one remaining chair. The prankster's moment in the sun, the joke's sadistic punchline. None of them met his eyes. Yet they did not seem about to laugh, not even at his expense.

"I called this meeting," said Abdurrahman, "to discuss our situation in light of the national emergency."

Hatim's fingers cracked methodically beneath the table as he listened, absorbing little of what was said, grasping only that a choice was in the offing: to go on working despite the federal government's recommendation to shelter in place, or to go home and await further instructions. Corporate had devolved the decision to the regional managers on the grounds that each office would face a distinct set of challenges. Abdurrahman, in turn, was devolving the decision to his employees.

They went around the room. Karim said that his elderly father-in-law was at home, and he would like to be there to look after him. Ibrahim nodded politely, but when his turn came, he said that he would like to stay, for he could use the money. Marie belched loudly. Abdurrahman glanced at Hatim as if seeking interpretation.

"We'll stay," Hatim mumbled. "God willing, we could use the money, too."

By 10:00 AM, it was decided: the center would remain open, manned by a skeleton crew, while about two thirds of their colleagues headed home to tend to relatives and other affairs. Back in his cubicle, Hatim clicked listlessly through emails on which he'd been cc'ed, none of which seemed to pertain to him. In the background, his colleagues spoke in hushed and anxious voices, echoing the social media posts they'd seen, the news reports, the messages from friends. They congregated in little groups around the room. Phones rang. No one answered them. Not even Abdurrahman seemed to mind. He joined his underlings at the water cooler, reading off his phone, sounding less like himself, thought Hatim, and more like the Uber driver from the morning.

Only Hatim and Marie kept their distance. As if to compensate for never having done an hour's work before, they now made a show of working hard. Hatim banged on his keyboard, highlighting random file folders on his desktop, opening windows, closing them again. From the space by his elbow, the sourdough obtruded forcefully into his consciousness, staler now, its ravished form a mute and damning testimony.

If these truly were the end times, reflected Hatim, then he might as well swallow as much bread as possible—though, also, if these really were the end times, he'd best not get caught with that bread in his belly when the angels to set about weighing their feather against his misdeeds. Soon, he began making little pilgrimages, back and forth, to and fro, from the cubicle to the restroom and back to the cubicle, from asceticism to indulgence to asceticism.

Returning for the third time, he glanced at the wall clock, which informed him that Asr Salah had just passed.

"In light of today's events," Abdurrahman announced ten minutes later in the conference room, where he'd gathered his remaining employees, "I've made a decision."

Starched cuffs and collars crackled. Men shifted in their seats uneasily.

"There's no way to know what tomorrow will bring," said Abdurrahman. "We only know what's going on right now. Uncertainty is always a difficult thing. Even me, you can see, I'm a bit frightened." He cracked a bashful smile, let it linger for a moment, then drew his composure back around himself and spoke with sudden, brash authority. "We've got one more hour together, brothers. One more hour. After that, God only knows how many days before we meet again. They're saying we may all be working from home soon. Every office may be closed."

Murmurs rustled around the room.

"I've just been on a conference call," he continued. "This is what corporate's saying. That's why I've decided that before we go our separate ways, we must take this opportunity, which God has given us, to come together as one in prayer, to ask for His mercy on behalf of this office, this city, and all Muslims everywhere."

Everybody was nodding now, even Marie, the brown dishtowel bobbing on her head emphatically.

"We must ask that He spare us," said Abdurrahman. "We must ask that He protect us. We must ask that He grant us the strength of will to face the unknown resolutely, without fear. We must—"

"But who's going to lead the prayer?" demanded Malek. "Has anyone here been trained?"

Silence fell over the conference room. Nervous glances darted to and fro.

"We don't need an imam," said Abdurrahman, not wholly unruffled. "Anyone can lead a prayer."

"It's one thing to say a prayer," Malek observed, "and another thing to lead it. I'll be more than happy to say it, but leading it … that's another matter."

"I've heard it done," said Ibrahim, "many times I've heard it done, but my memory's not what it used to be. I'm afraid I might mix up some words here and there. That's too big a risk to take, given the circumstances."

"And my voice," Fahad put in, "is a bit scratchy. My wife always tells me I sound like a record player. A vinyl record player."

"Those are supposed to have the highest sound quality," Nasir observed. "Better than digital. Maybe you should be the one to do it."

Everyone laughed, but there was an unnatural edge to that laughter, a sort of manic force behind it. Even Fahad laughed along raspily, but he sobered up before the others, shaking his head and mumbling, "No, no, no, it wouldn't be right. It wouldn't be right at all."

"I don't think I should do it, either," Marie chimed in, "because that would just be weird."

"Who here has the best voice?" Nasir asked. "Anyone can read the prayer, but his voice has got to be good. Really good."

"That's right," Fahad agreed. "The best."

"The very best!"

"Not me."

"Not me."

"You know who's got a real nice voice?"

All heads swiveled toward Marie, perched with her legs drawn up and tucked beneath her in her chair, a bag of Cheez-Its cradled in the crook of her arm.

"Hatim!" Half their eyes swiveled toward him, then back onto her as she went on, "He's always singing in the shower. He's got a voice like an angel. That's what my momma always used to say—voice like an angel! She used to hear angels gossiping, telling her shit about me and my brother, you know, all the bad stuff we was doing, but we weren't never doing nothing, so I guess that was just the meth talking. But she knew what they sound like. You know. The angels. She didn't know nothing about your-all's religion, but I bet all the angels pretty much sound the same." She popped a Cheez-It into her mouth and smacked her decisively. "I think he should do it."

They might as well have been halogen spotlights, the eyes that swung from every corner onto him, scorching his flesh, singeing the delicate hairs on his arms, leeching the moisture from his lips and tongue so that, when he opened his mouth, he was shocked to hear the words emerge at all, words he hadn't meant to say, though acquiescence was the only tactic that he'd ever practiced, the only game he'd ever learned.

"Of course," he croaked. "Of course, brothers. Just a minute. Just give me a minute. Just... but don't you think we ought to wash ourselves?"

This set in motion a lively discussion. Some, pointing to war-torn cities without intact plumbing, argued that ablutions could be waived in emergencies. Others observed that this wasn't that sort of emergency, though even these voices acknowledged that there were no showers in the office, and that they would have to make do with the sinks in the restrooms and breakroom.

"We must do our best, brothers," Abdurrahman said sternly. "Our very best. Otherwise, how can any of us expect our prayers to be accepted?"

With that, everyone agreed. Dutifully, they filed out of the conference room, took turns relieving themselves, then began removing their shoes and washing their hands and feet at the sinks. Hatim went through the motions, though it took all the contortionism he could muster to lift his foot into the sink between the coffee maker and the microwave, and he ultimately had to use a stool with Malek and Fahad steadying him.

In much too short a time, he found himself back in the conference room, before a makeshift congregation. The heavy table was shifted to one side. An app on Malek's phone determined that Mecca lay in the direction of the utility closet.

"All right," Hatim heard himself declare. "All right. Here's how we do it in my country. First... well, brothers... you see, the thing is... we begin first with a silent prayer."

Back home, whenever the droughts had come, he'd seen the solitary farmers seated in their fields, their faces upturned, imploring God for rain. Their minds, he'd imagined, must've churned with dark clouds. They'd been lucky. They'd trusted God to answer their prayers. More to the point, perhaps, they'd known precisely what it was for which they'd prayed.

What was *he* praying for?

For strength? Resilience? Good luck? Mercy? Or should he push the envelope still further, ask for even more, for restoration—but to what state? What status quo? This thing had come along and cast the world into disarray—so what? His world had always been in disarray. Perhaps he'd done this to himself, run his own useless life into the ground, or perhaps it had been done to him—what did it matter? Perhaps the world could be frozen, but the clocks could not be put into reverse. Apologies could be issued, but no deed could be undone.

When he closed his eyes, he found it waiting for him, suspended in the void, emitting a limpid glow—as if, having spent hours absorbing the fluorescent glare, it was re-releasing that frigid luminescence now, interrupting the darkness within him, casting its furious radiance into his soul. No longer torn by feeble human hands, but whole, immaculate, entire, realer than the rasping breaths behind him, brighter than the bulbs that guttered in the ceiling, pregnant with the force of something on the cusp of being, some edict, judgment, verdict, revelation still impending, yet no matter how he strained his eyes and clenched his fists, he couldn't force it to be any more than what it was. Exquisite, porous, hardy, spongy, golden-brown, but the bread was only bread. No more. No voice issued from the crack along its golden dome, no echo, no encrypted wisdom, no un-scripted supplication, no indication of beneficence or vengeance, no sign that he, Hatim, was any less alone.

And then a cold hand reached down into his stomach, seized a fistful of his guts, and squeezed. His body jerked as if kicked by a horse, his eyes snapping open in time to catch a watery arc of vomit slashing out into the air ahead of him while at his back, breaths were sucked in. He felt himself pitching forward, felt his lower body buckling out from under him, and then he was on his knees, mere inches from the carpet, face to face with what had once been austere gray, but was now a blossoming microcosm, multi-colored microfibers bursting red and green and blue before his eyes. The smell of his own vomit crept toward his nostrils. He felt himself shaking, wondered whether these were sobs.

He would never be forgiven. He'd desecrated something, and all the veils would soon come off, and his colleagues would identify him as the nonbeliever that he was, unraveling the only thread that bound him to this world.

Then what?

What, precisely, would he lose?

His loving wife? His stable home? The fruits of his labor? The years he'd poured into securing legal status in this country?

Delusions. Gaudy fictions. Each and every one.

He had but one thing left to lose, one final sacrifice, and that loss bore down like an oncoming train even as the smells feet shuffled near his ears, and voices murmured anxiously above, and colors burst behind his eyes, bright ribbons of plasma, and rainbows, and suns. It wasn't Abdurrahman's voice. It wasn't Malek's, Fahad's, Ibrahim's, Marie's. No. It was his mother's. His dear, old mother's, the woman who'd borne him, who'd baked his first loaves, worn thin from years of hardship, beseeching him over the phone, "But this is madness! Can't something be done?"

"It *is* madness," he'd agreed. "But it's out of my hands."

"This has been going on for years! They get richer, I get poorer—something must be done!"

"It's the postal service. It's this damn corruption. That's the problem, Yma. That's the problem with our country. This damn corruption. Every month, I send the cash. I swear. God willing, someday it will reach you. Someday these damn corrupt postmen will all drop dead, and someone new will take over, and they'll recover all the money that we've lost. I won't give up, Yma. I'll keep sending."

"And don't forget to pray."

"Of course, Yma. Of course. I'll keep praying."

His dear old mother, who'd never heard of Western Union. Who'd given him everything she had, life and breath and bread enough, but nothing useful or enduring. She still thought he was here in America legally, believed that he'd landed a Fortune 500 job, knew beyond a shadow of a doubt that every month, he sent her five hundred

American dollars in cash, and every month, the Moroccan postal workers found it, stole it, threw the empty envelopes away.

The deception had been for his mother's sake initially, or so he'd told himself. Perhaps it had been true. Now, though, it was the only precious thing he had to offer up, a pathetic lie soon to be lost among the billion-something other sacrifices rising like steam off the crust of this world: the jobs, the convictions, the futures, the lives, all soon to be wrenched from the billions of ordinary people who never saw the implacable, colorless, odorless specter coming to rip apart their lives.

It was paltry.

It was nothing.

It was all he had to lose.

The voices were not murmuring around him anymore.

The conference room was not revolving around him anymore.

The night through which he'd slogged in something like a fugue, the abandoned parking lots, the empty strip malls, were not around him anymore.

What was around him now—he recognized it—was a supermarket. But not a normal supermarket. Not a normal aisle.

Before him stretched bare metal shelves, as empty as his freezer, as bright and breadless as the day. Someone pushed roughly past him, moving as if hellhounds snapped at his heels, but Hatim barely registered the elbow to his ribcage, barely felt a thing. The day was finally at its end, and what is a place to sleep anyway, after all?

In those final, frantic hours of Friday the March 13th, as lockdowns rolled across the land, few shoppers, if any, had the presence of mind to glance down the bread aisle and notice the heavyset man getting down on his hands and knees, unhooking the second shelf up from the floor, leaning it against the rack across from him, and rolling himself onto the bottom shelf as if it were a berth. As close to bread as anyone could still get in that supermarket—unless, of course, one were to visit the gluten free section—on as good a horizontal surface as a man like him was likely to find, he sank into a sleep so deep that it could not accommodate a single dream, though somewhere deep, deep down he knew, and got no rest from knowing, that when he woke—and he would have to wake eventually—the world would be forever changed.

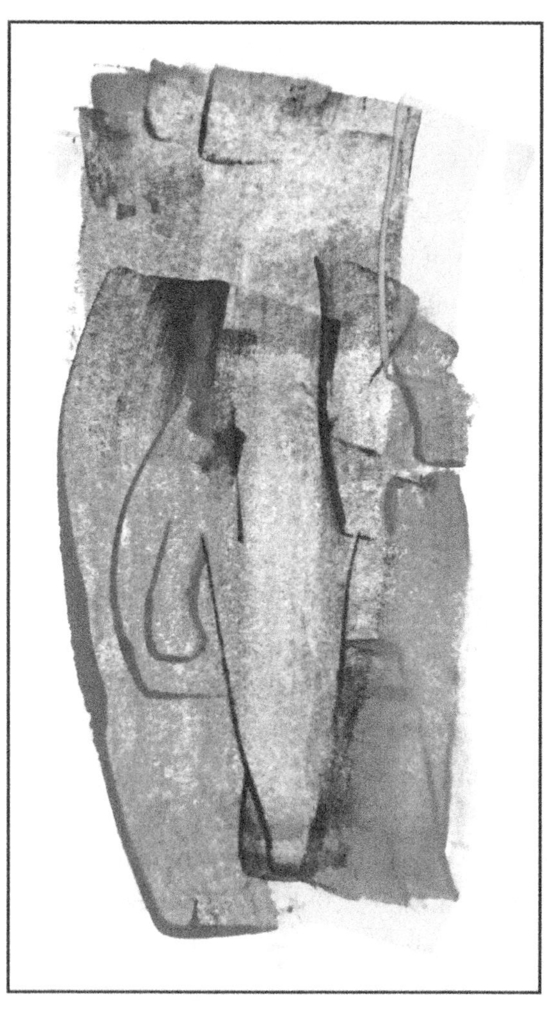

Observance
Michael Moreth

Dessert

KARIS PITT

Sweetness hides
inside my kitchen.

A pan of brownies tucked
under a tea towel,

vanilla ice cream playing
peek-a-boo in the freezer door.

The sugar, the honey, the cinnamon
all whispering behind the cabinet

while leftover Lindt truffles masquerade
as tools in a hallway basket.

But the popsicles don't hide.
Their warm, charming colors

blazing from the freezer, waiting
for our toddler to pluck them, one by one.

Glassblowing

KARIS PITT

I roll the sun against the workbench.
Like seraphim playing playdough
at a preschool table, it has a strangeness.

Like Moses at Mount Horeb
striking water from the rocks.
A cacophony of things that shouldn't be.

The goosh of bright orange,
smooth as a viper's egg, a molten yolk
that drifts to the siren song of gravity.

My arms, sunburnt and raw, tweezing
the yolk until it grinds out a squeak.

Grandma

KARIS PITT

My grandmother gripped the knife
between her wizened fingers,
and it flowed. Like watercolor,

juice bled from the apple's flesh.
The knife painted the table
in shining skins and seeded cores.

Smooth as carving Monet's
Lilies from the water.
She would slip apple crescents

into your palm as she asked
about your friends,
your friend's neighbors,

and the cute little Schatzi
three houses down, questions sliding
from her tongue like peels to the linoleum floor.

My apples are all elbows and angles,
awkward and stilted as my knife
slams down on the cutting board,
cracking the flesh
like a tremor through the earth.

I wish I watched her more closely,
asked her where she learned
her secret trade, mimicked
how she cradled the apples
and never once nicked her thumb.

Still, I know how to keep my door open.

One day, my home will be
the apple carving house,
to slip apples into my daughter's palm,

and ask her friends about their teachers,
their neighbors, and the calico
three houses down.

"Get it down. Take chances. It may be bad, but it's the only way you can do anything really good."

WILLIAM FAULKNER

5 AM Again

FABRICE POUSSIN

Makeshift lakes sing in their
concrete beds surrounded by
cypress knees transplanted
in these foreign grounds.

An orange glow tries to pierce the
horizon still in its nightly daze
but it will rain again this morning
as we play with the air

Little change will be seen
in this quiet edifice of trees
few natives dressed in feathers
and fur plan another day.

Darkness will certainly return
for a brief moment to lose
once more its desperate battle
when life joyful conquers all.

If I Had an Easel

FABRICE POUSSIN

If I had an easel
I might be out of control and
raid the local art supply shop
for paints and charcoal and acrylics
a few canvases and the best brushes.

If I had an artist's stool, I would place myself
comfortably before the blank surface
mix colors with much passion and of course
without a clue
I would begin to strike the fibers before me
and trace the lines of your eyes.

If I had a beret like Picasso, I would be so inspired
attempting to draw the shape of your kisses
with every trace of sweetness
dreaming about those warm moments
your smile coming to life on its own.

I am no Monet, nor Rembrandt or Michelangelo
so you will have to forgive me for my naïveté
as I continue to pencil in the form of your shoulders
those delicate fingers and artfully painted nails
your legs naked under the summer sun.

If I were a magician like Geppetto
you might begin to breathe under the flowers of silk
softly inhaling the whole universe
yours, princess ruler of oceans and mountains
and turn your head to the revelation.

If I were truly an artist my friend
I would recreate you with every gaze
and you would freeze in awe of your own image
reflected in my weary eyes longing for your embrace
and you might sleep upon my breast safe at last.

Lily of the Valley
image by Kaelen Felix

Little Girl

FABRICE POUSSIN

Little girl, I am sorry to say
that I never knew you until
I read your name in the news.

You dreamed I can assert
of those futures all design
within the walls of a fortified
neighborhood near the city.

What made you change your mind
on that somber Wednesday evening
at the onset of a promising new year
when you abandoned all your hopes.

I never knew you, yet we could have been friends
it is too late now, that you sleep in a world
perhaps better made for you whom I never knew
but I miss you little girl and give you my sorrow.

Messenger of Doom

FABRICE POUSSIN

Everything hurts for the sad man
what he sees in the early-day papers
the strange announcements he finds on
his computer feed and the cries of
a little boy who yet has to understand this world.

A way of life for the messenger of doom who
sees naught right with this planet
he dwells on the details so distant
the ugliness of his close surroundings
while the sun arises again in its fiery splendor.

Perhaps it is another grey hair, a toothache
or again a new spot on the aging forehead
nothing escapes him who hesitates to
feel at ease in a place where all could
go wrong at a moment's notice.

Dark thoughts are contagious, they
leave little room for enjoyment
when the child screams anew at midnight
and already he contemplates a tiresome day;
such is the life of the one who only seeks pain.

The Old Man and His Love

FABRICE POUSSIN

I spied him along the trail early today
beard white as the many days of winter
he has, just like this one, walked alone.

He stepped into the grass, a little lost
it seemed, but he was not alone
struggling to keep his love close.

Hair as light as his best friend
curly and less gray in many parts
with a little brown on his canine fur.

It was clear that the old man was glad
and I, lone traveler of the path
saw the treasure he held upon the leash.

I could see the glee when back in the car
they would return to the warm room
of a holiday season that just passed them by.

His best love would put its head on his lap
together they might watch some rerun
of their favorite Christmas pictures.

Then they would sleep past the ring of midnight
to awake in another year, with nothing changed
and the certainty of a lifelong bond of conscious love.

Valentine's Day

LAN QYQALLA

Lora
embroidered Valentine's Day
on the map of love
Egnatia-Naisus street
and in passing I also took
the honey flavor
from the hot ashes
of the estinguished fire.

Lora
like a blonde ladybug in the meteorite
nobody whispers
on the map of love
and the star twister out of exhausted longing
in the timeless feeling
brought the freshness of age
the kiss of the mountain like Hera from Olympus
departed in the endless today
night.

Lora
frozen in heat
slightly heated to the bosom of love
"I'm very cold
Lan takes me with him
tonight
I do not want flowers
a white rose
to have for Valentine's Day!"

Hello…

LAN QYQALLA

Hello! Hello!
the voice hums like in a cave,
I had forgotten the color of the voice
in this agn of late month.
Hello, hello…
the voice on the other side shuddered
in the raging river,
—Yes I am…
here.closed in the ego
"gnosi" the lip timbre,
turmoil of times
or late spring?!
Hello, I'm Lora,
nothing important
in me the shadow of longing
affects the absorbed nectar
in search of immortality…
I clutch the phone
I feel stuck in water, who revives my fire?
Mekur in late May?!
Hello, Hello… , listen to me!
I am the sin-ridden Danaide,
why don't you talk to me
why are you silent?
…I can hear you on the other side,
I was disturbed by this phone call in the last month.

Rain In My Eyes

LAN QYQALLA

The rainbow appeared
behind the lines of rain,
the worries and troubles of stis,
carved verses
where the west burned,
in the braided flower,
we put a wreath.

You can't see the rainbow
it didn't rain a little,
in my eyes… !

Autumn Love In Pristina

LAN QYQALLA

We met in the fall,
in the amphitheater you tweet…
the streets of Pristina,
in the cold night,
shoot me like a mountain fairy.
the stars were aligned
that summer evening in your tear,
we were both lost in the untouched oasis
and the lips stopped at the sounds FlokArtë.
Why did we travel, tell me why
in the cold winter and snow,
the beaming sun gave us a gift,
you ray of sunshine lit me siashra.
Why did we run to the meadows, why
in the early spring fragrance of love
we pray to the flowers of the green field,
embraced we felt exotic intoxication.

Dreams of Blue Whales

JASON RYBERG

Tonight the world is wild
with the erotic electro-
pheromonal micro-bursts
of linden trees

and the locusts are really jamming
(though the lone cricket
clicks and chirps
in horny, sorrowful longing)

and God's good eye is beaming
its silvery, mystical spotlight,
center-stage, down through the hole
torn in the top
of the dark circus tent
of clouds.

So, here's where we find
our bold (and here-to-for
missing) mis-adventurers,

sleeping out in the backyard,
so carefully and conspicuously arranged
amongst this atmospheric nocturne
of fireflies and empty beer cans,
moonflowers and Marigolds
and giggling garden gnomes;

a circle
of narcoleptic
synchronized swimmers

slowly
spiraling
down

through
layer
after churning,
swirling
oceanic
layer

into
the deep
undulant dreams
of blue whales.

Lesser Pieces of the Whole

JASON RYBERG

Look at that big, *phatt,*
yellow, fluorescent moon out
there, this evening,

just floating along
on a river of cloud-fluff,
and it's not even

seven o'clock, and
weirdly anthropomorphic
clusters of leaves are

doing strange, ghostly
pirouettes in the middle
of the road for the

car to suddenly
cut through and explode with its
bright, dual high-beam

laser cannons—*PEW!*
PEW! PEW! PEW!– only for them
to scatter and fly

into a thousand
lesser pieces of the whole
and reassemble

into something like
their former selves in the
rear-view mirror and

keep on keepin' on
down the road or crawl into
a ditch for the night.

But, Then Again

JASON RYBERG

The moon is grieving
behind a cloud for a star
that has fallen from

universal grace,
and moths are twirling around
the front porch light like

Sufi Dervishes,
and sheets left out all night on
clotheslines in the back-

yard are billowing
like ghosts in the wind, and some-
where, off in the woods—

the sound of what you'd
swear was a tree suddenly
cracking and falling

under the weight of
all that time and stillness, but
then again, you can't

remember if you've
ever actually heard
a tree fall in the

woods, but you're sure
none of the ghosts you've seen looked
anything like that.

Trails End

JOSHUA SASTRE

When I first saw the trailer in *Trails End,* I knew it didn't make sense for us to be there, for the ground beneath it to be ours, but I didn't know how to say that or why I would. I was nine.

We lived in a safe and secure (I never heard it described any other way) co-op building in one of the poorest areas of the Bronx. My father thought cashing in a chunk of his 401K to put a down payment on a weekend getaway in Milford, Pennsylvania, was a smart thing to do, to enjoy breaks from our safe and secure co-op as a family.

Yet, he complained about money constantly, about being unappreciated and misunderstood, about being caught in quicksand that punished good behavior, about traps everywhere. All that was infuriating to hear over and over, but I didn't know how to say that or why I ever would.

In *Trails End,* I could see all the stars after dinner and hear invisible crickets screaming nonstop about nothing. I never saw a single star in the Bronx at night, though I often heard my invisible parents screaming from their bedroom about multiple nothings.

You weren't allowed to live in *Trails End,* my mother told me. This kept it nice. It wasn't a trailer park, it was a recreational camping community. At its center was a community hub called The Clubhouse. It had a library, arcade games, a fitness room, and two large outdoor pools, one of them heated.

"What if we promise to be good?" I asked, knowing she would respect the question.

"It's nicer than home," she admitted quietly. "But no. We have to follow the rules. Everything special has rules."

I didn't understand. If we couldn't live in *Trails End*, each of its rules would feel like an insult. She looked at me and halfway smiled, knowing that I understood it wasn't up to her, like almost everything. My father gave his opinion, my mother gave in.

These were their rules. It's how I was born.

There was a bodega, or general store, outside the main entrance, about a quarter mile down the highway. There were plenty of dirt paths you could take to get to the highway from inside *Trails End*. Eventually, I found one I liked.

My father had bragged that here, a kid could ride his bike all day, all over, and not worry about catching a stray bullet.

Then, we should live here, I thought.

The general store was the brightest bodega I'd ever seen. The old man behind the counter wanted to know if I was alone. I answered him by looking around.

"I don't serve runaways. Sounds unChristian, but it sends a dubious message."

I told him I didn't know what that meant.

"Means your bullshit detector's got no batteries yet," said a middle-aged lady in a chair against a wall. She turned a skinny hand over in her lap with long nails painted glossy red. "If you were a little older, you'd see right through Pompous Pilate here."

"I didn't run away," I said to them. "My parents are in Trails End."

"They don't let little kids leave through the main entrance there alone," the man said. "You cut through the woods, then? You a sneak-away?"

"It's his thing," the lady looked at me, then went back to examining her nails. "Tries real hard to make an impression, then sinks like a stone in a lake."

"Speaking of rocks, judging by the one on your majesty's finger, I'm still treading your waters."

I wanted the woman to react to this, but she didn't.

A moment later she halfway smiled. "Tell him what you want, boy, before he falls asleep thinking about what he's gonna say next."

"It's my thing, right?" the man said and smiled at her, briefly, like it hurt his face. "Dreaming ways to disappoint you."

I could feel how different they were from my parents. That they'd liked each other a long time. It made me scared to move. "Big Red."

The man tapped the counter. "Right there. Grab it."

I could see the bright red fifteen-stick packs on the shelf of candies below him. "You don't have the five-stick pack? For thirty-five cents?"

"Just what you see, kid."

I asked if he could order the thirty-five cent packs. My allowance was small.

"That'll take a few weeks. You know you can't live in *Trails End,* right?"

"Yeah. But we're coming back."

"I'll think about it. That's all you want?"

"His allowance is small," the lady said. "There's nothing here that cheap."

He smiled at me, revealing a tar stain between his two front teeth. "Hey sneak-away, you wanna buy a ring?"

My father whined that driving up here in the snow would be too much trouble. My mother said winterizing and de-winterizing the place every year would be even more trouble. But she gave in after three or four beers, and in the eight years of *Trails End,* we never came during the winter. I pretended my father was right.

I made some friends in lots nearby. All their trailers were bigger than the one my father bought, a twenty-four-foot Corsair. Jack's was a thirty-five-foot Skylark and Frankie's a forty-foot Holiday Rambler. In Spring, they always shared embarrassing stories about sledding and, after a few years, snowmobiling. I knew they felt bad for me, but I tried not to care. Or I used it. Sometimes, when we went to the bodega. I stopped calling it that out loud, since it made everyone laugh. I asked if someone could buy me a fifteen-stick pack of Big Red. Not every time, but since the old man never ordered the thirty-five cent packs, it couldn't hurt to admit being poor. It wasn't my fault he didn't know how to run a bodega.

My first serious crush was Jack's sister, Tanya. My first minor crush was a girl named Rachel. She lived on the same floor in my co-op building, two doors down. We kissed twice, once in the hallway by her door and the next day in the elevator after the only adult got out. About a week later, I came home and saw someone, who wasn't her father, come out of her apartment. He was taking a garbage bag to the incinerator chute and left the door open. I peeked in as I walked past and confirmed it wasn't Rachel's apartment anymore. There were cardboard boxes everywhere. It stung my brain more than my heart.

My crush on Tanya almost killed me, but that was my fault. The second year, I asked to borrow her bike just to see what she'd say. But I should have also asked where the brakes were. Until then, I'd only ridden dirt bikes with pedal brakes. I'd seen ten-speeds before and was vaguely aware of handlebar brakes, but I thought they were optional. An alternative for riders who didn't want to put their legs to work. Girls.

But I forgot all about that option, once I was on the highway.

It didn't take long for me to be going faster than I'd ever gone before, since the highway sloped down for about a mile past the general store. I didn't know speed could sneak up on you like that, the shocked pumping of my heart demanding my legs spin, spin, spin backward, though there was no metallic catch. The car that hit me—or that I hit when I lost control of the bike—was how I learned about irony. Since it was a sports car and not a regular car, it had high-powered stopping for its high-powered engine. By the time I hit it, spinning over the hood and cracking the windshield with my shoulder, it had almost completely stopped.

"Lots of jalopies around here with drum brakes. God is good," the old man said, mostly to himself, after the young driver had rushed me in and explained.

"The boy's got people in *Trails End*," the old man continued, addressing the driver and pointing at me with a crooked thumb. "You should bring him to the security building at the front gate. Just try not to jostle him too much, I think. Luck like that might reconsider."

"The inability to commit to a single personality is graver than any mortal injury," the lady said. She was in a different chair against a different wall. Her nails were still painted red, but they weren't shiny like before. Or maybe, the paint had faded.

The old man sighed. "You needn't supplement your good deed for the day with this nonsense-maker," he said to the driver. Then he looked at me. "Good luck, sneak-away."

The driver tightened his grip around my legs and back. When he turned to move through the door, I glimpsed the old man and his pretty wife. They seemed to like each other less today.

I thought the old man not offering me a free pack of Big Red was the most unChristian thing imaginable. I hoped a regular car would hit him someday.

Tanya wasn't mad at me for destroying her bike. She said she hardly used it and was glad it went out in a blaze of glory. She asked if I knew that song. I told her I didn't. Bon Jovi was for girls.

My father was furious that I dislocated my shoulder. Mostly, I knew, because he couldn't beat me for wrecking Tanya's bike, at least, not, right away.

Tanya's father, a retired sheriff, would expect to be compensated.

When the beating came, it would have to be about something else. Probably grades, or being disrespectful. In the Bronx, two weeks later, I giggled, when he farted, while lecturing me about cutting school. The look on his face was almost worth the belt.

The third year, I kissed a girl named Lluvia. We were watching *Friday, the Thirteenth, Part Four or Five* in Jack's trailer. Jack went to the bathroom, and she looked at me for too long. It felt like she was asking an obvious question, and I gave her the only answer I had. Her father was friends with Jack's father and had a trailer here before anybody. They said her lot was close to the main entrance, and I'd probably seen it a bunch of times before. They said her trailer was bigger than all of ours, it was almost a house. I went looking for it a few times, but nothing stood out to me.

I was never alone with her again, which she seemed to require. She lived with her mother in New Jersey and only visited a couple of times a year. The next time I saw her, she barely looked at me. The number you dialed is no longer in service, I thought, feeling smart and stupid.

I used to think my parents enjoyed fighting. It was incredible how they could turn a missing sock or expired milk into a screaming match about basic human decency. But they never fought inside *Trails End,* which made me think it was something they could control. Like they'd made an agreement that first trip, fighting about whose idea it was on the way. I wanted to see irony in everything.

The fifth year, a dropped plate ended the agreement. The plate had no food on it, yet, and didn't shatter, but my mother's flippancy about dropping it on his feet sparked something in my father. It was the middle of the day, and the door to the trailer was open. From inside, I could sense how far their voices carried, as if hearing it two or three lots down. I pictured unbelieving faces. The embarrassment I felt was like the shock of seeing so many stars in the sky that first year. The walls in our Bronx co-op building were thick enough so that nobody had to worry about being overheard, nobody knew anything they weren't invited to know. But now, Jack, Tanya, and their father knew us without asking. Things would be different now, and that made me want to apologize not to them, but to the cloud-hazed stars that winked over *Trails End* and shunned the Bronx.

Jack and Tanya, it turned out, hated their father. They seemed energized by the new information they—and probably all the trailers on our street—now had about my parents, and behaved, as if they'd been released from some self-imposed NDA. Their father had only been retired for a few years and still acted like a sheriff most days. But I thought the privileges he allowed them made up for it. Jack had a motor scooter which Tanya used all the time, which was why she didn't care very much when I trashed her ten-speed—and even though I was the same age as Tanya and only two years younger than Jack, my father made it clear that I was not allowed to ride it ever. Even if the ex-sheriff approved, even if I was as old as Jack, my father wouldn't have budged. Like coming here during the winter, it was crippling to even consider.

Still, I never liked the ex-sheriff, because he hated seeing me with my hands in my pockets, hating seeing me pretend I was comfortable and thoughtful, but at least he let his kids do crazy shit. "Too bad they don't have pocket pool Olympics," he liked to say in front of everybody, "this kid would take the gold." Apparently, that was just the tip of a nasty iceberg they'd been dodging for years. Tanya was a slut, Jack was a homo, and their mother, who never came to *Trails End*, was the most selfish bitch alive. Tanya was a close second, seeing as she did nothing to reverse her brother's condition. "You could at least shake your titties in front of him now and then," she repeated to me and Jack and Frankie one night on the roof of Frankie's trailer. Frankie was only a year older than me but, somehow, didn't seem surprised, even though he was also hearing this for the first time. I told myself it was because he was from California. Because I heard somewhere that cold weather made people stupid. "My cousin's gay," he said, suddenly. "Lives in San Diego."

Nobody said anything. A minute later, Jack shrieked with laughter.

Frankie smiled. "You want his address?"

The seventh year, the differences between Trails End and the Bronx started to shrink. My parents were fighting just as much here as they did at home. One Saturday they argued for an hour straight, stopping only to watch me ride off with Tanya and Frankie. I was on my dirt bike and Tanya was on the back of Frankie's. When we got to The Clubhouse, Frankie said to me, "Just run out the clock. It probably won't be much longer." Tanya agreed. I said something embarrassing about time being relative, which I'd heard in a movie and which they seemed to accept. I don't remember when I stopped trying to impress Tanya, but talking was a lot easier when the stakes were low. It didn't matter that I never knew what Frankie meant.

Inside, we played arcade games for hours. Thunder Blade, After Burner, X-Men, Space Harrier—Tanya's favorite. We ate hot dogs and almost went swimming but decided it wasn't hot enough. The sun started to go down, filling The Clubhouse with orange light that made everything look wet. Tanya said Jack needed help with something and we left.

When I got back, my father was sitting frozen in a hammock he had hung the first year. My mother was inside making soup.

She had a bruise on her cheek. I could see it through her makeup. It was the first time she wore any in Trails End.

As far as I knew, my father had never hit my mother before; made her cry, yell, spit in public once, but that was it. Trails End had taken the lead. After that, the power of seeing so many stars at once was meaningless, like cops that bust through your door too late.

The next year we didn't come until July. It was for a whole week, the first time we had stayed so long, and without my mother. I don't know what my father told people, but I explained to Jack, Tanya, and Frankie that my parents couldn't handle the tight space of the trailer right now. Even our Bronx co-op, at eleven hundred square feet, was doing a shitty job keeping them apart.

"Should get a house," Frankie said.

"With a basement," Tanya said.

"And a shed," Jack said.

The way they smiled at each other, with quiet reverence for my situation, told me I'd gone as far with them as I could go. Frankie was clever, Jack was tortured, Tanya was Tanya. I would never fall into their strange rhythms, the winter kids, and knowing it hit me with the force of a high-powered sports car. I was sixteen.

It was supposed to be a cooling-down week for my parents.

But when we got back, my mother was gone.

Someone, probably Frankie, had joked this would happen. But honestly, I thought she would be there, ready to pick up where she and my dad had left off, some money-related squabble that was, like everything else, part of something bigger and older.

I wasn't surprised when my dad told me we weren't going back that year. In December, he asked me if I would be okay to spend the weekend alone. I was intrigued but not enough to ask why. When he got back, he told me that he had sold the lot in *Trails End*.

I stared. I didn't blink or breathe. The fact that he had gotten rid of the place after eight years at the start of winter felt like the most spiteful, unChristian thing anyone had ever done.

It didn't have to be true that I wouldn't see Jack and Tanya's thirty-five-foot Skylark or Frankie's forty-foot Holiday Rambler or the general bodega store's cautiously loving couple ever again, but I knew that it was.

Until Spring, it felt like my father had set a trap of some kind. I couldn't go anywhere. He refused to be alone all winter. We watched a lot of seventies TV.

I never saw my mother again. Wherever she was, I hoped it was nicer than our Bronx co-op.

I hoped she was following every rule.

I'm old enough and solvent enough to buy a lot for myself and my own Corsair or Holiday Rambler or Skylark—if they even make them anymore—though I own a small house with a basement and a shed in a safe and secure upstate New York town that *Trails End* cannot upstage with stars.

But I want to go back just once.

It was eight years of snowless unbelonging. There were better ways to remember that tract of childhood, but I couldn't see them. If I reenter that four-season recreational camping community, I'll probably see Lluvia's enormous trailer right away, if it's still there (I think it is). Staring at it like the billion stars that first year, like a sneak-away kid who couldn't trust his nine-year-old eyes, I'll consider that the number I dialed was never in service, even if the phone in my head is still ringing, even if the trailer-door opens, and Lluvia steps out and takes my call.

Conversation with God

RAMZI RIHANI

I have a few questions that I will be grateful if you could send down your answers to. I say "send down" because we've been taught that you are up in Heaven. God forbid, you cannot be down in Hell. That's where bad things happen. You are the Almighty, the most powerful, the most knowledgeable, intelligent, and capable, the kindest, and the fairest one of all. Your magic makes the best magicians in the world look like novices in their field. They can make tricks on stage and make things disappear and reappear, and we'd pay for expensive tickets to see them. You, on the other hand, created the entire universe, effortlessly, while sitting on your throne, and you offered it to us for free. But was it truly free?

BIRTH

You created us all equal. Or so it is claimed. Of the 7.9 billion people who live on your Earth, we were taught that all were created equal. How is it so that the baby born to a billionaire father in NYC is equal to the baby born in Anand Nagar, the poorest slum in Calcutta? You may say that we should not measure equality by wealth. True, but if wealth provides comfort and opportunities in life that are far beyond someone who survives on a bowl of rice per day, you cannot claim that they are equal. You may argue that despite the wealth, the former was born into, that baby may grow up to be depressed, on opioids, suicidal, and the latter born on the back alleys of Anand Nagar may be much happier. If so, why didn't you let us all be born in a world of slums but guarantee our happiness? I apologize if I sound argumentative. Some of your citizens down here believe there is a little bit of God in each of us. This is why I am allowing myself to ask these questions.

DEATH

You are the ultimate decision-maker of who dies, when, and how. This gets to be a little too harsh. If you can share your criteria with us, you will make our life a little easier and more understanding of death. You gave us 70–100 years to live yet sometimes you take people at a much earlier age and cause undue suffering to their loved ones. First, where did you get the 70–100 years from? Why not 25 or 250 years? Certainly not because of physical and health reasons. Remember, you, and only you, make these rules.

Further, your death sentence comes so abruptly. I didn't mean it in the earthly definition because you are above all judges and juries. So why don't you give notice to your candidates, like a standard two-week notice that most humans are used to in the workforce? This way you allow them to bid farewell to their loved ones, pay their bills, and try to finish items on their bucket list.

We cannot lobby for reconsideration for someone's premature departure as you, unilaterally, make this decision and we bear the consequences. Ok, I'll meet you halfway. Have you ever thought of introducing a visitation-of-the-departed program on an as-needed basis? You can charge a handsome amount per visit and limit the number of visits. But then, this would be a privilege for the wealthy who can afford it and who would write it off as a tax deduction and we would fall into the trap of wealthy versus poor who cannot pay for the program. So, people are not born equal. To us humans, this is absurd, but you may impose on us any rule that provides better solutions, and no one will contest it. The trick is that we need to make sure the rule is coming from you directly because down here, many people claim that they are your spokespersons. When this happens, things escalate quickly, and it creates havoc. You have to put an end to it. You are the leading superstar, and your reps here lose control more often than they should. You are more popular than the Beatles, Tiger Woods, Elon Musk, and Shakespeare combined. Don't hesitate. Do it, and I guarantee we will follow.

POLITICS

Here's a very controversial issue, and I hope you can put some law and order to it. I am sure you are aware of what's going on politically here. Wars are being waged against innocent people because of a piece of land, oil, gas, natural resources, or for some leaders to achieve personal and political gains. Only you can put an end to this. Yet, you stand by watching. I know you do not enjoy watching your citizens being killed en masse. Or do you? If you were a political leader here, you would get so much criticism for not interfering to stop wars. People tend to love you and believe in you. They pray to you. Some people pray to you five times a day. So, why don't you give us explanations, and solutions, and start treating people unequally by rewarding the good ones and making the bad ones accountable? Don't let us decide who's good and who's bad. This is your job. We trust your judgment until you start making mistakes! Sounds subjective? Sure! But this is on you!

Recently, you made some of your countries elect or appoint heads of States like Putin, Kim Jong-Un, and Assad. These guys haven't done any good on your earth. Wars are waged, nuclear arms are developed, oppression, lies, crushing any citizen who criticizes them, etc. All hell broke loose under their reign. Why did you let this happen? You can change all this in one minute after your morning coffee. It is admirable that most people still have the same reverence, love, respect, and belief in you. No matter how low your people can dig, you remain above all criticism, as if you were truly God. You make this happen so confidently and be sure that people still pray to you more times than they have food every day. Man, sorry I meant God, you are a real magician; the ultimate almighty magician who has the whole world wrapped around his finger. Did I say His finger? We are programmed to refer to you as male, not female. Honestly, I do not know who you are. We are used to picturing you as this old man with a big beard, exactly how Michelangelo painted you on the ceiling, which is precisely what God looks like. But perhaps, you are female, and we do not know it. If I were a painter, then I would paint the most beautiful picture of God, the female version: a tender woman, yet very powerful, beautiful, encompassing all passions for her people and the solver of all their problems.

Are you aware that in one of the most powerful countries on your earth, Presidents are voted in based on whether they are pro-life or pro-choice? You may be laughing at us for this, but this is the truth. I am sure small countries such as Gibraltar, Monaco, Maldives, and San Marino are not preoccupied with this. I never checked these facts, but we humans can be sure without checking and verifying! That's on you! Why don't you settle the argument of abortion and provide your undisputable decision once and for all, so we can let go of this argument and proceed with our lives?

LOVE

Oh, here comes a softy. You make us fall in love and out of love as if we were puppets. Most of your envoys to earth asked us to love one another. Yet you interfere out of nowhere and spoil an entire relationship. I am sure you have your reasons for this, but what the heck, are we just numbers down here? I know we do not measure up to your might and intelligence to comprehend your very sophisticated formulae, but this is on you to make us understand. Even Google's complicated algorithm is unable to decipher the way you manage around love. Have you ever been in a relationship? People may laugh that you are asked this question. But seriously have you ever been in one? Tell us about it. How long did it last? Did you have children? Are you alone up there, or do you have a family of Gods?

Years ago, I met an Indian guy who was about to get married. He told me that he had never met his wife-to-be. He had not even seen her picture. You know who I'm talking about. So, I asked him, "What if you marry her and then you discover that you do not, cannot, and will never be able to love her?" He answered, "Then, I will learn how to love her."

Was that the God in him who answered? I felt so at the time. You remember, don't you? You were there. And we were taught that you are everywhere all the time. "Here, There, and Everywhere." Did the Beatles write this song for you? Now, that is super magical. Unfortunately, this raises our expectations so much. You are everywhere, know everything and everyone by name—first and last—and your wish becomes our command. So why don't you make your wishes attainable by your citizens? Otherwise, we fail, and ultimately you fail. No one wants this.

ACCESSIBILITY

This becomes personal. People are afraid to ask about contacting you. But let me be—for a few minutes—the voice of the fearful citizens. Are you accessible to us? Are you available to answer questions or offer explanations on major issues whenever we need you? I ask because I often hear people say, "How can there be God, and this happens?" Don't get upset with them. They say this out of love and concern for you, and not out of hatred. They may be frustrated, but they still love you and admire you. So, can you be accessible to them? I know there are a lot of us here—7.9 billion people. But since you know us all and you are here, there, and everywhere, you can be accessible to us. I am not talking about customer support accessibility. They are only available Monday–Friday, 6 AM–6 PM Pacific Time, and if you call them after those hours, you get an overseas answering service that only you can understand. I am talking about providing comfort when comfort is needed. This doesn't cost you much time or effort. I am telling you that this will raise your ratings so that you will be the God of Gods.

Think about it.

Written after Attending Bob Dylan's Concert

RAMZI RIHANI

Despite his raucous voice, and 60 years of age, Bob Dylan still has this aura of a performer that very few rockers possess. He is capable of performing the same song over a span of 40 years and still producing 40 different versions, as if it were a new song each time. This is one of the many characteristics that make Dylan the legend he is today. This concert is part of a tour to promote his newest album *Love and Theft,* which came out last month. He played the majority of the songs on the album plus new versions of such classics as: "Just Like a Woman" (a most tender rendition), "A Hard Rain's Gonna Fall" (a very timely and prophetic song), "All Along the Watchtower" (a version that rocked the house), "Forever Young" (a most Dylanesque performance), "Blowing in The Wind" (believe it or not, still reverberating after all these years), and finally the *coup-de-grace* and my all-time favorite, "Like A Rolling Stone," which is, undoubtedly, a landmark in Rock 'n' Roll history. This was 2:15 hours of sheer creative music. You would listen at the beginning of a song and slowly discover what it is. It is like meeting an old friend, after so many years, and rediscovering this friend over and over again. This is Bob Dylan: a master at continuously re-inventing his music, and equally so, his audience. What a pleasure!

The Boomerang Child

RAMZI ALBERT RIHANI

They left suddenly between their fear and their anxiety,
their swagger stayed behind
to meet new souls, hoping to give them life

The boomerang child moved back,
but the old folks had departed.
Nothing was left except memories of lost perfume
and ghosts of the archbishops of anarchy.

He knew he would not go through life unharmed,
but the more he got scathed,
the more he could face new encounters.
Encounters that smell of future oblivion.

He knew that a bad day was not a lost day.
His patience was his strength sung in different languages.
His kingdom was filled with crowds singing his epitaph.

To reach happiness, he needed three things:
a listening ear, kindness, and solitude.
Masquerade was not one of them, but it flashed in his mind.
The war continued. He survived.

Never too Late

RAMZI ALBERT RIHANI

When the page stretches itself and becomes an epic
When the tear stretches itself and becomes an ocean
and laughter stretches itself to become a tear
It is never too late to reinvent, laugh, and cry

When fear stretches itself and awakens our strength
When noise stretches itself, and you start listening
and the beast stretches itself to become human
It is never too late to remember, wish, and fly

When a whisper thunders like a mighty storm
When the dove writes a poem
and the prayer becomes a lullaby
and the ink becomes a forever color
and the tree, the still lover
and the memory forsaken forever
and the sun's rays descend on us like a hundred Julys
It is never too late to sing, live, and recreate

Then, you start looking for the Man in God.

The Drifter

RAMZI ALBERT RIHANI

Many years have passed.
In his journey, he chased fulfillment
but caught wisdom.
Wisdom got him fulfilled.
A circle is complete.
Is it the process or the end?
Unable to separate both, his process never ends.
Fulfillment and wisdom become one.

He found out why he was born.
He went looking for himself,
then decided to recreate himself instead.
The stronger he was, the harder the encounter.
Sometimes, storms come to disrupt your life,
and other times, they come to start your life.

He never dwelled on his agonies in life.
He used them as the foundation for his strength.
What he does not have gives him his freedom.
What he has fades it away.

Even dreams take a little time.
The day he stops dreaming,
his dreams come alive.

Be Patient

RAINER MARIA RILKE

Be patient toward all that is
unsolved in your heart…

Try to love the questions themselves…

Do not seek the answers
which cannot be given
because you would not be able
to live them.

And the point is
to live everything.

Live the questions now.

Perhaps you will then
gradually
without noticing it
live along some distant day
into the answers.

Mother's Day

DREW ALEXANDER ROSS

"Can we have a nice day for a change?"

"Sure. Paint yourself in good lighting. The kids don't see you ninety-five percent of the week. You get to be mister perfect for the minuscule time you put in their lives."

I twisted the napkin in my lap. Patrick glanced over at me, gave a weak smile, and lightly punched my shoulder before staring at the paper placemat the waitress put in front of him. Our parents continued in hushed but aggressive tones. Patrick's eyes lit up, and he ducked under the table.

I glanced up at Mom and Dad, who were too busy arguing to notice Patrick rummaging in Mom's purse. He came up with a felt-tip pen. Patrick took the paper placemat and drew a three-by-three grid. After he finished, he drew a circle in the center box and passed me the pen. I drew an x next to it.

By the time our food arrived, our placemats were covered in Xs and Os, and I had tuned out our parents' conversation.

They seemed to have reached a temporary resolution, as we tucked into our brunch of pancakes and eggs. It was silent. Patrick and I knew when to keep quiet.

Patrick devoured his food, as quickly as a dust-buster sucking up a dust bunny. He choked after he downed half a waffle and an egg over-hard on top in two bites. I stared wide-eyed at my brother and saw both my parents reach forward. Patrick gave an almighty sneeze, and a piece of egg white flew out of his nose and landed in his hot chocolate.

A burst of laughter emitted from everyone around the table. I hoped it was a potential sign that the dark clouds from earlier had moved on.

Dad paid the check and pecked our mother on the cheek. Patrick and I got up and picked a side to hug our Mom.

"Happy Mother's Day!"

* * *

Patrick and I sat cramped in the small leather backseat of our family sports car and jostled our legs in a silent kicking match that didn't go unnoticed by Dad. His eyes flashed in the rearview mirror, and we both looked down and stopped our non-verbal pecking order scuffle.

I peeked out the window and watched, as the street shops of the small town gave way to the woodsy backroads beyond.

We passed large houses removed from the township by winding streets and front yards the size of basketball courts. The Victorian homes and modern mini-mansions became sparser, and longer stretches of woods and reed fields took their place.

Fifteen minutes more of driving and an oldies station playing The Rolling Stones and Fleetwood Mac in the background brought us to a gravel road with a wooden sign at the entrance. The sign read *Devil's Garden*. Patrick had his hand on his seatbelt buckle, ready to jump out of the car and run into the woodland trails that beckoned with jutting branches and green leaves.

Dad parked the car near the only other vehicle in the lot, a faded green minivan with a *Children Onboard* bumper sticker.

"Looks like that would be much more comfortable for a family."

Dad quickly unbuckled his seatbelt and jumped out of the car, as if Mom's comment could have been avoided by getting out of the proximity of the initial words.

Patrick and I hopped out of the car and tried to keep out of each other's arm's reach, as we played a game of *You're It*. I frowned, as Dad pulled my brother aside. Patrick always seemed to be able to keep enough distance between us with his few years of extra growth, and I knew the game was over with Dad's arm wrapped around him.

I tried to get the last touch in, but Mom grabbed my hand tightly and pulled me next to her, as we walked onto a path through the woods. We passed a bulletin board with trail maps, notices, and warnings about different plants and animals. There were pictures on the board I wanted to look at longer, but Patrick had already escaped Dad's grasp and darted up the trail. Dad quickened his step to keep him in sight, and Mom dragged me along.

Chirps and tweets of different birds mixed in with the crackle of leaves from the scurrying of squirrels in the brush. My shirt stuck to my back from the humidity, but the giant maple and elm trees overhead gave enough shade to keep the worst of the sun's heat at bay.

A deer nibbling on a shrub looked up, as we rounded a bend in the trail. It stared at us for a moment. Then, it bolted into the depths of the woods, as if it sensed a danger only it knew of. Dad held a hand out to keep my brother from chasing the deer.

Patrick didn't need too long to find a creature he could catch. A small lizard, probably enjoying a carefree moment basking in the sun, had its day interrupted by two twelve-year-old hands. My brother trapped the lizard and cupped his hands, so he could see his catch. He showed me his prize, and I squirmed. Patrick grinned and showed it to our parents.

"Very nice, Patrick," said Dad.

"Put it back. It's probably frightened to death," said Mom.

We continued on the narrow trail for another twenty minutes before overcoming a slight rise in the terrain and reaching a vista with a lake below it. The trail meandered down to the waterside, but the recognition of nature's beauty passed between us, as we looked at the scenery.

"Did you remember to lock the car?"

The moment passed.

"I don't remember. But I don't see why that matters out here."

"I left my purse in the car. What if someone breaks in?"

"There was only one other car in the lot. No one is going to break into ours."

I edged toward Patrick, as our parents resumed their verbal boxing match from brunch. Their quips became vicious, as they looked to land a punch that would draw blood.

"Do you want to go explore?" my brother punched me lightly on the shoulder before running off the trail and finding a deer path. "Let's go see what's on top of that cliff!"

Our parents stopped bickering to spot Patrick running along the deer trail to a cliff overlooking the lake. I didn't want to fall too far behind, so I ran in the wake of the crushed leaves, snapped twigs, and bent branches my brother left behind him.

"We're going back to the parking lot!" called Dad. "We'll head to the lake, once we've checked on the car!"

"Okay!" I shouted over my shoulder, already putting my parents out of thought and putting as much distance as possible from them.

* * *

Patrick clambered up the back of the cliff. I watched him hop from rock to rock, darting between enormous boulders, making his way up the crags.

I kept him in sight but had to look down occasionally to ensure my progress up the cliff. I might not have liked wild animals as much as Patrick, but I wasn't going to shy away from any physical feat.

Above me, I saw the silhouette of my brother climbing up the final holds to reach the top of the cliff. The sun shone through the canopy and crowned his conquering of the mountain.

I bit my lower lip, as I resumed climbing up the crags. The massive boulders were more challenging for me to navigate. I tried stepping between them, as Patrick did, jumping across a gap to continue my quest up the cliff. But as I reached the end of the boulders' crevasse trail, I realized I had to pull myself up to their tops to advance.

It felt like a hole appeared in my chest that began to suck everything from my surroundings. My vision started to tunnel, as if my eyes were drawn into my head. I could see the outlines of their sockets. My skin felt tight over my bones, and my shoes cramped. Even the air around me seemed to disappear into the void of my chest, which thumped erratically and sent shivers down my arms and legs.

I looked back across the gap I had jumped across, which now looked greater than the distance back to the parking lot. I reached feebly at the side of an enormous boulder, hoping to grab hold with an arm that looked as thin and small as a twig.

My panic paralyzed me, and I shrank down and hugged my knees. I looked up at the towering boulder above me and saw a shaggy head poke out from above.

"Need help?"

Immediately, my paralysis washed away like a desert flower receiving a sprinkle of water at the last moment. Quickly, I scrambled to my feet, scoffing as if annoyed that it took my brother so long to come back and help me. I scowled to convey that we were wasting precious adventure time with the delay.

Patrick reached his arm over the side of the boulder to grab mine. We didn't connect on my first jump. I felt the stabs of panic returning.

"Step on the other boulder before jumping up," Patrick said.

I straddled the two boulders with each foot and propelled myself a little bit farther so I could reach Patrick's arm. He pulled me up the rest of the way.

Once we peaked the boulders, the face of the cliff was the only obstacle left to overcome. Patrick was already scrambling up the back of the crag. I followed him and saw that the peak was broad enough for a path to walk on. The cliff overlooked the lake, with tiny shimmering stars dotting the surface from the sun's reflection on the ripples.

Patrick already marched across half of the cliff top, reaching out and touching the leaves on the branches overhead. I saw him in the distance and meant to follow, but something caught my attention out of the corner of my eye.

A flat piece of stone, the size of a placemat, jutted out from the cliff's edge. Coiled on top of the surface rested a giant, brown spotted snake. It almost looked too perfectly wrapped around itself to be real, but a blink of its eyelids showed that it lived.

"Patrick. Snake."

I don't know if Patrick would have reacted more quickly if I said ice cream. He skipped back over the peak's trail in seconds. He stared hungrily at the snake from above my shoulder and, without hesitation, moved his twitching fingers out to make another friend.

Patrick's body blocked his approach of the giant snake. He darted forward, and after a quick scuffle, he turned to me with his prize captured in his grasp. The body of the massive snake coiled around Patrick's arm, and the tail still reached past his kneecaps and twisted violently. Its head was grasped firmly between my brother's thumb and forefinger.

The eyelids of the snake narrowed, and the muscles in its body thrashed against my brother. Patrick's arm wavered in the air, as he attempted to control the reptile. In a second that would forever imprint in my memory, the snake twisted its head and lashed out with saber-like fangs that unfolded and sunk into my brother's hand.

"AHHHHHHHHH!"

Patrick let out a surprised wail and flung the snake from his grasp. It went over the cliffside. I turned to my brother and saw him staring wide-eyed down at his arm. It looked like he had on an inflated doctor's glove where his hand should be. Patrick's terrified and unfocused eyes found mine.

"Get Mom and Dad."

* * *

I scrambled back down the cliff, jumping on and between the boulders, to find my way back to the trail. I returned to the path so quickly that I wondered for a moment why it took so long to get up the cliff in the first place. But the thought was distant. My mind and body were focused on finding our parents. I needed to get to them. Everything else felt removed.

For a moment, I hesitated. I felt my chest begin to thud again. I didn't know if Mom and Dad were at the lake or if they would still be back by the car. After a slight pause, I rushed back down the trail to the parking lot.

My arms were sleek with sweat, and my hair was plastered to my forehead, as I sprinted through the woods. The trees and bushes passed in a blur. Each turn made me question if I made the right decision heading back to the parking lot. I should have met Mom and Dad after a few minutes of running.

I thought of how long it took to climb up the cliff, even though it took moments to get back down. The time that passed while I was stuck on the cliff felt longer the more I thought about it. Tears started to well up in my eyes and blur my vision, as I thought of Patrick's shocked face.

"Get Mom and Dad."

My legs almost didn't stop in time. I ran around a bend in the trail and nearly collided with Dad. I looked up at him and Mom. I could tell they immediately knew something was wrong. A silent message must have passed through the air. Their faces were mirrored displays of worry.

"What happened?" Dad's voice cracked.

"Patrick got bit by a snake."

Dad looked at Mom.

"I'll get Patrick. Get to the car."

Mom's eyes welled up with tears, but she nodded and rushed back to the parking lot.

Dad and I ran back up the trail. I led him at first, but soon he ran in front, holding my hand as I barely kept pace. Seeing the severity of determination in his gaze, as he raced ahead on the trail was scary.

"Where's the cliff?"

"The trail was right by the lip overlooking the lake."

As soon as the words left my lips, we rounded a bend in the trail and saw the lip. I stopped, and Dad turned to see where I was looking. The deer path was marked by the broken and bent branches from our journey. The cliff was in the distance above the boulders, but I didn't see my brother.

"It's up there," I pointed.

"Stay here."

Dad hurried and pushed through the bushes and low branches of the nearby trees. He bustled up the path and clambered up the boulders. I lost sight of him once he passed the nearer rocks.

I noticed the stillness of the forest when I realized I was alone. I didn't know if it was a trick of my mind, but I didn't hear any tweet or chirp from a bird. There wasn't even a breeze to rustle the leaves on the ground.

A long time passed, and I felt tears slide down my face.

Moans brought my attention back to the cliff.

Dad carried Patrick down the boulder path toward the deer trail. He turned his back to push through the bushes and trees on the path back to the main trail.

"Dad… It hurts."

Dad turned, and I saw my brother. The blood drained from my face, and a rush of fluid from my stomach tried to come up to replace the vacancy.

Patrick's arm looked as large as his leg. Dad brushed past me and labored back down the trail. I followed in shock.

* * *

HONK! HONK! HOONNNKKKK!

Mom whipped the steering wheel around, as she weaved our car through traffic. I could only see the tops of the cars pull out of the way. Most of my vision was blocked from the dashboard. I had never ridden in the front passenger seat before.

Patrick moaned in the backseat with each jerk of the wheel. I turned back to look at my brother. He was in Dad's lap. The cuff of his shirt sleeve looked like it gripped the arm of a major league baseball player.

The car jerked, and my brother wailed, as his arm jostled against the seat.

"How far?"

"Not far," Mom glanced at Dad in the rearview mirror. There was an emotion that passed between them I didn't understand. It made me happy and scared me at the same time.

Mom spun the wheel again, and honking horns surrounded our car. I looked out the window and saw a massive building in the distance. A large red plus sign shone out from the side of the building.

Our car beelined for that building. I didn't understand what happened next, but the car jerked to the left, and Mom pressed a hand down on the horn, which let out one long honk.

"Jesus Christ," said Dad.

I peeked behind my seat and saw him holding my brother with one arm, while clutching a handle on the roof over his door. I jerked back around, as my body slid in the front seat and smacked against the door. I heard screeches and honks from other vehicles, as ours zoomed up a ramp toward what I now knew must be a hospital.

Mom drove the car to a pair of sliding doors with *EMERGENCY* painted on them. She slammed the brakes, while Dad hurriedly unbuckled his seat belt and threw open the back-passenger door.

I watched, as men and women in blue and green uniforms rushed through the doors, and what looked like a cart with a tablecloth on top rolled in front of them. Dad gently put my brother down on top of the cart.

"He got bit by a snake."

"Do you know what kind of snake bit him?" one of the doctors asked.

Dad looked around, as if searching for the answer somewhere just out of sight. I remembered the photo on the bulletin board. I opened the door, and everyone turned to me.

"The snake was tan and had spots like a leopard but brown. It was really big. Copper-something."

"Copperhead," the doctor grimaced.

* * *

The batteries of the clock in the waiting room must have been dying. The second hand oozed slowly along, like it was fighting through muck. I counted Mississippi on my fingers and was scared to learn the clock was correct. I stopped looking at it after that.

Dad paced around the room and occasionally talked to the man at the check-in counter. Mom alternated between clenching my hand and going over to talk with Dad.

I was worried we would have to go soon. I couldn't see outside, but it must have been nighttime. Everyone else in the waiting room had already left.

Mom and Dad occasionally came to ask if I was okay or told me everything would be okay.

I didn't know how to answer the question, and the statement made me think it wouldn't be. I wanted to ask what would happen to Patrick, but I was frightened by how my parents behaved. I had seen them fight many times, but the discomfort this time was foreign.

A door banged open, and a doctor in a white gown came out. Dad and Mom rushed over. The doctor nodded, and my mother brought her hands to her mouth. Tears glittered on my Dad's cheeks, but he was smiling. He grabbed my Mom and hugged her tightly.

Dad beckoned me over, and the doctor led us down a hallway. She reached a door that a nurse had just exited and held it open for us to enter.

I saw Patrick lying on the bed with a bruised but normal-sized arm wrapped in a sling that was supported by a rig above his bed. He sported a dopey smile, and my Dad engulfed him in a giant hug. I walked over to the bed, and he tried to punch my arm but missed. I punched his good arm in return. He giggled.

It was then that I noticed Mom wasn't by the bed. I looked back at the door and saw her standing there with her hands back over her mouth and tears in her eyes. Patrick smiled.

"Happy Mother's Day!"

Dad released a roar of laughter.

Mom's eyes darted to him with sudden sternness.

Redbud Trees Spring Carpet
photograph by Marc Lund

Sneaking into Starlite

DONALD OSBORN AND
ANNA HENKENS SCHMIDT

Half the town's population must have snuck into the Starlite Drive-In Theater during its years of operation in Chadron, Nebraska.

The other half was conceived there.

Money wasn't the issue. It only cost a buck or two for entry, though a carload was around $5. There were no regulations against trying to bend the laws of physics. You could smash as many bodies as you wanted inside each vehicle, as long as you could get the door closed. Sneaking in had nothing to do with monetary constraints, however, but everything to do with entertainment.

Ingenious methods of sneaking into the drive-in became the stuff of high school lore. There was an unspoken rule of one-upmanship, of who could come up with the most incredible solution to watch the movie without opening their wallets.

Mike Carson had an old mail van. We fashioned it with a false back, so when the ticket taker would pull open the back door, he'd see an empty vehicle. But what he wouldn't see were ten kids compacted together, hiding behind the flimsy wall. Mike would pay for a single ticket, and then once we were parked, the rest of us would pop out and watch the movie.

Kenny Nixon drove a long, black car. Just before he pulled up to the ticket booth, the rest of us would exit on the opposite side. We'd crouch down and strain our knees, walking slowly beside the car, careful to keep our heads below the windows. As the car inched forward, we'd keep pace with the wheels, hidden from sight until we reached our space.

A lot of people hid in trunks, but the box office attendants caught onto that trick quickly. Cars in the 1970s were a lot bigger than they are now, so the floorboards and a blanket made for an easy cover. Plenty of people climbed the fence, but you had to be pretty sneaky about it. They had it set up so cars could only drive in through the entry and out through the exit. Just like a rental car company, the exit was fixed with spikes, which would blow your wheels if you tried to drive through the wrong way. Once, Kenny Groves and I laid a big piece of board over the spikes and entered in the back way.

But it turned out our most creative form of sneaking in first required us to sneak something out.

During my senior year in high school, my friends found a thick spool of speaker wire—at least three-and-a-half football fields in length—and it gave me an idea. Each drive-in space consisted of a post with a speaker. You'd take the speaker from its holster and slide it into your car, thereby providing you with sound. "You know," I said, "with a long enough speaker wire, you could run it all the way up that hill over there, and you could see and hear all the movies without having to go past the ticket booth at all."

Everyone loved my idea. The next time I entered the drive-in, it was with a legitimately-purchased ticket and a pair of wire cutters. By the time the second feature came to an end, I'd jerry-rigged the speaker to the new, longer wire, snaked it through the fence, and passed it off to my friends who walked it up the hill.

It worked beautifully. We tried to keep it a secret, but word got around, and it became a little party place. Kids would show up with blankets, beer, and watch movies for free past midnight. Sadly, it didn't last long. Someone must have gotten wise to the idea, because we showed up one night to find the speaker and wire gone. At least we were legends while it lasted.

Half the fun of the drive-in was sneaking in, but the movies weren't half bad either. It was at the Starlite I first saw John Wayne gallop across a rugged landscape. I tried to keep my cool when Alfred

Hitchcock's *Birds* turned the screen black. Ted Grant and I laughed until we couldn't breathe during Don Knotts's portrayal of a hapless astronaut in *The Apple Dumpling Gang.* The best was during *The Texas Chain Saw Massacre* when Kenny Groves started running up and down the aisles with his chainsaw going, all the girls screaming and yelling.

To an onlooker, we looked like a ramshackle car lot in a field on the edge of town, but to the people inside the drive-in, we were transported to other worlds. We'd sit in our cars with the windows open, or on blankets on the ground, the scent of freshly-cut summer grass mixing with butter and popcorn. The wind carried the dissipating smell of car exhaust and leaded gasoline, a sweeter smell than today's unleaded varieties. We smelled like youth, like Avon perfumes and nervous energy, like Ponds Cold Cream and Dial soap. Sometimes you'd get a whiff of a dill pickle purchased at the concession stand or the tempting scent of a chocolate candy bar.

But it was never about the movies or the concession food. The Starlite was the place where everybody would tell their parents they were going on the weekend. Since every movie was a double feature and didn't get out past midnight, it was the perfect alibi for stretched curfews. Besides movies, the Starlite provided another outlet of fun for us miscreants. Outside the theater, a massive marquee was updated by the staff using ladders and long poles. Each week, as we checked the new movie listings, our brains would buzz with anagrams. We'd cruise up and down Third Street, brainstorming the perfect letter combinations. It would be a good night's project trying to figure out how the letters of each word could be manipulated for our amusement.

When night fell—dark enough to avoid detection but still light enough for visibility—we'd monkey our way to the top of the marquee with no assistance from ladders. Since we didn't have poles or tools of any kind, it took several people to complete a job. One person would hold the letters, another would pop them into place, and yet another would direct from the ground. We took great delight in rearranging the letters into words that wouldn't be allowed in most Scrabble games. My favorite movie title of all time was John Wayne and the Train Robbers. With some creative spelling and a few upside-down letters, the marquee proudly displayed: Johns Rubber Weiny.

The owners of that movie theater must have hated us about as much as we loved using their place of business for our shenanigans. Sadly, the Starlite Drive-In Theater eventually flickered out. The marquee, once a canvas for our mischievous creativity, now only read "Closed for Good." We didn't even bother rearranging the words to spell "Cool doGs freed." It wasn't just a movie theater that closed, but the end of an era. I'm not sure it ever occurred to us that we'd probably quickened the closure of the theater, on the account that we cheated them out of so much ticket money.

Every now and then when I catch the fragrance of popcorn mixed with fresh Nebraska air or hear the distant hum of an old movie soundtrack, I'm transported back to those nights under the stars. The Starlite may be gone, but the memories that sneaked into our minds still shine bright.

I Have Been to Places of Great Death

NOLO SEGUNDO

I have been to places of great death:
Walking the battlefield of Gettysburg,
As a lusty young man of no firm belief
Who stepped between the great rocks
Of Devil's Den and felt his soul shudder
as though he had been a soldier there,
and died in fear a long, long time ago.

I taught my tongue to the gentle Khmers
As civil war raged and the killing fields
Were being sown—I left before the
Heartless murdering began, the killing
Of over a million: teachers and students,
Doctors and farmers, the old, the young,
Each with a photo taken before dying,
Their pictures taped to classroom walls.

And when I visited Hiroshima, now myself
Chastened by death's touch, and knowing
My soul real, knowing of meaning absolute
And of unseen forces that work good or ill,
As I stood at the first ground zero, I once
Again shuddered to feel the pull of madness
(though I knew not if it was my own or some
Remains of that evil which brought the fire
And brimstone of a world-wide war...)

But by then I knew I could pray, and so
Opened my desperate heart and sought
His mercy—and then I saw a sort of angel,
Who took me from that place of insanity,
Healing me while we wandered by the
Beauty of the Inland Sea as my storm
Calmed and left me, never to return…

I have been to places of great death, and
I have felt death's cold, careless hands.
But I know now what death itself fears:
The Light, the light eternal which carries
Souls beyond time itself, like the winds
Of a Love exceeding all understanding.

The Leap

NOLO SEGUNDO

I was half-mad with despair,
Hopeless in love and life,
At the end of my rope—
so I chose to drown,
To cease all pain in
Sweet oblivion, to be
No more, to be gone…

And when I flung my
Young and strong body
Into that swollen river,
I thought that's what
Awaited me—nothing!
But oh I was so wrong,
For my agnostic mind
Could not foresee the
Awaiting vast blackness,
The pain beyond pain,
And the utter aloneness—
No other souls, none
But my bodiless mind
That had spurned God
And love as well, and
Now roiled in torment,
Until I called out to Him
And was released
From hell to return
To the world I had
So recently spurned.

Some will discount
This as the ravings
Of a young man
Breaking apart—
It's only fear, just
Imagined terrors,
Be brave they say,
Neither heaven nor
Hell awaits us, our
Only fate, extinction.

I might wish them
To be right, but
They are deluded—
As I once was, for
Now I know there
Is no way out, no
Escape from oneself,
From one's mind,
From one's soul...

The Old Tracks

NOLO SEGUNDO

In my town and only
90 feet from my house
Run a pair of old tracks,
Railroad tracks older
Than my house, even
Older than me, and I
Am become old, very,
Very old, like a tree
Whose branches
Betray it with
Every strong wind
And fall to ground
Leaving less and
Less of the tree.

I used to walk in
Between those
Carefully laid
Iron rails, stepping
On the worn wood
Of the old ties as
Though they were
Made of glass…
I walked the length
Of my small town,
I walked the world.
I walked where
Passenger trains
Carried lives and

Their once warm,
Now cold, dreams
And I was part of
Each life, now gone
To ether and mist,
And so too my
Lonely soul will
Ride those rails
One bright day.
Still, a freight train
Comes by once or
Even twice a week,
And I thrill to hear
Its wailing horn as
it cries out for a
forgotten glory,
and the ground
still shakes a bit
as the old train
lumbers slowly
by my house and
I wait a holy wait
For the music of
Its rumbling and
The cry of its old
Heart as a young
Engineer pulls the
Whistle and sees
Not that he is
Driving eternity.

Beat Perfectionism and Start Creating

BERNADETTE STOCKWELL

My husband's grandmother, Ruthie, was a lovely woman.

She could make quahog chowder like no one else.

She made the best shortbread cookies.

She experimented tirelessly, often subjecting her husband, Edwin, to numerous botched batches—we called them 'rejects'—until finally, she arrived at the perfect recipe.

Edwin would say, "I made her the cook she is," patting his full tummy and wiping the corners of his lips with his linen napkin.

She could also sew really well. She crafted lovely stuffed animals and quilts, even her own clothes. She crocheted like a wiz, creating granny square afghans and more.

In department of home economics, she was a master.

But in her workshop, she was, well, an excuse maker.

I say this with all the love and respect I can muster for someone 60+ years my senior.

Still, if I have one regret for someone else, I regretted that Ruthie never finished a project out of wood.

Like many of us, Ruthie dreamed of doing more with her life than being a wife, mother, and excellent cook.

She dreamed of woodworking projects, like an end table, a chair, or a shelf unit.

Ruthie subscribed to *Fine Woodworking, Popular Woodworking,* and *Workbench.*

Over the years, she had procured the finest saw, drills, and sanders.

She went to lumber yards and carefully chose lengths of wood and sheets of boards to make these pieces of furniture.

But—she would not or could not begin any project until she cleaned her room.

And her room *never* got cleaned.

Therefore, she never started and didn't finish her dream projects.

Her room was not neat, but it was also not a hoarder's nest.

Her room, the last one on the left at the end of the hall, had closets full of clothes, other unfinished soft projects, books, magazines, and less used furniture.

I'm not sure what else was in her room because she often pulled the door closed so that no one could see the din of the dust and clutter.

But if this room was messy, it was certainly not dirty. It was not a health concern.

It was simply a collection of abandoned projects.

Probably other projects that she was reticent about carrying on with until her bedroom was more orderly.

This form of procrastination often becomes a self-fulfilling prophecy, usually stemming from perfectionism or idealism obscured by the flawless images seen in magazines.

The conundrum of "I cannot do this until I do that, and I cannot to that because I have not done this."

'Not until' is a cunning trap for the creative.

It's true that a cluttered workspace might represent a cluttered mind, and with power tools, that cluttering can be dangerous. I have seen photos of famous artists' studio spaces. Often, these rooms lack the order of an organizer's orderly touch.

And yet, the artist can compartmentalize in order to start and finish a project.

After all, we wouldn't be touring these spaces unless the maker had made enough stuff to step over that threshold from anonymity to fame.

As I write these words, I sit in my old master bedroom looking at piles of half-filled boxes, a closet where six or seven of my mother's empty picture frames lean against the wall. Large plastic storage bins, filled with my own sewing supplies, sit below a built-in shelf. A pile of clean sheets waits to be put back on a guest bed that will rarely have an occupant.

The room screams, 'Clean me. I'm a mess. I could serve you so much better, if...'

I am not going to be the one to cast the first stone. I know full well that I, too, can suffer from the "can't start until" syndrome. Shall we call this CSU? But when I do feel myself pulled away from creating because my space is disorganized, untidy, and dusty, I refrain from the desire to set things straight first.

Do Your ARt! first because doing your art feeds your soul.

It ignites your passion.

Doing your art just makes you feel better. Try this:

- Consider your typical workspace
- Are you in control of that space?
- For example, if you prefer to create in a coffee shop, the clutter that might be beside you doesn't belong to you. You're off the hook.
- If you work in an old bedroom, the basement, the attic, or even the corner of your garage that's still a garage, give yourself permission to make art anyway.
- Address that pile of boxes or those bags full of old clothes.
- Say, 'I'll get to you later. Maybe.'
- Don't be Ruthie.
- Don't keep putting off until...
- Take 20 minutes.
- Then, when the timer rings, take 20 minutes to neaten your space.
- But only *after* you have made art first.

P.S.: You can be Ruthie, or Phil, or Jesse, or Andy. You are ALL wonderful people. And Ruthie did finish many projects.

Art Imitates Life

ROBERTA BATORSKY

"What can a cat do in an empty apartment?"

A recent Polish radio interview
broadcast on Off Radio Krakow
with the decade ago-deceased poet
and Nobel laureate,
Wislawa Symborska
provoked the wrath
of its listeners
by using AI to create
a convincing replica
of the dead poet's voice,
representing it as
taking place in real time.

The station was accused of
sacrificing humans
on the altar of technology,
breeching journalistic ethics,
and losing the human,
or formerly human, factor.

The producer,
who was terminated,
fashioned a computerized
version of the dead poet's
actual sound and wry,
introspective manner.

In his defense he said
he would have invited her
on his program
if she had not died.

Symborska's estate
called the computer-generated
exchange "horrible," *
but was
encouraged because
it showed that
computers don't work
as well as humans,
which was also a frequent
message in her poetry.

Raven Reigns in its Territory
image by Kaelen Felix

Heaven on Earth

LISA TOMEY-ZONNEVELD

I believe that when nothing is said or done
about disparity
the soul cries

Love is all that we remember
when the angels call us home

I suppose that love is held in the soul
My soul is not worthy of this ascension
If he does not hold love for others

Then, there is the who we choose to emulate
Choices are ours to make
We have such freedoms
Only to be kept with love of fellow people

This causes pause for thought
Goals for heaven or a golden place
seem rather selfish
when love of others here on this earth
Is perhaps enough

Heaven on earth
I love that idea
Let's make it happen

Chance Meeting

RICHARD WEST

Today as I walk the mist-shrouded woods
I stop at a point where I sense I am watched

and I suddenly see him on the periphery
of my vision—motionless between two trees,

still as a tree root and silent as a stone—
his red hair and dark eyes

melding with the autumn foliage.
I stop, but avoid direct eye contact

and the two of us enter into the strange bond of
pretending we do not see each other—

till, bored or satisfied in some way, he slips
silently into the underbrush

and we go our separate ways.
He to his foxhole, and I back home—

both of us with memories of a species
intelligent, yet alien and enigmatically opaque.

The Edge of Dawn

RICHARD WEST

Here, on the edge of dawn,
I can see the reasons that brought me here.
A year is just begun, and all around me
well-wishes and resolutions swarm.
The latter, so often well-meant,
but then, sadly forgotten—like loved
but neglected children, or fading
stars in morning sky. This as the
memories of our better selves decline,
and we convince ourselves that we are just
too busy, or too tired, to improve.
But I do not look back or forward.
The silent shells of yesterday
offer no more consolation than
the misty maybe's of future time.
I look instead to time's true *terra firma*—now.
It is here, and here alone, that resolutions
may take root. It is now and only now
that new hopes breathe—in living colors
bright against the sky's pale ground—
and promises well made, and well
remembered, are at last, well kept.

Carousel

RICHARD WEST

The third act of my life begins,
and I have already forgotten my lines.
Faces without names, names without faces,
words without meanings, meanings without words.
So many links are gone—the mind's URL's lost among
the tangled synapses of age—
not consistently, but in a carousel of loss
that spins from gone to here and gone again.
But we are on this carousel together, love,
let us take solace in each other's laughter
and—before the music stops—
enjoy the ride.

The Albatross

RICHARD WEST

What is it to be the albatross?
To ride on never-ending winds,
to sail on atmospheric seas
formless,
shapeless,
boundless,
endless.
To navigate
seas without shores,
nights without stars,
stars without ending.
To see the distant storm
and to circumvent its path
so as to be always
untroubled
above the darkened waves.
To view the distant islands
and to avoid them—
so as to shun the storm of humankind
and be always alone with loneliness
in a life of pristine quiet
except for the slap of wavelets far below
and the song of the never-ending winds.

Unfinished Exit

CLAUDIA WYSOCKY

I keep thinking
about the time in high school
when you drew
me
a map of the city,
I still have it somewhere.
It was so easy
to get lost
in a place where all the trees
look the same.
And now
every time I see
a missing person's poster
stapled to a pole,
all I can think is
that could have been me.
Missing,
disappeared.

But there are no
posters for people
who just never came back
from vacation, from college,
from life.
You haven't killed yourself
because you'd have to commit to a
single exit.
What you wouldn't give to be your cousin Catherine,
who you watched

twice in one weekend get strangled nude
in a bathtub onstage
by the actor who once
filled your mouth with quarters at
your mother's funeral.
The curtains closed and opened again.
We applauded until
our hands were sore.

But you couldn't shake the image of
her lifeless body,
the way she hung there like a
marionette with cut strings.
And now every time you try to write a poem,
it feels like a
eulogy.
So even though you haven't
found the perfect ending yet,
you keep writing.
For Catherine, for yourself, for all the lost
souls
who never got their own
missing person's poster.
Because as long as there are words on a page,
there is still hope for an unfinished exit
to find its proper
ending.

Painless
Michael Moreth

CONTRIBUTORS

DUANE ANDERSON lives in La Vista, NE. He has had poems published in *Fine Lines, Cholla Needles, Tipton Poetry Journal,* and several other publications. He is the author of *On the Corner of Walk and Don't Walk,* and *The Blood Drives: One Pint Down, and Conquer the Mountains.*

DANIEL BARBARE: "I started writing poetry in 1981, after suffering from major depression. I have written a poem a day ever since. Of late, I love to write poetry about being a janitor and use the theme of "America." It means so much more than just writing about myself. I have something to say, even if it is being a janitor. I love to read Walt Whitman, who speaks with such authority. Writing poetry works for me, and it makes sense. It fits together in a nice little package. At least, that's how I see it."

DAVID BARNES: "I started my MLAS program in the 1980s and continued for several years, while working full time. I spent my adult life as a criminal investigator for the state of North Carolina. While conducting investigations, I often wondered how people got to the point in their lives where people who did what I did got involved with them. I began daydreaming stories during surveillances and stakeouts. I have published "Crosscut" at fictionontheweb, "The Mouse" on eastoftheweb, and several stories in *Fine Lines.* I tell stories of those who aren't in mainstream America."

DESIREE BATISTE graduated *summa cum laude* with her Bachelors of Science in Technical Management with Criminal Justice specialization in 2020 and a 4.0 GPA. She released her first book, *The Shaping of a Diamond,* which is a 27-year journey through her struggles and triumphs told through poems. She is a child abuse and domestic violence survivor, who uses poetry and writing to overcome past traumas and inspire others. Writing is its own form of therapy. She lives in Buckeye, AZ.

JOSEPH S BENSON is a Marine Vietnam Veteran, husband, father of two, and grandfather of six. He retired after thirty years as an educator in the Kansas public schools, followed by eight years as a blackjack dealer, and a two-year retirement job in a convenience store. He took up writing as an outlet for service-connected PTSD and now lives the good life in Hiawatha, KS.

BRET BROKAW writes for *Fine Lines,* is a professional phlebotomist, and is a world traveler.

JEREMY K. BROWN is a first time writer for *Fine Lines.*

SUSAN BRUMEL: "I retired from a thirty-five-year career in hospice social work a few years ago, at which time I began writing poetry. My work is inspired by the journeys of my patients, the compelling beauty of nature, and the human condition. I also enjoy music, long walks in the forest, flower arranging, and jumping in puddles with my grandchildren. I live in New Jersey with my husband and Bernese Mountain Dog, Dottie."

LIN BRUMMELS earned a BS in Psychology from the University of Nebraska-Lincoln and an MS in Rehabilitation Counseling from Syracuse University. She's a Nebraska licensed counselor. Brummels published poems in *Poet Lore, San Pedro River Review, Concho River Review, Plainsong, Nebraska Life,* and *Fine Lines.* Brummels' poem "Jerry's Hands" was awarded Honorable Mention in the 2021 Nebraska Poetry Society poetry contest. Her chapbooks are *Cottonwood Strong* and *Hard Times.* Her book of poetry is *A Quilted Landscape.*

MARY CAMPBELL a native of Omaha, NE, was a writer, musician, writing coach, and certified meditation instructor, whose award-winning poetry appeared in scores of periodicals, including publications of the Kansas Poetry Society and the Arizona Poetry Society. A longtime writer and editor at the University of Arizona, Mary was the author, co-author, and ghostwriter of more than twenty books. She wrote and co-wrote hundreds of songs, poems, stories, essays, news and magazine features, blog posts, and podcasts. Mary composed for and directed children and adult choirs; led church-school, preschool, and meditation classes, and taught in a nationwide children's ballroom-dance program. She gave *Fine Lines* permission to publish her work. We celebrate her wonderful ability to use words and compose artful images for our readers.

MARY CHIRNSIDE is retired from the State of NE, is an RN with a certification in Mental Health/Psychiatric Nursing, is passionate about gardening, reading, travel, observing life and other endeavors and Faith, the Border Collie. She did not pursue creative writing until several years after her retirement from the State, having worked at the Regional Center and before that with the Department of Corrections. Mary has always enjoyed putting her thoughts on paper. Life is interesting!

JENNIFER CHOI is a first time writer for *Fine Lines.*

ED CONNOLLY is a retired business executive, lives in Omaha, and enjoys writing memoir articles.

TERRI DREISMEIER is a graduate student at the University of Nebraska, Omaha.

ANNA FAKTOROVICH is the Director and Founder of the Anaphora Literary Press. She previously taught for four years at the University of Texas Rio Grande Valley, Edinboro University of Pennsylvania, and the Middle Georgia State College. She has a Ph.D. in English Literature and Criticism, and an MA in Comparative Literature. She published two academic books with McFarland: *Rebellion as Genre in the Novels of Scott, Dickens and Stevenson* (2013) and *The Formulas of Popular Fiction: Elements of Fantasy, Science Fiction, Romance, Religious and Mystery Novels* (2014). She has been editing and writing for the independent, tri-annual Pennsylvania Literary Journal since 2009, and the Cinematic Codes Review since 2016. She has presented her research at the MLA, SAMLA, EAPSU, SWWC, BWWC and many other conferences. She won the MLA Bibliography, Kentucky Historical Society and Brown University Military Collection fellowships. https://anaphoraliterary.com, director@anaphoraliterary.com

KAELIN FELIX lives in St. Louis, MO, where she writes books and illustrates them, too.

WENDY FETTERS has enjoyed her association with *Fine Lines* for many years (since the beginning of time!), enjoys writing poetry, and is currently working on a book. She has lived five or six lifetimes. This retired Spanish teacher recently participated in two local movies, performed at the Jewell Nightclub, and continues to play OMA in the *Nutcracker* each December. She continues traveling, reading, and spending time in nature. Her grandchildren are her world and provide many ideas for her poetry.

KRISTI FITZGERALD is a 3-time NaNoWriMo finisher and a long-time Willamette Writer's Member. She's been published in *Renaissance Magazine*; *Fine Lines* literary journal in Omaha, NE (where she's also an online Editor); and *Chicken Soup for the Soul* compilations, and featured in one of their podcasts. She has BAs in English and Theater and a MFA work in costume design. She taught English and Theater. She lives in Montana with her fly-fisherman husband of 30 years.

MARCIA CALHOUN FORECKI lives in Council Bluffs, IA. Her academic background is in the Spanish language. She earned a Master of Arts degree from the University of Wisconsin-Milwaukee. Her first book, *Speak to Me,* about her son's deafness, was published by Gallaudet University Press and earned a national book award. Her story "The Gift of the Spanish Lady" was published in the *Bellevue Literary Journal* and nominated for a Pushcart Prize. *Blood of the White Bear,* written in collaboration with Gerald Schnitzer, was a Willa Award Finalist in 2014.

CINDY GOELLER has a University of Nebraska at Lincoln Bachelor of Arts Degree in Education, specializing in math and computers. While nurturing a family of three children and farming with her high school sweetheart, she taught for both Northeast Community College and Wayne State College part-time and substitute taught at many northeast Nebraska area schools. She is a lifetime photographer and says she used her first 4-H ribbon money to buy her first camera, a Brownie Fiesta.

NANCY GENEVIEVE is a Special Editor for *Fine Lines* and an Emerita Associate Professor of English at the University of Illinois at Springfield (UIS). She taught creative writing for ten years at Eureka College (IL) before teaching for ten years at UIS. She retired in 2010. She and her husband live in Reading, MA.

JOHN GREY is an Australian poet, US resident, recently published in *New World Writing, City Brink and Tenth Muse.* Latest books, *Subject Matters, Between Two Fires,* and *Covert* are available through Amazon. Work is upcoming in *Paterson Literary Review, Amazing Stories,* and *Cantos.*

RICHARD HANUS: "I found *Fine Lines* on Duotrope. I have a large, large number of works, having been doing art for 20 years. Their eclectic mix in regard to subject matter and media is challenging and fun. Because I rarely sell my work and never put it on social media, so I am free to do what I want. I don't provide any clues or guidelines for interpretation (no titles), letting the viewer enjoy the freedom to judge. Art helps balance my life, being dominantly "right brain." On the "left," I am writing a study of *Macbeth,* having completed analogous work on *Hamlet* and *Othello* this summer/fall. In both "brains," I am surprised by what I find, no matter my degree of expertise at the outset. I live in suburban Chicago, am 81, and am a retired English teacher with a PhD in Late Renaissance Literature."

UMA IQBAL is a new writer for *Fine Lines.*

ZAN V. JOHNS is a Pushcart Nominee and 3-time bestselling author of Poetic *Forecast* and *After the Rainbow*. Johns is a contributing author in the Women Speakers Association's #1 international bestsellers *Voices of the 21st Century (2021 & 2022)*. Her poems are featured as the Dedication page in both collaborative books. Johns co-edited *Social Justice Inks* anthology with publisher Lisa Tomey-Zonneveld. She serves as an editor with the *Fine Lines Literary Journal* and administrator for the Passion of Poetry, an online platform for emerging and esteemed poets. She is a retired human resources leader who resides in Westminster, CO.

KAREN KADER: "I suffer from depression and agoraphobia. My family saw my frustration, trying to capture wildlife with an old point and shoot camera, and gave me a DSLR camera in 2013. That camera changed my life and opened up a new world for me. My work has appeared in the *Nebraskalife* magazine, the *Nebraskalife* calendar, *Nebraskaland* magazine, *Omaha Magazine*, the *Nebraska Ornithologists' Union*, and *Fine Lines*-the summer issue cover, Mesa, a Ferruginous Hawk, resides at Fontenelle Forest Raptor Woodlands in Bellevue, NE."

JILL SHARON KIMMELMAN was nominated for a Pushcart Prize, in Poetry and Best of The Net 2018. Publications include *Vita Brevis Press, Spillwords Press, Yasou! A Celebration of Life Ezine, Compositor, Writing in a Woman's Voice blogspot, Poetic Musings, Delaware Boots on the Ground, Love of Food,* and *Better than Starbucks.* Her passions include reading aloud, "cooking from the heart," and photography. She lives in Delaware with her husband Tim and is the proud mother of her son Jordan. Jill can be reached on Facebook at *You Are the Poem* and Instagram.

MARC LUND earned a Social Welfare BA from the University of Nebraska—Lincoln and a Juris Doctor from Creighton University Law School. As a past director of the Omaha Area Council on Alcoholism, Marc received an award from the National Council on Alcoholism for a treatment program he developed for children of alcoholics. Additionally, Marc developed and directed an outpatient alcoholism treatment program for Omaha Family Services in Council Bluffs, Iowa. After law school, Marc moved to St. Louis to practice criminal defense law as a trial attorney for the Missouri Public Defender Office. He served for 9 years before moving into private practice for 15 years. In both careers, Marc said what he found most rewarding was being able to help provide a second chance at life to those in a crisis situation. Marc is currently pursuing his interests in writing, art, music, travel, and nature adventures.

KATHY MALONEY has been the associate editor for over 20 years of the *Human Research Report,* a monthly digital newsletter whose goal is "protecting research subjects and researchers" for universities and hospitals. Kathy chooses to spend her non-work time writing poetry, reading, and creating art using mixed media. She writes monthly illustrated letters to her grandsons. She also designs and produces individual greeting cards for family and friends. Kathy taught English at Central High School, Omaha, NE for 20 years.

KRISTEN AND BRADLEY MARTIN: Kristen is an artist, writer, counselor, and professor who lives in Bend, OR. She is writing her first novel, *The Troll's Eye.* Bradley is a graduate of the University of Nebraska at Lincoln and a career wilderness adventure leader for the National Outdoor Leadership School (NOLS). They both would rather be poems than the poets.

DAVID MARTIN is the founder and managing editor of *Fine Lines,* a non-profit quarterly journal that has published creative writing by "young authors of all ages" since 1992. All writers are welcome to submit their poetry, prose, photography, and artwork. This publication has printed work by authors from all 50 states and 100+ other countries. The website (www.finelines.org) has more information about submission guidelines and a sample journal to view. He has published two books of essays and poetry: *Facing the Blank Page* and *Little Birds with Broken Wings.*

VINCE MCANDREW is retired from the Omaha Public Schools, where he was a teacher, counselor, and administrator. He is now giving full attention to his grandchildren and his poetry.

IVY MOON is a graduate of the University of Nebraska, Omaha.

MICHAEL MORETH is a recovering Chicagoan living in the rural, micropolitan City of Sterling, the Paris of Northwest Illinois USA.

RIC NUDELL is a first time writer for *Fine Lines.*

ISAAK OLSON is a high school sophomore in Canton, MI and is interested in architecture and fashion design. He is presently taking a sewing class to further explore design options.

ITTO AND MEKIYA OUTINI are first time writers for *Fine Lines.*

JOHN PALMER graduated from Carleton College (Northfield MN) in 1965 after spending more time on the identity crisis than on his studies. He attended Chicago Theological Seminary from 1965-67, before realizing that church ministry was not for him, but he loved economics. He transferred to Iowa State

University, where he received a PhD in economics in 1971. That same year, he became an Assistant Professor at The University of Western Ontario, and he retired in 2011. His hobbies include acting, music, hiking, photography, and writing about economic policy.

KARIS PITT is a poet and Early Childhood educator residing in Papillion, NE, with her husband and daughter.

FABRICE POUSSIN is a professor of French and World Literature. His work in poetry and photography has appeared in *Kestrel, Symposium, The Chimes,* and hundreds of other publications worldwide. Most recently, his collections *In Absentia,* and *If I Had a Gun, Half Past Life* were published in 2021, 2022, and 2023 by Silver Bow Publishing.

LAN QYQALLA graduated from the Faculty of Philology in the branch of Albanian language and literature in Prishtina, from Republika of Kosovo. He published numerous books. He is the Director of the Association of Writers "Naim Frashëri" in Fushë-Kosovo, a member of the presidency of the Association of Writers Of Kosovo, editor-in-chief at *Orfeu Magazine* and Website, a member of the Editorial Board of the *Magazine of World Historians* based in Switzerland, a vice-president of the Union of Albanian Writers and Critics. He works as a Professor of Albanian Language and Literature at the Gymnasium. He lives and works in Pristina.

JASON RYBERG is a first time writer for *Fine Lines.*

RAMZI RIHANI is a Lebanese American writer. His poems have appeared in several publications in the US, Canada, UK, Ireland, South Africa, India, and China, including Linnet's Wings Magazine, ArLiJo, Goats Milk Magazine, Poetic Sun, Last Leaves Magazine, Cacti Fur Journal, Ariel Chart International Literary Journal, Poetry Potion, The Piker Press, Active Muse, Ephemeral Elegies, and The Silent Journey Anthology. He is a published music critic. He published a travel book, "The Other Color—a Trip Around the World in Six Months." He lives in Washington, DC.

DREW ALEXANDER ROSS resides in Los Angeles, where he works as a script analyst. Drew has over ten short story publications, including short stories featured in The British Fantasy Society's Horizons Magazine, Mythic Magazine, and Door=Jar Magazine.

JOSHUA SASTRE has published short stories in the online journals *Scarlet Leaf Review, The Writing Disorder, Open: Journal of Arts & Letters,* and *The Adirondack Review,* and the print journals *Adelaide Magazine, AHF Magazine,* and *Down In The Dirt Magazine*, as well as the online publisher bookstogonow.com. His short story "Finished" was nominated for a Pushcart Prize by *The Writing Disorder*. He is currently working on his first novel.

ANNA HENKENS SCHMIDT AND DONALD OSBORN are a brother-sister writing duo. It has been said that the first-born sibling in a family is the most likely to become a CEO or president; whereas, the last-born child is most likely to end up as a comedian. Somehow, the roles were reversed in this family. Donald tells the stories, Anna writes the words, and together they chronicle a career in the clouds. Donald lives in Omaha, Nebraska, where he plays in a band, spends a great deal of time in his hot tub and massage chair, and flies a Dassault Falcon 50 jet. Anna lives in Durham, North Carolina, and homeschools her three children, while attempting to keep her big brother from getting into too much trouble.

NOLO SEGUNDO pen name of L.J. Carber, 77, became a published poet and essayist in his 8th decade in some 200 literary journals in 15 countries on 4 continents. A retired teacher [America, Japan, Taiwan, the war zone of Cambodia, 1973-74], he has been nominated for the Pushcart Prize and thrice for Best of the Bet. Cyberwit has published 3 poetry collections in paperback: The Enormity of Existence [2020]; Of Ether and Earth [2021]; and Soul Songs [2022]. These titles like much of his work reflect the awareness he gained over 50 years ago when he had an NDE whilst nearly drowning in a Vermont river: That he has—IS—a consciousness predating birth and surviving death, what poets since the Psalmists and Plato have called the soul.

BERNADETTE STOCKWELL teaches expository and research writing, public speaking, and fashion technology at UMass Lowell and Fitchburg State University. She coaches artists/creatives/makers and writes about creativity. Dr. Stockwell regularly posts articles on *Psychology Today*'s blog and is finalizing edits of *Do Your ARt! 10 Simple Steps to Enhance Your Creativity and Elevate Your Mood*, a book on process and practice. She collects patches from National Parks, sprinkles, buttons, and socks. Find more of Stockwell's valuable resources at www.doyourart.org.

WISLAWA SYMBORSKA is a first time writer for *Fine Lines*.

LISA TOMEY-ZONNEVELD is a poet and writer from Raleigh, NC. Publications include *Heart Sounds* chapbook, *Heart Beats* anthology of poetry (2021), *Silver Linings* collaboration with LaVan Robinson (2021) other anthologies, and several literary publications. She is on the editorial team for *Fine Lines* and a Gold Ambassador of *Garden of Neuro*. Lisa believes in life-long learning and tender, loving care of one's work. She is the manager of *Prolific Pulse Press* LLC.

RICHARD WEST was Regents' Professor of Classics in a large public university and has published numerous books, as well as many articles and poems, under his own name or various pen names. He now lives with his wife Anna in the American Desert Southwest, where he enjoys learning to cook and attempting to add flavor to his poems.

CLAUDIA WYSOCKY is a first time writer for *Fine Lines*.

PLEASE SUPPORT OUR SPONSORS

Est. 1992
Where Writers Grow!
fine-lines@cox.net www.finelines.org
(402) 871-3682 9905 Rockbrook Road, Omaha, NE 68124

Fine Lines is dedicated to the development of writers and artists of all ages and interests. Our publication started out as a newsletter. It has now turned into an international writing network and a 501 (c) (3), non-profit, educational organization. The first publication issue was 4 pages long and allowed students the opportunity to show readers their clear thinking and proper written expression. Today, each quarterly issue is 300 pages of fiction, nonfiction, poetry, and art.

Fine Lines receives submissions from people of all occupations: prose articles, reflective essays, what one learns through the writing process, and poetry in all forms. We have printed writing from a six-year-old, a 94-year-old great-grandmother, ministers, janitors, doctors, lawyers, scientists, teachers, and students of all educational levels. Our writers and artists come from all 50 states in the USA and 100 other nations.

To paraphrase George Orwell, good writing is like a window pane, and the editors of *Fine Lines* hope to assist writers see through their windows more clearly. We help people develop their potential and value your participation in this endeavor.

- Submissions: https://finelines.org/wp-content/uploads/2020/11/Call-For-Submissions.pdf
- Donate to *Fine Lines:* https://finelines.org/wp-content/uploads/2021/11/2022-Fine-Lines-Donation-Letter-1.pdf

- Intern: https://finelines.org/wp-content/uploads/2021/04/Internship-Job-Posting.pdf
- Where are our writers? https://finelines.org/Countries/
- *Fine Lines* blog: https://finelines.org/2016/07/mondays-with-martin-a-writers-prayer/

Write on,
David Martin, Managing Editor

Now Available:

Print Edition at Amazon.com
Full-Color PDF Edition at FineLines.org

FINE BOOK FEATURE

AVAILABLE NOW AT ONLINE STORES

May He Bless My Name by Carla M. Cherry

With grace, candor, and wit, Carla M. Cherry deftly narrates her unfolding as a young woman and mother in her expansive poetic memoir, *May He Bless My Name.* Cherry lyrically details her journey as she revels in the joys of watching her son grow, strives to overcome economic struggles, balance family life and career, assure her son's education, and contend with a lack of privacy and a desire for romance as she battles imposter syndrome. And when mental illness affects her family, Cherry leans on her pillars of faith, family, and heritage as she pursues hope and triumph.

ABOUT THE AUTHOR

Carla M. Cherry is a veteran high school English teacher. Her work has appeared in *Random Sample Review, Anti-Heroin Chic, La Libreta, ISLE,* and *Raising Mothers.* A Best of the Net and Pushcart Prize nominee, she has authored six books of poetry, *Gnat Feathers and Butterfly Wings, Thirty Dollars and a Bowl of Soup, Honeysuckle Me, These Pearls Are Real, Stardust and Skin,* and *May He Bless My Name* (iiPublishing), and two chapbooks: *Clap Your Hands, Stomp Your Feet* (Grandma Moses Press) and *Sundays and Hot Buttered Rolls: A Granddaughter of Harlem Speaks* (Finishing Line Press). She holds an M.F.A. in Creative Writing from the City College of New York.

REVIEWS

"This memoir book of narrative poetry by Carla Cherry is an extraordinary authentic literary work of the anguish and love an African American mother has for her son. From a letter to Oprah about beauty to the fears of police brutality and mental health, the themes of this book will have readers crying as well as laughing, always with the feeling of hope. This book provides opportunities for discussions on the social issues that often affect and impact African American families."

JUDY ANDREWS

"I wasn't sure what to expect. This played out like a movie but it's real life. With my busy schedule I could only read a bit at a time. I kept returning to it like they were family. I had to check on them. To make sure everyone was safe and ok. I could relate to a lot of this story. Told is such an accessible way. I felt I was right there with these characters."

MIKHAIL WHITWORTH

www.carlacherrybxpoet1.com

www.finelines.org

Made in United States
Orlando, FL
08 July 2025

62751016R00184